D1757062

The Moral Life

Also by Nafsika Athanassoulis

MORALITY, MORAL LUCK AND RESPONSIBILITY: FORTUNE'S WEB

PHILOSOPHICAL REFLECTIONS ON MEDICAL ETHICS (*editor*)

Also by Samantha Vice

ETHICS IN FILM (*co-editor with Ward E. Jones*)

The Moral Life

Essays in Honour of John Cottingham

Edited by

Nafsika Athanassoulis
Keele University, UK

and

Samantha Vice
Rhodes University, South Africa

First published 2008 by
PALGRAVE MACMILLAN
Houndmills, Basingstoke, Hampshire RG21 6XS and
175 Fifth Avenue, New York, N.Y. 10010
Companies and representatives throughout the world

PALGRAVE MACMILLAN is the global academic imprint of the Palgrave
Macmillan division of St. Martin's Press, LLC and of Palgrave Macmillan Ltd.
Macmillan® is a registered trademark in the United States, United Kingdom
and other countries. Palgrave is a registered trademark in the European
Union and other countries.

ISBN-13: 978-0-230-52756-0   hardback
ISBN-10: 0-230-52756-6   hardback

This book is printed on paper suitable for recycling and made from fully
managed and sustained forest sources. Logging, pulping and manufacturing
processes are expected to conform to the environmental regulations of the
country of origin.

A catalogue record for this book is available from the British Library.

Library of Congress Cataloging-in-Publication Data

The moral life : essays in honour of John Cottingham / edited by
    Nafsika Athanassoulis and Samantha Vice.
        p. cm.
    Includes bibliographical references and index.
    ISBN 0-230-52756-6 (alk. paper)
    1. Cottingham, John, 1943– 2. Ethics. 3. Religious ethics. I.
    Cottingham, John, 1943– II. Athanassoulis, Nafsika, 1973– III.
    Vice, Samantha, 1973–

    BJ604.C683M67 2008
    170—dc22   2008011739

10   9   8   7   6   5   4   3   2   1
17 16 15 14 13 12 11 10 09 08

Printed and bound in Great Britain by
CPI Antony Rowe, Chippenham and Eastbourne

Contents

v

Notes on Contributors

Nafsika Athanassoulis is Lecturer in Ethics at Keele University. Her work focuses on normative theories and in particular virtue ethics. She is the author of *Morality, Moral Luck and Responsibility: Fortune's Web* (Palgrave, 2005) and editor of *Philosophical Reflections on Medical Ethics* (Palgrave, 2005).

John Cottingham is a well-known authority on the philosophy of Descartes and seventeenth-century rationalism, and has written numerous books and articles on the history of philosophy, with special reference to the early-modern period. He has also published extensively in the field of moral philosophy and philosophy of religion, with special reference to the theory of the good life and the relation between philosophy and spirituality. He is currently Professor of Philosophy at the University of Reading, where he holds an Established Chair of Philosophy. He is also an Honorary Fellow of St John's College, Oxford. He has held the Radcliffe Research Fellowship in Philosophy and has served as Chairman of the British Society for the History of Philosophy, as President of the Mind Association, and as President of the Aristotelian Society. He is (since 1993) Editor of RATIO, the international journal of analytic philosophy. In 2002–4 he was Stanton Lecturer in the Philosophy of Religion at Cambridge University, and in 2008 he was elected President of the British Society for the Philosophy of Religion. John Cottingham is co-translator of the standard three-volume Cambridge edition of *The Philosophical Writings of Descartes* (Cambridge, 1985–91). His other books include *Descartes* (Blackwell, 1986), *The Rationalists* (Oxford University Press, 1988), *Reason, Will and Sensation* (OUP, 1994), *Western Philosophy: an anthology* (Blackwell, 1996, augmented 2nd edn 2007), *Descartes's Philosophy of Mind* (Orion, 1997), *Philosophy and the good life: reason and the Passions in Greek, Cartesian and psychoanalytic ethics* (Cambridge, 1998), *On the Meaning of Life* (Routledge, 2003), and *The Spiritual Dimension* (Cambridge, 2005). He is editor of *The Cambridge Companion to Descartes* (1992) and the Oxford Readings volume on *Descartes* (1998), and is general editor of the *Oxford Philosophical Texts* series.

Roger Crisp is Uehiro Fellow and Tutor in Philosophy at St Anne's College, Oxford. He is the author of *Mill on Utilitarianism* (1998) and

Reasons and the Good (2000), and has translated Aristotle's *Nicomachean Ethics* for Cambridge University Press.

Maximilian de Gaynesford is Reader in Philosophy at the University of Reading. He was formerly Fellow and Tutor at Lincoln College Oxford, Humboldt Research Fellow at the Freie Universität Berlin, and Associate Professor at the College of William and Mary in Virginia. He is the author of *I: The Meaning of the First Person Term* (OUP, 2006), *Hilary Putnam* (McGill-Queen's, 2006) and *John McDowell* (Polity, 2004) as well as of papers on the philosophy of mind and language, epistemology, metaphysics and moral psychology.

Brad Hooker has been at the University of Reading since 1993. His book *Ideal Code, Real World* was published by Oxford University Press in 2000.

Michael Lacewing is Senior Lecturer in Philosophy at Heythrop College, University of London, and researches in the philosophy of psychoanalysis. He has published in *Ratio, Philosophy, Psychiatry and Psychology* and *Philosophical Psychology.*

Thaddeus Metz's research focuses on the meaning of life and on respect-based approaches to ethics, politics and law. His work has appeared in journals such as *Ethics, Philosophy and Public Affairs, The Journal of Political Philosophy, Law and Philosophy, The Oxford Journal of Legal Studies, APQ* and *Religious Studies*. Metz is Professor of Philosophy and Diretror of the Wits Centre for Ethics at the University of the Witwatersrand.

Seiriol Morgan is Senior Lecturer in Philosophy at the University of Bristol. He works primarily in moral philosophy, and has interests in metaethics, moral theory and various areas of applied ethics, particularly sexual morality. He has published in *Philosophy and Phenomenological Research, Philosophical Review, Ethical Theory and Moral Practice* and the *Journal of Applied Philosophy.*

David S. Oderberg is Professor of Philosophy at the University of Reading, England. Among other books, he is the author of *Moral Theory: A Non-Consequentialist Approach* (Blackwell, 2000) and *Applied Ethics: A Non-Consequentialist Approach* (Blackwell, 2000), as well as co-editor, with Jacqueline A. Laing, of *Human Lives: Critical Essays on Non-Consequentialist Bioethics* (Macmillan/St. Martin' s Press, 1997) and, with Timothy Chappell, of *Human Values: New Essays on Ethics and Natural Law* (Palgrave, 2004). His latest book, *Real Essentialism*, appeared with Routledge in 2007.

Samantha Vice is Lecturer in Philosophy at Rhodes University, South Africa. She is co-editor, with Ward E. Jones, of *Ethics in Film*, forthcoming for Oxford University Press, and has published papers on the self, goodness, self-judgement and the work of Iris Murdoch.

Acknowledgements

We are very grateful to all the authors in this volume who so enthusiastically responded to our call for contributions in honour of John Cottingham. We are particularly grateful to Brad Hooker, the source, it seems, of all good ideas, for suggesting this project in the first place, and of course to John Cottingham, whose work has provided the inspiration for everything that followed.

A big thank you is also due to both our families for their love and support while we worked on this project.

Introduction

Nafsika Athanassoulis and Samantha Vice

Few philosophical careers have been marked by as great a range of expertise and interests as that of John Cottingham. Making his name as a translator and scholar of Descartes, he has ranged over rationalism, ethics, the philosophy of law and most recently, into the terrain of spirituality, psychoanalysis and the pursuit of meaning. This volume, which honours Cottingham's contribution to moral philosophy as he retires from full time work as Professor from the University of Reading, concentrates on this later work in ethics and religion, for two reasons. Firstly, it seems fitting that a volume in honour of a philosopher should also honour the direction in which his work has moved, and that it should explore those topics which, at the height of a successful career, are currently important to him. Secondly, it is the editors' belief, and as will be apparent, also that of our contributors, that Cottingham's most recent work revisits ancient debates in ways which revitalize them and open new paths for philosophers to explore.

The spirit of Descartes, so great a presence in Cottingham's career, can in fact be discerned in the direction his work has recently taken. In *Philosophy and the Good Life*, he develops a conception of philosophical ethics he calls 'synoptic', a conception which links 'a vision of the good life with an overarching world-view',[1] and which continues to occupy him in *On the Meaning of Life* and *The Spiritual Dimension*. Ancient philosophy in its various manifestations strove for such synopsis, albeit without ultimate success. But it is in the rationalism of Descartes that Cottingham finds the real 'challenge' to this 'integrative project'.[2] The universe so influentially described by Descartes is one which

> ... from the human point of view, is 'poker faced' – a universe which operates autonomously and largely without reference to our human

1

concerns, governed by abstract and immutable laws whose ultimate rationale, resting on the unconstrained and inscrutable will of its creator, is finally opaque to human reason.[3]

The destiny of human beings then lies 'not in attunement with the natural order', but rather in their ability to 'manipulate and control it'; 'in the new age, technological power replaces harmonious submission as the guiding vision for human life'.[4] In the face of this influential challenge, it has been Cottingham's project to return persons and their concern with living a worthwhile life to the centre of the philosophical enterprise. Over the three latest monographs (*Philosophy and the Good Life*, *On the Meaning of Life* and *The Spiritual Dimension*), he has been building a systematic account of human nature and flourishing and most recently, has articulated this against the backdrop of a theistic world-view. The project is to bring the different aspects of the human condition into some coherence, and to find a place for such creatures as we are within a natural world that yet contains intimations of the divine. His philosophy itself is an exercise in synthesis and accommodation; wide-ranging and inclusive, it eschews the narrow specialisation that characterises so much current academic practice. And the characteristic tone of this exercise is also appropriately inclusive: Cottingham's philosophy has always been notable for its charity towards his opponents rather than antagonism, and for an articulate and sensitive appropriation of sources beyond the analytic philosopher's typical reach.

The recurring theme within this project is that theories of how best to live must be premised on a realistic view of the human condition. We are creatures whose lives are bounded by physical frailty and mortality, who are essentially partial in our concerns and outlook, whose motivations and reasons are opaque even to ourselves. At the same time, however, it is just as much a fact about us that we 'cannot live wholly and healthily except in responsiveness to objective values of truth and beauty and goodness'.[5] Ethics must take both aspects of our nature into account, and Cottingham's various works on partiality, the limits of reason in self-knowledge, the truths of psychoanalysis, and the spiritual realm are unified by this common concern.

As early as 1986, in his first influential paper on partiality and the modern moral tradition ('Partiality, Favouritism and Morality'), we find this insistence that moral philosophy must take human nature into account. If we remember our nature, we are led to reject moral systems that demand too much of us. Accusing theories that require stringent impartiality from us of being 'hypocritical', he reminds us in a later paper that while the 'standard moralist urges us to transcend our selfish nature and adopt the life of universal agape', still, 'few or none of the proponents of that life have [ever] come remotely near to putting it into practice'.[6] And he concludes that if a theory gives us a vision that is impossible for us to achieve, 'then its coherence as an ethical ideal collapses'.[7] Cottingham's turn to Aristotelian virtue ethics as a realistic and humane theory, which has partiality built into the foundations, is a fruitful addition to the ever-growing work on virtue ethics. In turn, it has stimulated those belonging to the impartial moral traditions to articulate and defend their positions in new ways and has initiated a new debate on 'the ethical credentials of partiality', to use a title of another paper.

The emphasis on human limitations has continued and deepened in *Philosophy and the Good Life*, in which the role of reason in regulating and setting the standard for the good human life is placed under pressure by the notion of the unconscious. The Freudian insight is that our deepest motivations and desires lie beyond the reach of reason, so that to live a reflective life requires the kind of self-examination and personal archaeology typified by psychoanalysis. Again, we have a call for humility: this time, a reminder to philosophy of the limits of reason, and the insistence that a good life is not one that is fully encompassed by reason's rule. Philosophy requires a psychology, and in particular, a rich enough account of the role of the emotions and one's personal formation, if it is to play the ancient synthesizing role of its best proponents.

As his work on partiality, value, spirituality and meaningfulness all insists, philosophy also requires a subtle *moral* psychology to make sense of moral experience and the way we respond to a vision of objective value. While our limitations are such that moral philosophy must give us a moral vision we can in fact attain, still our nature is not entirely limited, and in his latest work on spirituality, *The Spiritual Dimension*, Cottingham has made a turn to the transcendent. But even here, he insists that we can find traces of the divine within ordinary, natural life.[8] In a sense, the retreat from all-encompassing reason which began in *Philosophy and the Good Life* is present in Cottingham's latest work in the philosophy of religion. We must acknowledge that 'human beings, in their vulnerability and finitude, need, in order to survive, modes of responding to the world, which go beyond what is disclosed in a rational scientific analysis of the relevant phenomena'.[9] Already in *On the Meaning of Life*, he agrees with Pascal that 'a religious idea can work on us without its cognitive credentials being first secured'.[10] The spiritual dimension is most centrally the domain of *praxis*, in which primacy is accorded to 'prescribed practices and techniques such as those of meditation, prayer and self-purification'[11] rather than the codification of obligatory beliefs.

Analytic philosophy of religion has tended to focus on the traditional arguments for the existence of God and with explaining His attributes, rather than concerning itself with spiritual *experience* and its role in our judgments about flourishing, meaning and value. *On the Meaning of Life* and *The Spiritual Dimension* provide the conceptual resources to make such an exploration respectable within the analytic tradition. Of course, that life's meaning requires a 'spiritual dimension' at all is a position that is out of favour in much philosophy today. Cottingham's emphasis on *praxis* and spiritual exercises, rather than belief and the traditional arguments for the existence of God, however, opens up new resources for theists and revitalizes the very old debate between atheists and believers.

All the themes so far mentioned are taken up in the course of this book, and their ongoing discussion is evidence of how Cottingham's work has made them fresh. Disagreement is rightly taken amongst philosophers to be a sign of respect and affection, and it is their respect and affection for John that the nine writers for this volume wish to express with their contributions. The aim of philosophy, he writes in *Philosophy and the Good Life*, is 'to enable us to lead better lives through a reflective understanding of our human nature'.[12] John's work puts this thought into practice and we – his students, friends and colleagues – have found our work and our lives enriched by engaging with his work.

Notes

1. Cottingham, 1998, p. 31.
2. Cottingham, 1998, p. 60.
3. Cottingham, 1998, p. 71.
4. Cottingham, 1998, p. 72.
5. Cottingham, 2003, p. 103.
6. Cottingham, 1991, p. 800.
7. Cottingham, 1991, p. 801.
8. For example, Cottingham, 2005, p. 133.
9. Cottingham, 2003, p. 99.
10. Cottingham, 2003, p. 93.
11. Cottingham, 2003, p. 93.
12. Cottingham, 1998, p. 4.

Bibliography

Cottingham J., *The Spiritual Dimension: Religion, Philosophy and Human Value* (Cambridge: Cambridge University Press, 2005)
Cottingham J., *On the Meaning of Life* (London: Routledge, 2003)

Cottingham J., *Philosophy and the Good Life* (Cambridge: Cambridge University Press, 1998)

Cottingham J., 'The Ethical Credentials of Partiality', *Proceedings of the Aristotelian Society* XCVIII (1997–8) 1–21

Cottingham J., 'The Ethics of Self-Concern', *Ethics* 101, 4 (1991) 798–817

Cottingham J., 'Partiality, Favouritism and Morality', *The Philosophical Quarterly* 36, 144 (1986) 357–73

Part I Partiality, Spirituality and Character

1

The Insignificance of the Self: Partiality and Spirituality

Samantha Vice

The context of this paper is the relation between an impartial conception of morality and the domain of partial concerns, relationships and projects around which so much of a worthwhile life is built. It seems obvious to many that morality must in some way accommodate the special force of our partial concerns, that it cannot simply demand that we treat them as we would those of any other person, or lay them aside when moral principles require it. That it seems obvious has not prevented modern ethics from forgetting it, and we have the work of John Cottingham to thank for bringing its deep importance back to our attention. Here I am reminded of Iris Murdoch's remark that one of the movements of philosophy is back 'towards the consideration of simple and obvious facts',[1] and Cottingham's work is just such a return.

The return to the obvious is difficult given the impartiality of the modern moral tradition. As Adrian Piper writes, consequentialists and deontologists alike 'do not permit you to accord any special privilege to your personal requirements, merely in virtue of the fact that you are the agent whose behaviour you are evaluating'.[2] So morality apparently requires us to treat the interests of everyone concerned as having equal value, and not to favour anyone because he or she stands in a certain relationship to you – of friend, child, partner, member of your group, or yourself. The moral point of view is the point of view of a benevolent, disinterested, impartial spectator, and so we must strive to rid ourselves of the biases, ignorance and favouritism that lead to unfairness and injustice.

As attractive as this view is on the face of it – and any conception of morality must in some way incorporate these insights – it seems to ignore most of what we think makes our lives worthwhile: the commitment to and pursuit of projects that matter *to me*, as well as relationships of love, friendship and parenting. These are special *to me*, even if from the point of view of Hare's Archangel or Firth's Ideal Observer, they are no more special than any one else's concerns.[3] This varied realm of what I shall be calling 'partial concern' is both self-directed and other-directed; I can be as intensely attached to someone else's interests, for her own sake, as I am to mine. The domain of the partial is therefore large: it includes concern for my own self-interest, goals and projects – and these can be directed towards myself or others – and concern for the well-being of those I care about, *for their own sake*. What all these concerns have in common is, as Cottingham writes, that the description and reason for my favouring in all cases includes 'a non-eliminably particular, self-referential element'[4] – that child is *my daughter*; it is *my* life-work or moral purity at stake. In currently fashionable parlance, the reasons or principles governing this realm are *agent-relative*: a full specification of an agent's favouritism must include a reference to that agent. Partiality is thus special concern for one's own projects, or the interests of people who have a certain relation to you – of parent, friend, self. As a contrast, think of the utilitarian principle of benevolence, which is *agent-neutral*: any agent – it doesn't matter who – has a reason to help others in need when she can, regardless of their relation to her.

This paper will not address the questions of whether morality *is* essentially or fundamentally impartial, or just how the apparently reasonable demands of some partial concerns should be incorporated; it will, however, assume that at least some moral demands are impartial. Instead, against the background of this debate, my aim is to explore the phenomenon of spirituality, which is plausibly thought of as a paradigmatic instance of the partial. Such an exploration brings together the two themes that have come to dominate John Cottingham's recent work: the relation between morality and partiality, and the spiritual dimension, to use the title of his latest monograph. I will argue for two main claims, one rather restricted, one more general: firstly, that despite appearances, certain conceptions of spirituality are not partial at all; and secondly, that the distinction between the partial and the impartial is ultimately unhelpful in understanding spirituality generally. If true, these rather specialised claims are important, I shall argue further, not only because they shed light on the relation between the self and the spiritual quest, but also because they encourage us to rethink a standard criticism of utilitarianism.

1. Spirituality

What, to begin with, is spirituality? I use the term 'spirituality' in a broad sense that incorporates both a religious and non-religious concern with activities of self-reflection, contemplation and self-purification, and with moral progression governed by objective value. Spiritual aspirants generally also manifest suspicion towards the mundane world of commercial and social aspiration, and seek a deeper and more meaningful relation with some value beyond that world. Cottingham writes that the spiritual dimension covers 'forms of life that put a premium on certain kinds of intensely focused moral and aesthetic response, or on the search for deeper reflective awareness of the meaning of our lives and of our relationship to others and to the natural world'.[5] In general, he continues, the label 'spiritual' refers to 'activities which aim to fill the creative and meditative space left over when science and technology have satisfied our material needs'.[6] Using religious terms for a moment, it seeks both 'inner transformation' as well as 'outward saintliness'.[7] The spiritual tradition characteristically takes self-directed, 'inward' attention to be at least instrumental in securing outward transformation and in reaching an end that is valuable independently of the agent. Spirituality is an ongoing project, and whatever its end, it requires some work that just is irreducibly self-directed. The end might be pure altruism or submergence of the will in God, self-forgetfulness or even self-annihilation, but at least instrumental self-concern or 'care' of the self is a prerequisite.[8]

In this sense, not just any forms of life that 'put a premium on' reflection and self-transformation will count as spiritual. It is true that sometimes the term can connote a concern with pure *authenticity*, with fashioning a unique way of being, whether or not that way is moral or even reasonable, a kind of aesthetic self-concern explored by Michel Foucault and Alexander Nehamas (after Nietzsche).[9] As I will use it (following Cottingham), however, spirituality is concerned, firstly, with reaching what is (taken to be) really valuable and, secondly, with doing what is right and becoming a person of moral virtue. I will therefore assume that obviously immoral ends are already ruled out of the spiritual quest.[10] So it is in this morally sensitive as well as value-sensitive sense, rather than in the ethically neutral 'aesthetic' sense, that I will usually use the term.[11]

Now, in the context of the debate on partiality in ethics, what status does spirituality have? For those who undertake the activities of inner exploration and self-transformation, it is obviously an intensely important project that structures one's future and upon which one's assessment of the past depends. It is, furthermore, important as *my* attempted transformation, the work on *my* self; in fact, the redemption of my soul or the final verdict on my life depends on the success of this project. It is a project that only I can undertake and which matters precisely because it is mine, so on the face of it, it is a paradigmatic instance of partial concern.

In a recent paper, Cottingham insists that ethical transformation is a 'legitimate moral undertaking' that 'by its very nature requires me to adopt a perspective that ... accords my own life a special importance, or centrality'.[12] This perspective he calls 'auto-tamieutic' (self-stewardship): the perspective

> ... from which I acknowledge the special and unique responsibility I have for understanding and properly developing my moral character, and the unique set of abilities that have been given to me. I am in an important sense steward of my own personal resources. This means, in the first place, that I am responsible for developing my own moral character and talents in a way I cannot be for anyone else's. ... In the second place ... the idea of self-stewardship means that I cannot and should not view the allocation of my time and energies in this respect as something that could be determined entirely from an impartial perspective. ... For my duty of self-discovery and self-perfectioning carries with it, as it were, an *automatically implied pre-assignment of time and energies*: the goods in question are ones that are achievable only by me, and by my investments of time and energy.[13]

From the auto-tamieutic perspective, in sum, 'each of us can discern a set of personal goals that are ethically immune to wholesale dissolution in the name of some externally defined goal'.[14]

Now, there are many questions we could ask: For example, is spirituality in any sense special in this regard, or is it just one of many partial concerns which imply such assumptions? Is it ever appropriate to lay aside the spiritual project for the sake of the demands of impartial morality? Although I shall return briefly to this second question, my focus is prior to such issues: Is it correct to think of spirituality *per se* as essentially partial at all?

2. Normative theories and the Good

Cottingham is correct, I think, that one must consider spirituality to carry a presumptive weight in one's relation to the same world one is hoping eventually to inhabit more deeply and afresh. The responsibility one has to oneself in this regard is distinctive and carries a weighting that is, in Samuel Scheffler's words, out of proportion to the 'weight of those concerns in an impersonal ranking of overall states of affairs'[15] (in this it is like any partial concern which, from the 'point of view of the universe', is no more important than any other). But I think that there is a plausible conception of spirituality in which, ultimately, the notion of partiality is unimportant or drops out of the picture altogether. This is worth exploring, because while this may not be the case for any conception, spiritual self-concern seemed to be a central case of partiality. Furthermore, while spirituality is not much explored in the debate about partiality and morality, still, most of us think that if any personal project carries presumptive weight in the face of moral demands, it is the spiritual quest – especially in religious forms. This intuition then gives support to the claim that morality *can* legitimately be laid aside if at least some partial concerns require it.

We can start by recalling the assumption of objective value in the notion of spirituality that we began with. Spirituality is a project aimed at realising or approximating what is taken to be objectively valuable. That, at least, is a crucial dimension of the *phenomenology* of spirituality. The aspirant seeks to reorient his life around something of value, which precisely because it is independent of his life, has a force that can be motivating, justifying and meaning bestowing. There are different candidates for this value, ranging through some notion of an impersonal Good or self-transcendence, to religious conceptions of a benevolent and all-powerful God. I will use the term 'the Good' to refer, neutrally, to all these potentially spiritual ends.

Furthermore – and this important for my strategy in this paper – it is not entirely inappropriate to include in this context familiar values from normative theories: the welfare of the dedicated utilitarian, the rational humanity of the Kantian, or Aristotelian *eudaimonia*. We are used to the idea that Aristotelian virtue will require work on character, but becoming a dedicated and successful utilitarian or Kantian will also, I think, require the kind of ongoing work on the self and dedication to an end that is characteristic of spirituality. If spirituality can sensibly be thought to exist without belief in God, then it should be able to incorporate sincere attempts at fashioning a self into the ideal utilitarian, Kantian or *Phronimos*.[16] Although applying the label to them might sound a bit strained, I hope to reach my claims about more core instances of spirituality through a familiar exploration of normative theories. Those who are unhappy with the label 'spiritual' in that domain can take my discussion as an analogy of what goes on in spirituality proper.

I want to put aside virtue ethics and focus on the Kantian and utilitarian – later I will narrow down further to utilitarianism. I am assuming versions of both these normative theories that are realistic and subtle enough to consider self-directed work appropriate and, indeed, required. It is very difficult to imagine a utilitarian or Kantian becoming morally successful in her own terms without some pretty radical self-transformation.[17] So consider a utilitarian or Kantian whose most fundamental commitment is to become the ideal moral agent and whose life is guided and structured by this commitment. Even if one is an 'indirect' utilitarian, or a Kantian who considers the Categorical Imperative a higher-order or 'limiting' condition on action rather than a first-order motivation for it,[18] the self-directed activity must be structured around the commitment to moral perfection in the requisite sense. If the successful moral agent is one whose character steadily and reliably issues in right action, then the aspirant to right action has an incentive to take the spiritual path to personal change.

Now, it has been argued persuasively that because impartial morality[19] can be integrated into subjects' motivational and value structure, its demands needn't be felt as 'destructively intrusive'.[20] Morality can matter personally and be felt as part of people's identity, contrary to what its critics often assume. This is quite correct but still, the commitment to spiritual progression is ultimately for the sake of a conception of moral perfection given by the theory. And both these theories are impartial, permitting and justifying from the impartial perspective the partiality inherent in spirituality. The spiritual project is valuable *insofar as it leads one to moral value*, and it is justified by that moral value. Here we have an instance of a familiar move in the impartiality debate: the justification of a partial commitment from an impartial perspective.[21] One needn't, however, think that spirituality is *only* instrumentally valuable in these conceptions; the kinds of activities required to become morally good might in themselves constitute what it is to be good. The sensitivity required to notice who is in need and to know how best to meet it; the knowledge of when one's proposed actions need testing via the Categorical Imperative procedure – these skills are both causally required to become moral and a constitutive feature of the moral agent herself. So we can note two things: firstly, that the spiritual process is justified by an impartial theory; and secondly, that spiritual activities and growth are instrumentally valuable for, as well as constitutive of, what it is to be a successful moral agent. Neither should sound surprising.

We can now ask further: What is the role of the agent in this pursuit and what relation does she have to the process and its end? Here, it seems that the theories can in principle part company. The Kantian's spiritual concern is to become a person of good will, who is characterised by a fundamental commitment to doing what duty requires. While having the advantage of allowing agent-centred principles, the Kantian picture has, however, also been criticised for displaying an obsessive concern with one's own purity – what matters is that *my* will be good, though disaster be all around. I'm not now going to investigate whether this is correct (though I happen to think the criticism misplaced);[22] what is relevant is that it is at least a possibility. Because of the complexity of Kantianism on this point, however, I will from now on focus on utilitarianism, where my concerns are better brought out.[23]

Whether appropriate to the Kantian or not, the utilitarian certainly cannot be criticised for moral self-indulgence: her concern just is to be the kind of person who will promote good states of affairs, and this – notoriously – need have nothing to do with the agent's own well-being, purity or lingering (non-utilitarian) scruples. The notion of the autotamieutic perspective reminds us that spirituality, so to speak, begins at home – that one must set one's own house in order before rearranging the world's furniture – but that it must remain there is a thought that hard-nosed utilitarians will find morally repugnant. The perfected utilitarian has left behind any concern for *her* self besides that of becoming the kind of self that would be the perfect utilitarian. Attention to the particular self may be a necessary starting point, but it is not the end and may have to be transcended if one is to realise the utilitarian goal. It really cannot matter that it be *I* who brings about the best state of affairs or that it be *my* soul that stays unsullied. This is just the kind of self-centredness, say these utilitarians, that prevents deontologists from being prepared to perform one bad action to prevent more bad actions of the same kind – and this is a stance that deontologists have found notoriously difficult to defend. Agent-centred restrictions, in Scheffler's terms, can, from the lofty purity of consequentialism, appear to be mere self-indulgence or squeamishness.[24] From the other point of view, of course, this purity is usually criticised because it seems to view people as 'mere conduits' of value, whose particularity and relations have no fundamental moral significance.

I have used this excursion into familiar terrain primarily in order to get to a notion of spirituality that might be considered rather too alien to merit discussion. If we understand and feel the force of utilitarian self-effacement, that should help us to understand the notion that I shall now explore. At the end of this paper, however, I shall return to the debate over utilitarianism.

3. Impersonal spirituality

So let us put aside normative theories of the right for the moment, and think about spirituality in a more ordinary sense, as the intensely personal quest for the Good. The suggestion that I want to explore is that one version of this project shares utilitarianism's disregard for the self. This element, commonly used against utilitarianism, is in fact integral to certain reasonable conceptions that belong firmly in the spiritual tradition. It follows from this, I shall argue, that the description of spiritual success in these conceptions will not contain the essential reference to the agent that marks the partial realm.

At this point it is worth remembering what the person undertaking the spiritual journey (any spiritual journey now) is in danger of: a sterile, idle 'fingering of the self', in Montaigne's nice phrase, or the morbid fascination with one's own faults that Iris Murdoch diagnosed so perspicuously.[25] This danger reminds us that the 'inward turn' to care of the self that exemplifies spirituality is in the service of an ultimate outward turn, to a value independent of oneself – whether God or morality or the Good.[26] It is this aspect of spirituality that prevents it from becoming immured in the fantasies and intrigues of the self. Murdoch, for instance, writes that the 'argument for looking outward at Christ and not inward at Reason is that self is such a dazzling object that if one looks *there* one may see nothing else'.[27] And she speaks in detail of 'techniques for purification and reorientation of an energy that is naturally selfish',[28] techniques which require a 'just and loving' *attention*[29] towards a reality outside of one. We can be helped in the moral quest 'by focusing our attention upon things which are valuable: virtuous people, great art, perhaps the idea of goodness itself'.[30]

Now this, I submit, is a perfectly conceivable task, and one that fits most accounts of spirituality. The person who has achieved spiritual success *is* one who knows a reality beyond herself, whose concern and attention is directed outward and who considers the self on which her attention was originally bestowed to be no more important than any other. However, the picture I am interested in takes this familiar thought further: the self is now consumed entirely by the outward attention towards the Good. There is a purity, a transparency from motive to end, and an impersonality that is familiar already from utilitarianism, and that we find elsewhere too – in Plato and the Stoics, and, more to the point here, some Christian conceptions of goodness. Simone Weil, for instance, writes:

> Joy within God. Perfect and infinite joy really exists within God. My
> participation can add nothing to it, my non-participation can take

nothing from the reality of this perfect and infinite joy. Of what importance is it then whether I am to share in it or not? Of no importance whatever.[31]

On this conception, the self seems to have evolved out of the picture. Writing in a different context, Antony Duff gives us a portrait of the spiritually flourishing person we are interested in. The attention of this person 'is focused not on himself and his benefit but on the Good. Nor does this Good consist in his own virtue, for that is egocentricity'.[32] Fundamentally, 'what is important is the Good, not his own moral perfection; *he* matters, if at all, only as an agent of the Good'.[33] Caring that *I* have achieved the good is an instance of 'egocentric service of the Good', a phrase he takes from Kiekegaard. Here is the passage from which Duff cites:

> Suppose a man wills the Good simply in order that *he* may score the victory, then he wills the good for the sake of reward, and his double-mindedness is obvious. ... Actually he does not care to serve the Good, but to have the advantage of regarding it as a fruit of conquest. When, on the contrary, a man desires that the Good shall be victorious, when he will not call the outcome of the battle 'victory', if *he* wins, but only when the Good is victorious: can he then, in any sense, be called and be double-minded?[34]

In more technical terms, the agent-centred demands of spiritual progression seem to have changed into the agent-neutral demand that anyone do what is required by the Good, and do it simply because it is required by the Good. This is not just from the point of view of the agent, nor is it a claim only about the phenomenology of self-forgetfulness. Rather, it is that a complete description and reason for this person's spiritual pursuit does not include a reference to her being the one to undertake the project and achieve the end – from any point of view. We have come, again, to a familiar idea: that of being a *conduit* or vehicle for value. The spiritual aspirant offers himself to the Good as a tool or a vehicle through whom it may be manifested or may fulfil its purpose. Standardly used to criticise utilitarianism, here we see it in the guise of spirituality where it seems to be more comfortable, and, in fact, entirely appropriate.

Two things are important for my point: firstly, the spiritual undertaking is (if things go well) one of continuous *progression*; one moves from a less perfect spiritual state to a more perfect state and it makes sense to talk of one's desiring to reach perfection. However, fallible human beings – even saints – only reach a state of perfection relative to their character, abilities and intelligence. Only the Good is perfect absolutely.[35] Borrowing a phrase from Martha Nussbaum, there is an 'ascent to the Good',[36] as one grows emotionally and volitionally, and acquires a deeper understanding of the final end. In this conception of ascent to perfection, the concern with one's own self is certainly the starting point and a necessary concern if one is to progress. However, one's attention does not remain on the self because what is of final and absolute value is the Good, not *one's own attainment of the Good*. As one ascends, partiality towards the self and its own self-referring projects must be left behind, as are all of one's earthly attachments. So it is important that this view of spirituality *begins* with partiality – otherwise in my claim that partiality disappears, I would simply be changing the subject.

Secondly, it is not just that an impartial Good allows or requires partial concern for one's spiritual state and justifies one embarking on the spiritual path. This would, again, be the familiar defusing strategy of incorporating partiality from the perspective of a higher-order impartial theory. Rather, the claim is that in both the full description and the justification of the spiritual project, the irreducibly personal, agent-centred element slips out of the picture. Admittedly, this is difficult to imagine if the thought that the agent remains the instrument and logical subject of change takes up all the space. However, something can happen *through* one, without the success being in any ethically significant way related to the self at all: 'There is music', says the conductor; not, 'There is music *through my agency*'. The music, the art, is the end, and it is enough. One's causal relation to its existence or success is not ethically relevant or relevant to how one feels upon achieving it or reflecting later upon it. It is not essential to a complete explanation; in fact it might make the explanation false if it were included. What is important and desired is that 'God was made manifest', not that 'God appeared *to me*'. This partly explains the uncomfortable, alien purity of certain paradigmatically spiritual figures: Socrates' utter disinterest in the mundane world and his own death, the self-forgetfulness of saints, Gandhi's singleness of purpose. Their vision is transparent: what they see directly, unclouded by the self, just is the Good.

None of this means that one cannot have self-directed thoughts during moments of insight or reflection into one's spiritual status – for example, feeling grateful that one has been chosen or knowing that one has, through grace, been granted a privileged experience.

The *phenomenology* of spirituality need not, and probably couldn't without madness, retain at every moment the fierce purity that characterises moments of contemplative insight, union with God or self-transcendence. What it does mean, again, is that at the level of justification and description, this kind of spiritual success makes no essential reference to the particular self. One's end is to live in a deeper, more clairvoyant relation to the Good; what structures, provides the impetus and justifies the attention one turns on one's own development is just this end. Of course self-concern is important in the sense that it is through one's own agency and progressing consciousness that the goal is achieved; it is important that one become the kind of person who has the desired relation to the value – because there is no other person one could be. So self-concern will be essential as a starting point to the journey. But what really matters is that the Good be realised in the world, and this is the thought that generated the project to begin with and justified the inward turn. Saying 'what is to be achieved' or 'when one is successful' brings in a subject *logically*, as does any talk of experiencing anything: there is one who is successful or one who has achieved or experienced the desired end. But this self-referentiality is not how spiritual aspirants experience it, nor how they have to explain the project.

The phenomenology might be analogous – in a shadowy, inadequate way – to the more familiar experience of 'flow': experiences in which 'you lose yourself in an activity or a line of thought', where there is no sense of self at all.[37] Joel Kupperman, who discusses the centrality of such experiences to subjective well-being, writes that 'one reason why it is claimed that many saints and mystics experience joy' is, paradoxically, the felt *loss of self* in such experiences.[38] This reminds us, once again, that this is not an impossible experience, even though it might sound alien to us.[39]

What of the auto-tamieutic perspective, which appeared so intuitively attractive? It seemed correct to say that we have a unique responsibility for cultivating our own talents and refining our own moral sensibility. From this point of view, we are stewards of ourselves and must assign resources to the project of self-development. There is no one else who could do it, and no one else we could be. In fact, the core sense of 'stewardship' reminds us, as does Cottingham himself, that our talents and moral journey are not entirely autonomous, created *ex nihilo* from an untrammelled will. Whether given to us by nature, upbringing or God, we find ourselves with abilities for which we then become responsible.

However, what I will call 'impersonal spirituality' is consistent with this notion of stewardship. Part of my strategy in this paper was to take as the natural starting point of spirituality a partial concern for one's own development. As a spiritual apprentice, it *does* matter that one's own talents and character be worked on and perfected, and one is justified in concentrating on this task. But stewardship can also allow that one makes oneself a suitable vessel for the Good to work through, and this might require extensive personal work before one is morally and epistemically prepared. What one is preparing for then, however, is that '*the Good be realised*', rather than that '*I experience the Good*'.

I am not arguing that this is the only view of the spiritual end. Earlier, I put aside aesthetic models of spirituality, which would probably not be impersonal. Someone purely interested in ridding herself of psychic tangles and personal unhappiness, someone interested fundamentally in forging a distinctive self-creation, might not experience this transparency, nor, accurately, describe the project in those terms. And as I discuss in the final section, besides these aesthetic or psychological conceptions, spirituality in the Aristotelian tradition and in some Christian traditions might also formally lack transparency (though I shall also suggest that insisting upon the terms 'partial' and 'impartial' is still apt to mislead). What I am describing is a particular kind of spirituality, one that is firmly embedded in the spiritual tradition and that puts pressure on the label 'partial'. However overwhelming the work on the self required, however deep the acknowledgement that this self requires radical transformation, this self-concern is, on the impersonal conception of spirituality, merely a starting point and a camouflage for the real enterprise.

What, now, is the relation between the demands of spirituality and impartial moral demands (assuming, reasonably, that there are some)? This, after all, is one of the questions Cottingham addresses in his discussion of the *partial* credentials of spirituality. Well, it depends on the content of one's spiritual end. If forms of utilitarianism or Kantianism, for instance, can be understood as spiritual, then the perfected agent will be the ideal utilitarian or Kantian. There can be no tension because the values of the theory and the aims of the spiritual quest are the same. For the substantial goals of impersonal spirituality, on the other hand, there may be a difference between the spiritual end and the moral end, although, if I am on track, it will not be felt as a tension between the partial and impartial. At certain heightened levels of achievement, when it is no longer important that it be oneself who is in those airy regions, one might be aware of a tension between conventional impartial morality and one's own vision and certainties. But this will be between different *impartial* commands on one, not between an impartial moral command and a partial value. In this kind of conflict, it is very difficult to see how this person, who has reached what she takes to be the ultimate truth and reality, *could* give up the spiritual end for the moral value. She will feel it as not just unreasonable, but in all respects the worst thing that could be done. And given that her judgement comes after long and intense work and self-abnegation, it would be very difficult for morality to insist upon it, especially as so often much of this quest is thought of in moral terms. We have here a clash between different conceptions of ultimate value, both impartial. But in fact, given the previous discussion, it is just not that helpful to keep the distinction between the partial and impartial here. Humility seems a fitting response when one has grasped ultimate reality in the Good. Whether or not it is *I* who has grasped this impartial good is just not important in describing the experience, even though *I* would, of course, be radically changed by it.

What we see here is that intensely personal and self-directed projects need not remain partial, despite their starting point having this character. While the auto-tamieutic perspective rightly insists on one's own responsibility for one's projects, success in those projects need not be related, either ethically or descriptively, to the particular self. What is important is the nature and functioning of the values towards which one strives. These can demand from one a project to change one's life; they can structure the verdict on one's own life and demand that one spend energy and time on it. Yet, they might not be ultimately a matter of one's own life at all. Their influence on us may display all the markers of partiality without the principles or reasons they give us being partial.

I want now, in the final section, to suggest how partiality might remain within the spiritual project, and to indicate why this exploration of spirituality is important – in part by taking another look at the criticism that utilitarianism makes us mere conduits for the good.

4. Conclusion: partial spirituality and the case against utilitarianism

There are at least two ways that spirituality could remain partial.[40] Firstly, if, with utilitarianism and Kantianism, we can think of *Aristotelian* self-progression as spiritual, then we'll have a good example of a spiritual self-concern that remains partial 'all the way down'. As Cottingham argued in a series of influential papers,[41] Aristotelianism gives a secure place for partial preferences because it does not take morality itself to be essentially impartial, and because it begins with the thought that a plausible ethics must give each person prudential reason to strive for virtue. A quest to become fully virtuous might then remain partial all the way to the end (though, of course, whether one is successful or not is partly out of one's control).

The criticism that virtue ethics is problematically egoistic is probably misplaced, and its defenders have argued that it can secure justice or fairness or benevolence quite adequately.[42] However, Kant's central insight, that morality has *categorical force*, does not seem to be captured in virtue ethics. Philosophers attracted to the idea of the categorical are not going to be content and will think that virtue ethics gives the wrong kind of grounding to morality. They might also be more attracted to the kind of impersonal spirituality I have explored here, though of course, they needn't be. The thought is that if something entirely divorced from one's own interests is recognised and pursued as the final Good, one's own place in the project might strike one as being less important than in conceptions in which self-interest is fundamental.

Secondly, religious conceptions of a loving God might guarantee partiality as well (though they also needn't, if they can support impersonal spirituality, as earlier argued). The partiality could be grounded in God's love for each of His creatures, for each unique particularity. It matters to Him that each of us becomes as perfect as she can, given her limitations. As each person matters to God, so we should matter to ourselves; we must care for our spiritual state because that is God's will, given His love for us. Without this love, why each of us should ultimately matter to ourselves in the face of the immeasurably greater Good is more difficult to grasp. So here it is the *impartial* love of God that justifies the continuing self-concern of the spiritual quest. Relatedly, the spiritual quest might be conceived as the realising and perfecting *in and through a particular life* of God's plan for each person.[43] This might require the cultivation of properly partial projects and loves. Once again, the impartial love of God is the ground of such a plan, and it is therefore only a form of virtue ethics that can justify partial concern in its own (partial) terms.

Certainly, then, we can find a sense in which Aristotelian and Christian conceptions of spirituality may retain partiality formally, though they may differ in the ultimate justification for this partiality. Having said all this, however, for conceptions of value-dependent spirituality other than virtue ethics, the distinction between partiality and impartiality still seems unhelpful and ultimately unimportant. Why is this? Spiritual aspirants value something that is not made valuable merely by (their own) fiat, which is independent of what they might think (and of course, this is also true for Aristotelians). This seems to be born out by a characteristic common to all spiritualities not in the 'aesthetic' mode – their self-forgetfulness, humility and outward attention. These traits can naturally develop into a purity of mind in which, really, the person doesn't matter much to herself, even though her project is to redeem her own soul or perfect her life. To the question, 'Do you want to be good for your own sake?' the answer could very well be 'yes', but equally, it could be that this isn't the point, that the point is to do as God wills, or simply to be good. And this seems reasonable. It is not clear how we could reject these as the real reasons and insist that the explanations must contain some hidden reference to the self, even if the phenomenology is otherwise and the person sincere in her reports. So at the limit of success, non-prudentially based spirituality is pushed naturally – and in a way that seems to be progress – away from the concern with the self that I have allowed to be formally retained.

Some personal accounts of spirituality, in which the boundaries between the self and the Good are very fluid and the sense of self-presence very complex, support the intuition that the distinction is unimportant. Thomas Merton for instance, writing of the self in contemplation, says: 'In such a world the true "I" remains both inarticulate and invisible, because it has altogether too much to say – not one word of which is about itself'.[44] Talk abounds of the necessary 'death' of the self, in order for a new self to emerge through Christ. But at the same time, 'It is now no longer I that live but Christ that lives in me'.[45] Contemplation 'is a deep resonance in the inmost centre of our spirit in which our very life loses its separate voice and re-sounds with the majesty and the mercy of the Hidden and Living One'.[46] So even a project which is premised on the knowledge of a loving God who cares for each person, and in which one's own salvation is one's responsibility, blurs the boundaries of the self and diminishes self-concern. As such, it is doubtful even on these conceptions whether spirituality is still usefully seen in terms of the partial concern for the self.

In fact, one can see how a stronger claim might seem attractive from this perspective: that spiritual quests seeking the attainment of an objective, non-prudential value (unlike Aristotelian virtue ethics) risk collapsing into an egoistic or aesthetic mode if they do not ultimately leave self-referentiality behind. Concern for fashioning the self, for being the one who is pure and perfect, too easily falls into an impure relation to what is ultimately important. It is once again here, in the realm of the spiritual, that familiar utilitarian complaints against non-utilitarians become apposite. It is difficult to imagine any circumstance in which exclaiming, 'I did it!' or, 'Now I've got it!' when facing the Good or God would be appropriate or, more strongly, even be possible to experience. The horizon of one's experience would be wholly taken up with the terrible presence. We find this vision in the work of Simone Weil, who writes: 'Perfect joy excludes even the very feeling of joy, for in the soul filled by the object no corner is left for saying "I"'.[47] This impersonality is a fundamental fact of one's relation to the ultimate value. Murdoch, deeply influenced by Weil, speaks of the need for *detachment*: we must learn that 'real things can be looked at and loved without being seized and used, without being appropriated into the greedy organism of the self'.[48] What is needed, on any conception of spirituality, is renunciation of the demands of the 'greedy self', and a natural progression of that, it might be thought, is a renunciation even of one's need to claim spiritual success as one's own. There is here, again, an echo of that purity of spiritual figures already mentioned, and André Comte-Sponville, influenced here by Weil, writes of this virtue: 'Nothing that can be owned is pure. Purity is poverty, dispossession, renunciation. It begins where the self ends, where the self does not venture, where it ceases to exit. Pure love is the opposite of self-love'.[49] It seems that a spirituality that remains personal cannot be pure, though it may have many other virtues.[50]

Of course, concerns immediately arise about the effects of this kind of success on other things we value, especially within the partial realm. Does impersonal spiritual success, or the plausible movement to greater impersonality, not render relationships in the more mundane regions impossible? Does 'leaving the self behind' entail leaving friendship and love behind too? How could love for any particular limited person survive that kind of intense vision of ultimate value? Perhaps, then, the virtue of purity is attained at too great a price. If this is true, and the accounts of the personal lives of saints are hardly encouraging here, then we have a reason to reject such conceptions and to hinder the movement to greater impersonality that I suggested is internal to other modes of spirituality. Too much that is good would have to be sacrificed for this spirituality to be an aspiration for any but the truly, terrifyingly, saintly.

This is a deeply difficult area which cries out for the kind of subtle and complex moral psychology that Murdoch tried to deliver.[51] Just what is it like to be someone whose self is extinguished in pursuit of the Good? What happens to the commitments of everyday loves and lives? While this is a deeply obscure region, a few things can be said. To begin with, impersonality or self-forgetfulness does not, as far as I can see, entail that no other person can be cherished as special. *My* friends or children or husband can be special even though success at cherishing them will not refer to *me*. Partialists have always rightly insisted that partiality is not selfishness and that one's partial projects can concern the well-being of others for their own sake. This is equally true for impersonal spirituality. For all that has been said, the content given to the notion of the Good *could* be caring or intense engagement with the lives of certain, special people. The projects that matter intensely to one could be the welfare of particular others. The worry that impersonal spirituality is inimical to the goods of special relationships is only apposite if one thinks it *impossible* to care for particular people without a reference or attachment to the self that cares. But this does not seem obvious.

So it is by no means clear that impersonal spirituality must be barred from special relationships. That said, however, impersonal spirituality is probably restricted to certain substantive conceptions of the Good and is less comfortable with others, and to admire it is not to say that everyone should pursue it. Even if it is true that special relationships sit uncomfortably with impersonal spirituality, it is not clear that a person should be denigrated for not having such relationships, if she is in other respects admirable. *Agape* or universal love, for instance, which might be more easily associated with impersonal spirituality, is not obviously less valuable because only a few can achieve it.

Why does all this matter? There are at least two reasons that give this discussion a rather wider significance. The first returns us to the old criticism against utilitarianism – that the particular, unique identity of each person is made morally irrelevant because we are viewed essentially as mere 'vehicles of the Good'. If impersonal conceptions of spirituality are coherent and reasonable, then there is nothing in the idea itself of being a conduit for the Good that is distasteful. Critics of utilitarianism have tended implicitly towards this view, I think, but the criticism is probably better restated in a way that takes different contexts of being such a conduit into consideration. It is not, in the abstract, being a conduit for the Good that is morally problematic, but considerations like the following: first, how we ought to think of our own agency in relation to others. The utilitarian commands us to treat others as if they were mere conduits for one's own production of the Good – that is, that one ought to, *by one's own agency*, produce good through the medium of other welfare-desiring, welfare-producing creatures and see the moral significance of persons in these terms. Here one regards oneself in relation to others as a good-maximiser and sees people as instrumentally rather than intrinsically valuable. A second consideration, closer to the debate about the space of partiality in morality, is raised by the psychological and ethical difficulties of seeing loved ones only as (i.e. in no other way than) conduits for the production of the good. These worries have to do with the autonomy and individuality of agents and the conditions for loving relationships. A third relevant fact is the content given to the utilitarian notion of the good and the maximisation condition that on most accounts, at any rate, is deemed essential to consequentialism. If the Good is the welfare that must be promoted through one's actions, then one is left with the rather unpleasant prospect of diligently producing, in an impartial way, a good that can only attach to particular people. And, furthermore, one is to do this with no clear idea of how other goods are to be incorporated and weighed in ways that recognise their own apparent intrinsic value.

However, if these problematic commitments are set aside, the very idea of the Good working through a person or being desired by a person in the impersonal way I have explored does not in itself seem repugnant, at least without further substantiation of the nature of the Good. All three of the considerations that may be taken as problematic are, for instance, silent about one's own personal orientation to the Good and so are neutral regarding the attractiveness of allowing oneself to be a conduit to the Good, or conceiving of that as one's ultimate ethical end. And if this is correct, then it is not the notion of an impartial relation to the Good and its impartial normative work that is the issue between utilitarians and their critics. It is, rather, the way in which a particular conception of the impartial Good is connected to how each one of us ought to treat and respond to *others*, and this connection can be cashed out in very different ways.

The second reason for finding the notion of an impersonal spirituality of wider importance is this: it seems to me that we have less of a grip on the terms 'impartial' and 'partial' than the debate supposes. In certain areas, the distinction is clear enough. We have a fairly reliable sense of when bias, self-interest or undue favouring mark a decision or a choice of principles in the public sphere. We know clearly that *our* children, friends and projects matter to *us*, without thereby insisting that they matter more from some impersonal or impartial perspective. However, in one of the most intensely felt and ethically important of projects, the distinction is unhelpful. Spirituality may begin as a partial project without clearly remaining one, and even if it retains partiality in its formal description, the development of humility and outward focus makes it unhelpful to insist upon the term. The relation of the self to the Good is complex, and in the face of at least some conceptions of ultimate value, maintaining a distinct regard for the self and its success is deeply misguided. Responsibly orienting one's life around an impartial Good can take one beyond oneself to something that has nothing at all to do with the self. Here, the self which mattered enough at the start to care for, by the end, no longer matters much at all.[52]

Notes

1. Murdoch, 1970, p. 1. The other 'movement' is 'towards the building of elaborate theories'.
2. Piper, 1987, p. 105.
3. See Firth, 1952 and Hare, 1981, Ch. 2; also see Taylor, 1980.
4. Cottingham, 1986, p. 359.
5. Cottingham, 2005, p. 3.
6. Cottingham, 2005, p. 3.
7. Cottingham, forthcoming, 2008, p. 2.
8. I take the phrase 'care of the self' from Michel Foucault, 1984. He uses it to characterise the kind of work on the self that was accorded so much importance in ancient Greek philosophy. For a different – and better – interpretation of this, see Hadot, 1995.
9. Foucault's interpretation of the ancient injunction to 'care for the self' as aesthetic, is, I think, mistaken. See his 1984 article, and also Nehamas, 2000.
10. Of course, those on the spiritual path may very well be wrong about their ethical commitments, seeing value where there isn't any. This paper says nothing about how to know whether their axiological commitments are correct or not.
11. Cottingham ties his conception of spirituality and ethical formation to value in this way. Furthermore, we both agree that only a realist account of value can do the job, but this paper does not need that stronger claim. It is enough if those on the spiritual quest consider the value they are pursuing to be independent of them (that is, experience it as independent).
12. Cottingham, forthcoming, 2008, pp. 3 and 4.
13. Cottingham, forthcoming, 2008, p. 6.
14. Cottingham, forthcoming, 2008, p. 12. This paper refers to 'ethical formation', rather than 'spirituality', but it is clear that the notions are substantially the same. In *The Spiritual Dimension*, 'spirituality' is used probably because the concern is explicitly religious and the term is usually associated with religion.
15. Scheffler, 1994, p. 9.
16. Recent work on character centred utilitarianism makes this sound less odd than it would have previously done. For example, see Railton, 2003, and Crisp, 1992. And new work by Sherman, 1997; Herman, 1993; Baron, 1997; and O'Neill, 1998, have shown the resources within Kantian ethics for developing conceptions of character.

17. See the papers by Railton and Crisp in note no. 16. We might also think of Susan Wolf's conceptions of the Kantian and consequentialist moral saint, in her 1982 article.
18. See 'sophisticated consequentialism', in Railton, 2003; for this conception of the Categorical Imperative, see Baron, 1984.
19. In what follows, when I refer to morality, I mean impartial morality, unless otherwise indicated.
20. Conly, 1985, p. 285; and see Piper, 1987.
21. This strategy of incorporating partial concerns from a 'higher-order' impartial perspective is standard in work on deontology and consequentialism. See for example, Baron, 1991, and Railton, 2003.
22. Hill's interpretation of the Good Will avoids this problem, see Hill, 2002.
23. Two different criticisms of Kantianism pull in different directions: Williams's 'one thought too many' criticism (1981) encourages us to think of Kantian ethics as disturbingly impersonal, ignoring what matters to oneself. On the other hand, the charge that the Kantian concern with the good will is a self-indulgent obsession with one's own purity pulls in an opposite direction, of being too concerned with what matters to the self.
24. In Bernard Williams's words – see Williams, 1973 and 1976. On agent-centred restrictions, see Scheffler, 1994.
25. Montaigne, 'On Practice', in 1580, II. 6, p. 426. Murdoch, 1970, for example, p. 68.
26. For an historical account of the 'inward turn', see Taylor, 1989, esp. Ch. 7.
27. Murdoch, 1970, p. 31.
28. Murdoch, 1970, p. 54.
29. Murdoch, 1970, p. 34.
30. Murdoch, 1970, p. 56.
31. Weil, 1947, p. 37.
32. Duff, 1976, p. 301. Duff argues that only on this conception of virtue can the good person conceivably be invulnerable to harm.
33. Duff, 1976, p. 303.
34. Kierkegaard, 1847, p. 87.
35. Thanks to Francis Williamson for clarifying this for me.
36. Nussbaum, 1994.
37. Joel Kupperman, 2006, p. 5.
38. Joel Kupperman, 2006, p. 5.
39. That it is very difficult to imagine is no obstacle to its being possibly true or valuable. As I have argued elsewhere, union with God or an intense relation to the Good *would* be utterly alien, difficult to render attractive and plausible. See Vice, 2005.
40. I am not qualified to speak of Eastern conceptions of philosophy, some of which seem to require a literal death of the self. Whether this is because the self is not important, or hinders attainment of what is important, or is really an illusion, would need to be clarified. Note that in this paper I have avoided ontological commitments about the nature of the self and what happens to it when it is 'left behind'. Whether or not the self really perishes or was only an illusion to begin with, were matters left aside.
41. For example, Cottingham, 1986, 1991 and 1998.
42. See, for example, Annas, 1993, Sect. 3.

43. Thanks to John Cottingham for reminding me of this.
44. Merton, 1972, p. 6.
45. Merton, 1972, p. 4.
46. Merton, 1972, p. 3.
47. Weil, 2002, p. 31.
48. 'On "God" and "Good"', in Murdoch, 1970, p. 65.
49. Comte-Sponville, 2001, p. 179.
50. This is not a conceptual claim about purity; if so, the claim would be trivially true. It is a substantial claim about the quality of one's attention and awareness in the light of pursuit of the Good.
51. And that Lawrence Blum (1988) calls for.
52. My thanks to Nafsika Athanassoulis, Pedro Tabensky and Francis Williamson for helpful comments.

Bibliography

Annas J., *The Morality of Happiness* (Oxford: Oxford University Press, 1993)

Baron M., 'Kantian Ethics', in M. Baron, P. Pettit and M. Slote, *Three Methods of Ethics: A Debate* (Malden, MA: Blackwell, 1997)

Baron M., 'Impartiality and Friendship', *Ethics*, vol. 101 (1991) 836–57

Baron M., 'The Alleged Moral Repugnance of Acting from Duty', *The Journal of Philosophy*, 81:4 (1984) 197–220

Blum L.A., 'Moral Exemplars', in P.A. French et al. (eds), Midwest Studies in Philosophy, vol. 13, *Ethical Theory: Character and Virtue* (Notre Dame: University of Notre Dame Press, 1988)

Comte-Sponville A., *A Short Treatise on the Great Virtues*, trans. C. Temerson (London: William Heinemann, 2001)

Conly S., 'The Objectivity of Morals and the Subjectivity of Persons', *American Philosophical Quarterly*, 22:4 (1985) 275–86

Cottingham J., 'Impartiality and Ethical Formation', in J. Cottingham, B. Feltham and P. Stratton-Lake (eds), *Partiality and Impartiality*, forthcoming, 2008

Cottingham J., *The Spiritual Dimension: Religion, Philosophy and Human Value* (Cambridge: Cambridge University Press, 2005)

Cottingham J., 'Partiality and the Virtues', in R. Crisp (ed.), *How Should One Live? Essays on the Virtues* (Oxford: Clarendon Press, 1998)

Cottingham J., 'The Ethics of Self-Concern', *Ethics*, 101:4 (1991) 798–817

Cottingham J., 'Partiality, Favouritism and Morality', *The Philosophical Quarterly*, 36:144 (1986) 357–73

Crisp R., 'Utilitarianism and the Life of Virtue', *The Philosophical Quarterly*, vol. 42 (1992) 139–60

Duff A., 'Must a Good Man Be Invulnerable?' *Ethics*, 86:4 (1976) 294–311

Firth R., 'Ethical Absolutism and the Ideal Observer', *Philosophy and Phenomenological Research*, 12:3 (1952) 317–45

Foucault M., *The Care of the Self: History of Sexuality*, vol. 3 (Harmondsworth: Penguin, 1984)

Hadot P., *Philosophy as a Way of Life* (Oxford: Blackwell, 1995)

Hare R.M. *Moral Thinking* (Oxford: Oxford University Press, 1981)

Herman B., *The Practice of Moral Judgment* (Cambridge, MA: Harvard University Press, 1993)

Hill T.E., 'Is a Good Will Overrated?' in *Human Welfare and Moral Worth: Kantian Perspectives* (Oxford: Clarendon Press, 2002)

Kierkegaard S., *Purity of Heart is to Will One Thing* [1847], trans. D. Steere (London: Fontana, 1961)

Kupperman J., *Six Myths About the Good Life: Thinking about What Has Value* (Indianapolis: Hackett, 2006)

Merton T., *Seeds of Contemplation* (Wheathampstead, Hertfordshire: Anthony Clarke Books, 1972)

Montaigne M., *The Complete Essays* [1580], trans. and ed. M.A. Screech (Harmondsworth: Penguin, 1991)

Murdoch I., *The Sovereignty of Good* [1970] (London and New York: Routledge, 2000)

Nehamas A., *The Art of Living: Socratic Reflections from Plato to Foucault* (Berkeley and Los Angeles: University of California Press, 2000)

Nussbaum M., 'The Ascent of Love: Plato, Spinoza, Proust', *New Literary History*, 25:4 (1994) 925–49

O'Neill O., 'Kant's Virtues', in R. Crisp (ed.), *How Should One Live? Essays on the Virtues* (Oxford: Clarendon, 1998)

Piper A.M.S., 'Moral Theory and Moral Alienation', *The Journal of Philosophy*, 84:2 (1987) 102–18

Railton P., 'Alienation, Consequentialism, and the Demands of Morality' in S. Darwall (ed.), *Consequentialism* (Oxford: Blackwell, 2003; Originally published in *Philosophy and Public Affairs*, 13:2 [1984])

Scheffler S., *The Rejection of Consequentialism* (Oxford: Clarendon Press, 1994, revised edition)

Sherman N., *Making a Necessity of Virtue: Aristotle and Kant on Virtue* (Cambridge: Cambridge University Press, 1997)

Taylor C., *The Sources of the Self: The Making of Modern Identity* (Cambridge: Cambridge University Press, 1989)

Taylor P., 'On Taking the Moral Point of View', in P.A. French, T.E. Uehling Jr., Howard K. Wettstein (eds), *Studies in Ethical Theory*, Midwest Studies in Philosophy, vol. 3 (Minneapolis: University of Minnesota Press, 1980)

Vice S., 'On the Tedium of the Good', *Ethical Theory and Moral Practice*, 8:4 (2005) 437–57

Weil S., *Gravity and Grace* [1947], trans. E. Crawford and M. von der Ruhr (London: Routledge, 2002)

Williams B., 'Persons, Character, and Morality', *Moral Luck* (Cambridge: Cambridge University Press, 1981)

Williams B., 'Utilitarianism and Moral Self-Indulgence', in H.D. Lewis (ed.), *Contemporary British Philosophy* (London: George Allen and Unwin Ltd, 1976)

Williams B., 'A Critique of Utilitarianism', in J.J.C. Smart and B.Williams, *Utilitarianism: For and Against* (Cambridge: Cambridge University Press, 1973)

Wolf S., 'Moral Saints', *Journal of Philosophy*, vol. 89 (1982) 419–29

2
Contempt and Integrity

Maximilian de Gaynesford

1.

John Cottingham is strongly associated with that approach to moral philosophy which challenges deontological and consequentialist paradigms by drawing attention to the role of virtues and character. His fine-grained work describing the structures of the ethical landscape and the complex sensibilities they sustain has focused particularly on the interrelations between integrity and human living. Since he regards 'wholeness or integrity' as 'our most precious human potential', developing an appreciation of this relationship is vital to the project he underwrites.[1] Essential aspects are revealed when the relationship is placed under stress or breaks down completely. We tend naturally to adopt certain attitudes to the loss or lack of integrity, to what Aurel Kolnai calls 'wilful inability to stand the test'.[2] Contempt is a standard example of the kind of reactive attitude called up in response to inadequacy or failure of this sort. So one way to pursue the inquiry into integrity is to examine its relations with contempt.

There are broader reasons for this investigation. Contempt is ignored or badly misunderstood in the literature. Kant's view that it is simply to be identified with disrespect has gone almost unchallenged. Cottingham has made this ignorance and confusion seem predictable: it is what we would expect given the dominance of moral philosophies that systematically misidentify the nature and role of virtues and character. But even moral philosophies which privilege these factors have tended to ignore contempt for the sake of attitudes that are less harsh, nicer, more comfortable. It would be a pity if what began as a commendably revisionary project deprived itself of its proper source and stimulus: the principle that we should 'keep before our minds ... what it is actually like to be involved in ordinary inter-personal relationships, ranging from the most intimate to the most casual'.[3] Once contempt has attracted the attention, it can be recognized as strikingly widespread, a regular, some-times regrettable, often intense feature of interpersonal relationships and of their representation in literature and drama. If it would be a good thing to direct our complement of sharp-honed sensibilities away from the usual safe-dealing towards less homely concepts, contempt would be a good candidate. For it is certainly not nice, prim or precious, it plays widely and deeply in our ethical lives, and it has received minimal attention (even less attentiveness) in moral psychology.

If the aim is to identify what is distinctive about contempt, we are obliged to address questions about human experience in an inquiry that integrates the emotional with the intellectual, the practical with the theoretical, the inner world of self-reflection with the outer world of empirical inquiry, using literary and other potentially emotive allusions to focus conceptual precision. Cottingham has called this approach 'the humane turn' and pursued it resolutely in his own work, countering trends towards scientistic dogmatism with an insistence on the variety of tools necessary to address human self-understanding and self-discovery, all in an attempt to persuade interlocutors rather than to corner opponents.[4] So I try to follow that lead in what follows.

Two reasons make me focus on contempt in a paper inspired by admiration for John Cottingham's philosophizing, and in particular by his constant generosity of thought. One is quite general and part of the argument of the essay itself: fully appreciating admiration and generosity means contrasting them with contempt and scorn as well as comparing them with esteem and charity. The other is special and part of what con-strains the argument of the essay: focusing exclusively on admiration and generosity is liable to render us powerless before various species of humbug against whose genus Cottingham argues we should set our face.

2.

Contempt gives rise to various questions. We will be less likely to distort our inquiry if we keep in mind an idea of their nature and range.

What *is* contempt: an act, or an episode, an attitude, or an agitation? Is it an emotion, a character trait, or a judgement? How does it differ from derision, ridicule, scorn, or loathing? Must it involve disdain, hau-teur, or pride? Is it possible without insolence, conceit, or superiority? How does it differ from disrespect, disregard, disgust, or indifference? Can one be truly averse to what one holds in contempt; can one mock, despise, or disparage what causes aversion?

What are the possible objects of contempt: persons only, or can it be directed on properties, non-mental objects, non-physical entities, institutions, rules, states of affairs? What are its possible subjects – which items on the previous list can have contempt? Is regarding someone with contempt different from treating him or her with contempt? Does being the object of contempt differ from being contemptible, and how does either differ from being beneath or beyond contempt?

If we cannot have courage without being courageous, how can we have contempt without being contemptuous – or *can* we? Must contempt make those who feel it despicable, rendering the subject as low as the object? Is self-contempt what the phrase suggests, contempt that is self-consciously self-directed? Or is it another sort of attitude or feeling altogether, like shame?

3.

Philosophers have never allowed themselves to be overly troubled by these questions. And while Aristotle, Hume, and Kant at least regard contempt as significant, recent philosophers have tended to ignore it.[5] It is rather as if they believe it should be treated with the aversion and distaste characteristic of the attitude itself.

The few exceptions have tended to go in one of two directions. The first emphasizes the affective aspects of contempt at the expense (and often to the exclusion) of its cognitive aspects. The second emphasizes the cognitive at the expense (and often to the exclusion) of the affective. The first group universally condemns contempt; the second is generally willing to approve of it, under certain restrictions. These results are sufficiently widespread to suggest that decisions on the moral question (whether to condemn or give limited approval) are heavily influenced if not entirely determined by decisions made in the philosophy of mind (that is, whether it is a state or attitude and of what sorts). So there is empirical and not just theoretical reason to achieve clarity about contempt. It is important not *even though* but *precisely because* our ultimate aim is to evaluate its place in an overall conception of human flourishing.

There are background lines of thought which would explain why moral philosophy has followed the philosophy of mind in this way. If regarding others with contempt were simply an emotional state, a short-term affective disturbance, there would be little to be said for it and much against. For it would be a state one could only act *in*, like acting *in* shock or *in* anger, or horror or surprise. As in these cases, contempt would not be acting as a motive but, as we might say, a mere cause; any resulting action would have the unpredictable and hence dangerous aspect of a reaction. Now acting in contempt differs in one vital way from acting in shock: the former is voluntary in ways that the latter is not (which is intuitively why one can be praised or blamed for the one, not the other). But that drives us on to the conclusion: given that it *is* up to us whether we act in contempt, and acting in this manner has undesirable consequences, it is up to us *not* to.

By contrast, suppose that regarding others with contempt were a cognitive attitude, something that reflected and employed our capacity to judge. It would be something one does, like approving or disapproving, liking or not liking – things over which we wield the two-way power of deciding and intending to do or not to do. As in these cases, contempt would then be something we might act *out of*; it might be a genuine motive for action and not a mere cause. We could think of it as warranted or not by the circumstances, something a person ought or ought not to encourage in themselves, something for which we are sometimes, in some ways, and to some degree responsible or answerable. Hence contempt is not to be condemned *tout court*. It becomes something we can approve of, under certain restrictions.

But neither tradition bears up under scrutiny. The problem with one side is that it makes emotion essential; the problem with the other is that it excludes emotion. One difference between feeling contempt for someone and judging they are contemptible is precisely that one need be in no such emotional state for the latter. Sometimes contempt includes the affective disturbances characterized and required for an emotional state (the person emotionally caught up in their contempt), but it is often, perhaps even paradigmatically, poor or even lacking in emotional content. In these instances, it is condemnation without disgust, denunciation without indignation, a form of loathing that allows itself no refreshing show of irritation. The point and achievement of such disdain lies partly in the surprise that a movement of such intensity should be a movement of the cool hour, a repugnance so lacking in excitement that it might otherwise be indistinguishable from indifference. That is why the paradigm subject is the 'coldly' contemptuous person and why we would find it paradoxical to describe anyone as 'warmly' contemptuous.

There are good reasons why contempt does not fit easily in either category to the exclusion of the other. To take the simple case in which we say Abelard is contemptuous, for example, we might mean at least three quite different things:

a) that he is constantly liable to feel contempt; that he has a general, non-discriminatory tendency of contemptuous feeling;

Here we are referring to a character trait. Abelard is liable to regard certain (or any) kinds of persons or things as contemptible or to treat them with contempt. If this trait is developed so that the circumstances which promote this regard or treatment occur very commonly, we may say Abelard is a contemptuous type.

b) that he regards some person (for example, Bernard) or action (for example, lying) or institution (for example, the benefice system) etc. with contempt; that he has an ongoing contemptuous regard for some particular thing;

Here we are referring to a stable and discriminating response that is not itself a character trait, though it may express or be based on one. Both (a) and (b) will include episodes of contempt-experience, thoughts and judgements of certain sorts, bodily changes of certain sorts, dispositions to behave in various ways, dispositions to experience further episodes, dispositions to have further thoughts or make further judgements.

c) that he treats some person or thing with contempt.

Here we are referring to a particular episode on a particular occasion which may involve an emotional disturbance, a perturbation or agitation, plus changes in bodily state.[6]

Note that Abelard may be described as contemptuous because he satisfies any one of these descriptions even though he also satisfies the other two. But there is asymmetric nesting here. Abelard could have episodes without stable responses of contempt to any particular person or type or a contemptuous character (they would be described as Abelard's 'lapses' perhaps). Abelard could also have stable responses without a contemptuous character. But to have such a character plausibly requires stable responses plus episodes. And to have stable responses plausibly requires episodes.

4.

Outside philosophy, the standard account of contempt settles on action. The Oxford English Dictionary (OED), for example, gives the primary meaning of contempt as 'the action of contemning or despising'.[7] Now we certainly do talk of 'acts of contempt' and 'attitudes of contempt'. The question is whether we mean by this what the OED invites us to suppose: that speaking of an act of contempt is like speaking of an act of murder or arson.

And this seems quite wrong: contempt in this respect is not itself an action but a mode or manner or way of acting. That is why we say 'A acted *with* contempt', and why saying this is not enough to tell us *what A* did—compare 'an act of mercy'; why we can do murder but we cannot do contempt (or mercy); why we can murder someone but we cannot contempt someone (or mercy someone); why the sense in which we may describe an act of murder as being done with contempt (or mercy) is not the same as that in which we might (in certain remarkable circumstances) describe an act of contempt (or mercy) as being done with murder.

Indeed, it may be that the whole extended family of contempt phrases should be treated as a means of verbal and nominal modification. This is straightforward in the case of adverbs and adjectives like contemptible, contemptibly, contemptuous, contemptuously (and the now obsolete contemptfully, contemptedly). To call a person or institution contemptible, for example, is to describe the mode or manner or way in which they exist or act.

The word 'contempt' itself is trickier since it is often situated within a 'with-' construction – for example, I treated him with contempt; I regarded him with contempt and so on. So it is tempting to equate such cases with others in which the 'with-' construction implies a relation between an action and an object or other entity – that is, 'I treated him with contempt' is equated with 'I treated him with medicine'.

But this seems quite wrong: contempt is not an entity with which I treat someone but a mode or manner or way in which I treat someone. In this respect, the phrase 'with contempt' is like the phrase 'with care', 'with glee', 'with politeness'. The point seems obvious in these cases since we can paraphrase them: 'to treat carefully, gleefully, politely'. By exposing an adverbial form behind the misleading 'with-' construction, we are cured of the temptation to think of care or glee as being entities to which an act relates us. And the same point holds for contempt: though the word has been little used since the 18th century, we can paraphrase 'to treat with contempt' as 'to treat contemptfully'. Being explicit modifiers, these uses of language have no tendency to mystify or mislead us in matters of metaphysics.

One way to capitalize immediately on these linguistic points about modes and manners is to note the close links between contempt on the one hand and specific patterns of intentional action or manners of behaviour on the other. The link with action explains how contempt provides motives for action. The link with behaviour explains how contempt is exhibited in the manner in which one does what one does, in one's demeanour and tone of voice. We express these features when we say that contempt 'colours one's thoughts' or 'pervades one's reflections'. Contempt is a way in which we manifest what is important to us. It also requires reflection on what matters to us; that is why it has its motivating power for us.

A final linguistic point. There is a straightforward transitive verb for contempt – to contemn – but it is, if not obsolete, now wholly reserved for literary use.[8] In *Daniel Deronda*, George Eliot writes, 'It lay in Deronda's nature usually to contemn the feeble'.[9] The archaism of the word evidently appealed to her: it neatly condemns as it conveys what is unappealingly snobbish in this aspect of Deronda's character.

The gradual disappearance of 'contemn' is striking, since it is this simple verbal form which is the root of 'contempt': Latin *contemptus*, the past participle of the verb *contemnere*.[10] Why is it that we now prefer more complex constructions like 'to regard with contempt', 'to treat with contempt'? Presumably because we prefer exactness to economy in so potentially threatening a matter. There is, after all, a duelling-difference between regarding someone with contempt and treating them with contempt, and the simple verb 'to contemn' smudges that. Without the specificatory addition of prepositions, the simple verbal form would obliterate vital distinctions and thus be too blunt an instrument for the purposes we would have in using it. If someone says 'Abelard contemns Bernard', after all, does that mean Abelard regards Bernard with contempt, or regards Bernard as contemptible, treats Bernard with contempt, or treats Bernard as contemptible – one, none, or all (in some necessarily vague sense that does indeed embrace each) of these?[11]

5.

In *The Metaphysics of Morals* (1797, 579–80), Kant condemns contempt outright on the grounds that to be contemptuous of a human being is to disrespect him, something which is clearly contrary to duty.[12] Of course, Kant has a specialized notion of respect in mind: it is that which is 'owed to human beings in general', which is not something a particular human being can do anything to win or lose – it is owed to him whether or not he is worthy of it. Kant is perfectly explicit about this:

> I cannot deny all respect to even a vicious man as a human being;
> I cannot withdraw at least the respect that belongs to him in his

quality as a human being, even though by his deeds he makes himself unworthy of it.[13]

We might respond: it is precisely *because* I cannot withdraw the respect owed to human beings in general from the object of my contempt that I can regard him with contempt. It is not a respect he could have won or lost, but it is the background against which I judge him as despicable. Were I to find he was not owed the respect due to human beings in general, for example, because I discovered he is a mere automaton in the guise of a human being and under someone else's control, I would not, *could* not, regard him with contempt. Far from being disrespectful in this precise sense, or simply neutral with regard to respect, regarding someone with contempt may actually be a sign of respect. To see this, consider someone who says 'You are beneath contempt'. They mean to convey something like the following: 'You are not even worthy of the respect which my regarding you with contempt extends to you'.

Contempt and disrespect should also be distinguished in more standard usage (where respect may or may not be earned, but can certainly be lost). The opposite of contempt is esteem, not respect. In Sophocles' *Ajax*, Odysseus says that the Greeks cannot show contempt for Ajax without injustice.[14] And the Greek here – *atimazoito* – holds a clue about contempt; it is to withdraw *timē* (that is, what it is to honor, respect, value, or prize) from someone; to deprive them of it, nullify, or negate it. When Ajax describes himself as contemptible, he uses the same form: *atimos*, deprived of honor.[15] Shakespeare's Coriolanus offers another case. He feels terrible contempt for the plebeians to whom he must appeal for support, but he does not disrespect them – indeed he *could* not, as citizens of the Rome in whose, *for* whose, honor he acts.

The logical distinctions are perhaps easier to see when we consider what it is to disrespect or have contempt for oneself. Someone who cringes before the powerful for the sake of advancement, for example, has self-disrespect but not necessarily self-contempt; he may esteem himself very highly and feel he is worthy of the goods such abasement might bring (Justinian's historian Procopius is an example; the poisonous *Secret History* makes clear that the sycophantic early works were written by a person of considerable self-esteem). Conversely, someone who works obsessively in despair at the results, like some philosophers, may be wholly lacking in self-esteem and yet not lack self-respect. There is a quick way to make these points: dignity is to self-respect as pride is to esteem: their expression. The person who cringes has pride but no dignity, and the obsessive has dignity but no pride. That is how contempt and disrespect can come apart.

6.

Like Kant, philosophers who deal with contempt tend to focus on the question of whether it is or is not morally justified or permitted.[16] This has had a considerably distorting effect on discussion of the issues. It is important not to over-moralize contempt, as if the only contexts in which it arises, or might justifiably arise, are those in which moral obligations exercise their competence as legitimately binding constraints or as proper determinants of choice and conduct.

Diderot took advantage of the fact that contempt can operate in non-moral contexts and with a force that is non-moral. Writing to John Wilkes in June 1776, he congratulated him for his speeches criticizing the American War and suggested that he should say this in Parliament at the next opportunity:

> I am not going to speak to you at all about the justice or injustice of your conduct. I know very well that this word is nothing but noise, when it is a question of the general interest. I could speak to you about the means by which you could succeed, and ask you whether you are strong enough to play the role of oppressors; this would be closer to the heart of the matter. However I will not even do that, but I will confine myself to imploring you to cast your eyes on the nations who hate you: ask them; see what they think of you, and tell me to what extent you have resolved to make your enemies laugh at you.[17]

The situation was such that no *moral* argument would have carried sufficient weight in Parliament. Only a strategy which flamboyantly ignored moral considerations would be effective. Hence Diderot suggests a strategy based around the threat of contempt.

A second example occurs in Act I Scene vii of *Macbeth*, immediately before Duncan's murder:

> LADY MACBETH – Art thou afeard
> To be the same in thine own act and valour
> As thou art in desire? ...
> MACBETH – I dare do all that may become a man;
> Who dares do more is none. ...

LADY MACBETH – When you durst do it, then you were a man;
And, to be more than what you were, you would
Be so much more the man.[18]

The temptation to over-moralize contempt is great. Terry Eagleton, for example, reads this passage as the inflection of an old debate: some, like Macbeth, see the constraints of human nature as creative ones; others, like Lady Macbeth, see being human as a matter of perpetually going beyond such constraints.[19] For Macbeth himself, to overreach those creative constraints is to undo yourself, becoming nothing in the act of seeking to be all. Lady Macbeth regards him with contempt because she recognizes no such constraint in nature: humanity is free to invent and reinvent itself at will, in a potentially endless process.

But this is entirely to miss the sexual contempt in Lady Macbeth's words and presumed tone. She is not interested in courageous notions of man-as-humanity being (in)capable of overcoming limitations, but in taunting notions of man-as-male being (in)capable of achieving an erection: being 'more than what you were' is to 'be so much more the man'. That idea can be used as a taunt – Goneril, for example, rounding on her husband: 'Marry, your manhood, mew', where the repeated 'm'-sound mercilessly exposes his flaccid state.[20] Or it can be used as a more tactful incitement to violence – Henry V, for example, rousing his soldiery: by contrast with them, 'gentlemen in England now abed' will 'hold their manhoods cheap'.[21] In missing the non- or extra-moral aspects of contempt, Eagleton's reading is blind to the play on the ambiguity of 'man' ('human being'; 'male'; 'manhood'). And there is a price: Eagleton misses the insight in Macbeth's speech, that the one who dares more simply is no human being—he does not *lose* his humanity in the attempt or as a result; he would have to have been no human being to have been able to bring himself to the point of attempting it.

Philosophy also has uses for contempt which we will overlook if we over-moralize the subject.[22] A familiar alternative to refuting the sceptic is to refuse his questions in such a way as to treat with contempt the debate he invites us to enter. Samuel Beckett offers a quick dramatization of precisely this move in his *Endgame*:

CLOV – Do you believe in life to come?
HAMM – Mine was always that.[23]

The interchange plays on the ambiguity of 'life': does it mean existence merely (will we go on existing?) or meaningfulness, the preconditions of significance (will life ever be significant, worthwhile?). The question is whether Hamm takes himself to be answering Clov's question (whether he 'takes Clov seriously' would be the usual paraphrase; but it is interestingly inappropriate here), or whether he is treating it with contempt and merely taking the opportunity to make a joke, or whether there is something of both here – contempt and an answer.

If he is answering the question, what he seems to be saying is this: you ask about existence after death, but that is not serious; what is serious is meaning right now; and I'll tell you that we have as good grounds to expect a meaningful life right now as we do to expect existence after death; and you know how seriously I take that option: I've just ignored your question about it. Better, since I haven't exactly ignored your question, I've just 'overlooked' your question about it; I've looked it over and found it wanting; I've looked over it so as to address a different, better question.

Wittgenstein regularly adopted this same strategy, refusing a question out of disdain for what prompted it. Very occasionally, he explains that this is what he is about; for example,

> To the philosophical question: 'Is the visual image of this tree composite, and what are its component parts?' the correct answer is: 'That depends on what you understand by "composite"'. (And that is of course not an answer but a rejection of the question.)[24]

7.

With these historical and linguistic points in place, we may start to make progress. But how? Not, it seems, by offering a 'theory of contempt'. Though interested in what we mean by the concept, its intricate relations with other concepts and the psychological attitudes they name, there is little or no temptation to say that we are or should be offering such a thing. In this matter, contempt (jealousy, gratitude, admiration) contrasts with goodness, or justice, or the right. Perhaps this is characteristic of the thicker concepts and what distinguishes them from the thinner: the extent to which theory-talk is or is not appropriate. In any case, we should be prepared. In talking of contempt, we may not be dealing in platitudes exactly, in simple reminders of what we all do or should know. We may disagree passionately about how a precise discrimination is to be made and marked, about whether a distinction corresponds to a difference, about how it is most aptly to be expressed. But we will expect little or no room for courting the kind of deep disagreements about what it is or how it is to be discovered which would justify proposing one theory as counter to another.

If not by theory, it seems appropriate to proceed by piecemeal comment and commentary. First, then, we could gain purchase on contempt by thinking what might occlude it in the aspect-perception way, what it might in turn occlude, what it might exclude. If some feature *F occludes* another feature *G* (as in the famous duck–rabbit illustration), though it is not possible to regard an object as both *F* and *G* simultaneously, it is necessary that one think of it as something which it might be possible to regard as both *F* and *G*. If *F excludes G*, on the other hand, it is not possible to regard an object as *F* and think of it as something which might be possibly regarded as *G* as well.

For example, it seems that regarding someone with pride excludes regarding them with contempt. But regarding someone with certain sorts of annoyance may simply occlude regarding them with contempt. Similarly, regarding someone merely as a means excludes regarding them with respect. But regarding them with contempt occludes regarding them with respect (at least in the more standard, non-Kantian sense). Regarding someone with contempt excludes regarding them with indifference, with pride, or as uninteresting, as praiseworthy, admirable, beneath contempt (that is, with bottomless disdain). Regarding someone with contempt neither excludes nor occludes regarding them as a source of comedy or amusement, with shame (that is, to oneself), as shameful (that is, them), as interesting. Regarding someone with contempt requires regarding them with disdain; it may require despising them too. Treating someone with contempt requires withdrawing from them, seeking to harm them by the withdrawal.

This final point leads to a second observation. Abelard can regard Bernard with contempt without treating him with contempt. But the converse does not hold. If it is genuinely with contempt that Abelard treats Bernard, then that is how he must regard him. This remark enables us to sidestep an unnecessarily complicating appeal to the inner/outer metaphor which occurs often in philosophical treatments of contempt. Thus Berkeley speaks of '[a]n outward contempt of what the public esteemeth sacred' (1993, 1.4), and Kant appeals to the same distinction when he tempers his condemnation of contempt under any form and in any circumstance with this acknowledgement:

> At times one cannot, it is true, help inwardly looking down on some in comparison with others (*despicatui habere*); but the outward manifestation of this is, nevertheless, an offense (*Beleidigung*).[25]

It is unclear in either case which of two options either author would endorse: that there is an inner and an outer contempt (that is, that there are some forms, the outer ones, which do not consist of feelings, emotions, etc.); or that there is contempt, which is inner, and the expression of contempt, which is outer. But we can adequately describe the phenomena without such bother. There is treating someone with contempt and there is regarding someone with contempt. The former is always perceptible and the latter need not be – the contempt with which Abelard regards Bernard may be visible ('I can see it in his eyes') or it may not.

Third, a similar asymmetry distinguishes being contemptible from being an object of contempt. One might be contemptible and yet no one, not even oneself, recognizes this. But if one is contemptible to oneself or others, that is to say (at least) that one is an object of contempt.

Fourth, it is possible to regard things other than persons with contempt. Some writers assume that contempt can be accounted for by concentrating exclusively on persons. Kolnai seems to take this position when he writes, 'Contempt is a possible reaction only to someone who is capable of and in the habit of making judgements'[26] (I say 'seems' because it is just possible to interpret the passage as a constraint on the special case of *contempt for persons* rather than on contempt as a whole.). Mason clearly takes the exclusive view and speaks of contempt as having a 'person *focus*'.[27] This seems false. It may be that occasions for contempt are usually restricted to those where persons are involved, responsible even. But its *focus* is on its objects, and its objects need not be persons. Thus one might regard an institution with contempt, or a particular action, or the kind of which various actions are instances, or a particular situation or state of affairs.

Fifth, and as these earlier points illustrate, contempt is overall or at least in its central cases essentially intentional: it takes objects (whether or not they actually exist) which it is about or directed on. There may be an exception to this: perhaps being contemptuous may sometimes describe a mood, one that is non-intentional. So someone might say that he is feeling contemptuous but not *of* anything, just as he might describe himself as feeling cheerful but not *about* anything. If there are such examples, and if they are not always vulnerable to redescription as boredom or ennui, they certainly appear to be limiting cases or variants. Acedia can take the form of a sour aversion, and this may provide the best example of a genuinely contemptuous mood. In the chapter which stimulated much medieval debate on the nature and causal properties of the vice, John Cassian (360–435 AD) writes: 'It produces dislike of the place, disgust with the cell, and disdain and contempt of the brethren'.[28] But the evidence is unclear. First, it is consistent with the passage to deny that the mood is identical with contempt; it merely gives rise to that attitude. Second, even if acedia is a mood and identical with contempt, it is equally consistent with the passage to insist that it takes intentional objects (in this case, 'the brethren').

Sixth, contempt has an affective component; it is, as we tend to say, something we *feel* (for a person, or activity, or situation). More specifically, regarding or treating some one or thing with contempt is to feel averse to them, and the character and intensity of this aversion varies, perhaps greatly, being dependent on the individuals involved and the situations in which they find themselves. Thus, on occasion, this affective component will have little or no emotional content; on occasion, the emotional content will be rich and have a distinctive phenomenology. For example, Abelard might regard or treat Bernard with contempt and yet be almost untroubled emotionally by him, being able to distance himself sufficiently. But he might lack the capacity to take up such a stance of cool detachment. Alternatively, though he has that capacity, he might lack the opportunity to exercise it. In either case, he may find being in the company of Bernard not simply distasteful but painful, his contempt being aptly describable in ways that extend to bodily sensations, such as that his contempt is something he can *taste*. His contempt for an activity or situation might similarly be limited to cool aversion, or it might involve feelings of hurt and grievance at engaging in the one or being involved in the other.

Seventh, contempt has comparative forms. One can regard *A* as more contemptible than *B*. And here it is a scaling term: that is, unlike regarding *A* as more square than *B*, regarding *A* as more contemptible than *B* is consistent with continuing to regard *B* as contemptible. These proposals are also consistent with the fact that contempt has superlative forms: one can regard *A* as the most contemptible of *F*'s.

Eighth, two persons can have contempt for one another even though they think they are of equal (that is, low) worth. Milton describes various characters – the fallen angels, Adam and Eve – as having precisely this attitude in *Paradise Lost*.[29] Thus Hobbes goes wrong in saying, 'Contempt is when a man thinks another of little worth in comparison to himself'.[30] The standards against which an object is recognized as contemptible need not be set by the person feeling contempt.

8.

Given what we now know about contempt, I propose to characterize the central cases as follows.

To *regard* someone or something with contempt is

a) to judge the object (for example, a person, *A*; or an activity, *V*-ing; or a situation, *S*) to be of little or no worth or account, to be looked down on, regarded as low, inferior, prone, either *tout court* or in relation to some standard (not necessarily oneself or even set by oneself);
b) to feel averse to the object in ways whose character and intensity depend on the character of the circumstances and of the persons involved (including oneself).

(a) is an attempt to characterize the central *cognitive* features of contempt and (b) the *affective*.

To *treat* someone or something with contempt is to satisfy (a)–(b), and in addition

c) to withdraw or distance or disengage oneself from the object;
d) to intend or desire to cause injury, hurt, or pain by so withdrawing; and
e) (often) to intend or desire that the injury cause the object to change (for better or worse).[31]

This characterization differs in important ways from those explicit or implicit in the literature. Some of the more important have already been defended. Contempt is not here regarded as exclusively cognitive or affective; it is not confused with indifference or mistaken for disrespect; it is not taken for a moral attitude (without prejudice to the possibility that it might be evoked in a moral context, or that it might, in certain circumstances, be morally justified to adopt it); its objects are not limited to persons. In the rest of this paper, I will attempt to motivate and defend other features of my characterization.

9.

This analysis recognizes the difference between regarding an object with contempt and treating it with contempt. A further advantage is that it explains why they differ as they do. It is because one cannot genuinely withdraw or distance or disengage oneself *from* oneself that self-contempt is limited in all but the most drastic cases to the mode of regard rather than treatment. It is partly because the option of withdrawing from others (or from activities, situations, and so on) is not always possible, available, advisable, desirable etc. that other-contempt is often limited to the regard mode. It is also partly because the option of intending to cause hurt or pain or injury to others is not always possible, available, advisable, desirable, and so on. The object may be a person who is dead, or fictional, or someone with whom one's own life is too intimately related and interdependent. It may be an institution from which one cannot withdraw, or which one cannot intend to hurt by so withdrawing. It may be an activity one cannot disengage from, being an ingrained habit, tradition, routine or addiction.

Condition (a) takes care of the fact that contempt need not play on metaphors of height differential alone (that is, the object of one's contempt is 'low', and that of one's esteem is 'high').[32] It also plays on metaphors of position and location: the object of one's contempt is prostrate, prone, supine, and that of one's esteem is upright, upstanding. It is precisely because these background assumptions are common that Auden can play against them, in his characteristic disconcerting-amusing way:

> Let us honour if we can
> The vertical man,
> Though we value none
> But the horizontal one.[33]

It is tempting to say that regarding someone with contempt is to regard them as nothing ('less than nothing' as we sometimes say; a phrase that is no less illuminating for being logically comic). But notice that the same might be said of indifference, which is a quite different matter. In indifference, the object and the state caused in us by the object are 'as nothing to us'. In contempt, however, we care both about the object and the state caused in us by the object. These things are 'something to us'. So we need to add to the definition: to regard someone with contempt is to regard them *as* nothing, though it is something to us to do so.

Contempt is a kind of presence-in-withdrawal. The air of paradox can be extracted if we say that it is a way of making one's absence felt, or recall what it was like to be or experience a door-slamming teenager. It is the main reason why a contemptuous disregard has a vitally distinct character from a disregard that proceeds from ignorance or indifference.

George Eliot muddies the pool here: in *Adam Bede*, she describes a character as having 'an air of contemptuous indifference'.[34] But perhaps this is not too problematic. Surely the best reading of this line is as containing a creative tension – the character is uncertain in himself as to whether to be contemptuous (that is, caring somewhat about the effect of his attitude) and being genuinely indifferent (that is, not caring about the effect of his attitude). This seems to me to capture something psychologically true about contempt: that someone who feels contempt for someone else is very often uncertain about whether to make their withdrawal count, or just to withdraw. Regarding or treating another with contempt can seem not worth the trouble.

10.

Conditions (a) and (b), the cognitive and the affective, account for the ways in which contempt is both like and unlike attitudes of liking/disliking; approval/disapproval. It is both something one *does* (one can decide and intend to regard or treat someone with contempt; one may be able to order someone to do so) and something one *feels* – making it like an emotion (that is, one may be in its grip, or full of it; it may come over one or overcome one).

What makes contempt unlike most other feelings is that it is something one can try to feel, succeed in feeling, get better at feeling. One cannot get better at feeling anger, love, pity; one can only become more irascible, loving, compassionate. Getting better at treating or regarding someone with contempt is certainly not (or not necessarily) the same as becoming more contemptuous; it could mean becoming more discerning or judgmental, less tolerant or lenient or forbearing and so on.

Another way in which contempt differs from attitudes like love/hate can be marked by noting how odd the familiar advice, 'Love the person, hate the deed' would sound in reference to contempt: 'Admire the person, be contemptuous of the deed'. Here, the issue is not one of language but of conceptual implication. It seems that we cannot both admire a person and be contemptuous of their deeds as we can love one and hate the other. One possible explanation is that contempt is much more firmly rooted in the constants of character, that it becomes meaningless when dissociated from such rooted features of its object.

Contempt is also something we say a person (sometimes) ought or (more frequently) ought not to feel, that his contempt is warranted in the circumstances or that he has reason to feel contempt. We blame people for their excessive or unreasonable contempt. It is unclear whether we can feel contempt at will or to order, but we can certainly cultivate and refine this response. We can give way to it or bring it under control, give expression to it or suppress it. All this suggests that contempt is an attitude-feeling that is in some (quite strong) sense voluntary. It is something for which we are sometimes, in some ways, and to some degree, responsible or answerable.

Contempt is informative – not about the state of one's body, like sensations, but about the state of a person or thing, the object of one's attitude. Indeed, it is *essentially* informative since it is an attitude of assessment (like pride, shame, humiliation, regret, remorse, guilt). It is not a localized feeling (like sensations, of hunger etc.). Like many emotions, it does have characteristic facial expressions and tones of voice. Contempt is not the name of a specific bodily sensation (as itch, qualm and pang are). It need not be accompanied by any bodily sensation at all, and when it is, it need not be of a particular sort or felt in a particular place. That is one way of distinguishing it from disgust (though contempt may be accompanied by disgust) which, in paradigmatic cases anyway, certainly does name bodily sensations, and in quite a specific range (its base being in the gastro-intestinal, with possible effects in the gorge – it is not felt in the hands or feet etc.).

Connections between contempt and shame shed further light on condition (b). Shame results from being (or feeling one is) *observed*.[35] In contempt for others, one is the *observer*. In contempt for oneself, one is both. The language of looking, gazing, is intimate to all these occasions. One has difficulty in facing others or oneself. One loses face with others; what is made to matter is how one appears in their eyes, or before their eyes. In all cases, being observed (or feeling one is, feeling that there is a watcher or a witness of oneself) brings about a feeling of inadequacy or failure, a sense that one's loss or lack of power or control has been exposed. In shame, this is accompanied by emotions of self-protection. In contempt for oneself, such emotions can be absent, or seem out of place if present. Contempt may be provoked by situations involving guilt as well as shame. One may feel contempt for oneself whether one has done something of which one is ashamed or about which one feels guilty. One may also feel contempt for another if they do something of which they may feel ashamed or guilty.

Contempt and shame can come apart as Sophocles' *Ajax* illustrates. Having been driven mad for a short time by the gods, Ajax sets about killing people he takes to be his enemies; when he awakes, he finds himself a laughing stock, since all he has actually killed is a herd of sheep. The play turns upon this point: he feels deep shame for the ridicule he has heaped on himself, but he does not feel contempt for himself. He has been observed, his weakness and nakedness has been uncovered, but he feels no contempt for himself, largely because, as he points out, it is not he but the gods who have brought about this situation. Hence

he feels the comforting emotion of self-pity, but his contempt and lac-
erating hatred are directed at the gods rather than himself.

11.

Condition (c) encourages us to ask whether anyone can treat anyone
with contempt. My proposal makes this a complex question, but no
more complex, I believe, than the phenomenon itself.

We can take the question both absolutely and relative to the agent of
the attitude. Absolutely, we can say that not everyone can feel contempt: obviously one has to have the requisite cognitive and affective
capacities for taking that attitude and feeling that emotion. And perhaps absolutely we can say that not everything can be the object of
contempt: obviously it has to have the (passive) ability to be regarded
as 'low' and so on.

Relatively to the agent of the attitude, we need to draw a circle around
the candidate objects: those who fall within and without the boundaries of entities for whom it is possible to feel contempt. It is probably
not possible for psychologically healthy and morally educated adults to
recognize as contempt any attitude they might have towards children,
animals, the severely mentally handicapped, and so on. But note the
sense in which this is relative: children are the possible objects of
contempt for other children.

Condition (d) makes clear that treating someone with contempt has
a potentially retributive aspect: it involves a desire to hurt or cause pain
to the object of contempt. Some writers seem to deny this. Michelle
Mason, for example, claims that 'contempt might quite often be accompanied by retributive feelings' but that 'such feelings are not essential to
contempt'.[36] Perhaps if such writers distinguished between regarding
someone with contempt and treating them with contempt, they would
be more prepared to accept that potentially retributive notions are essential to the latter. The only reason I can think why they might continue
to resist would be that they think that *instead of* involving the desire to
hurt its object, contempt is a withdrawing from or turning away from
its object.

This would not be a good reason. First, because the one *need not*
exclude the other. Withdrawing or turning away from an object can be
a way of realizing the desire to hurt that object. Second, because the one
standardly *involves* the other. What distinguishes the particular kind of
desire to hurt its object which is characteristic of contempt, at least in
standard cases, is precisely that it *is* achieved in withdrawing or turning

away from its object. Without this desire, we would no longer be treating someone with contempt but moving towards anger (at one pole) or indifference (at the other). In standard cases of anger, the desire to hurt the object is achieved in *turning towards* it, in *confronting* it. In cases of *genuine* indifference (that is, not those in which one is frequently moved to *say* one is indifferent), withdrawing and turning away express the *absence* of any desire to hurt or otherwise affect its object. When someone treats Abelard with contempt, however, they want their withdrawal or turning away from him to be felt by him, precisely as an aversion to him. And there is in this a desire to cause Abelard pain, or at least to bring about states that may be expected to cause him pain.

12.

Condition (e) encourages us to ask whether contempt might be excused, permitted, required even, given that the injury caused by withdrawal can transform its object for the better. On this question, it may be worth asking what would be expected of a virtuous person—the person who is, as Michael Smith puts it, 'especially careful and thoughtful in the formation of their moral beliefs', having 'a demonstrated ability to be open and sensitive to a range of important considerations that others are inclined to overlook'.[37]

We would not expect such a person to treat opportunities to regard others with contempt as he would treat occasions for feeling the heat or the cold: something to which he is merely vulnerable or susceptible, and is hence relatively passive and blameless about feeling it. But nor would we expect him to regard others with contempt in the way that he may regard them with kindness or generosity; something he should be constantly prepared and ready to feel. Perhaps it is not something he must be averse to feeling, like hatred. But nor is it like esteem, something which, in certain circumstances, he should be keen to feel, geared up for. Even less is it like love: something he might justifiably search for, or search for the opportunity to feel.

Part of the reason for this is that regarding or treating others with contempt is to risk making oneself contemptible. One's choice of object alone can make one's contempt contemptible. This seems to have been John of Salisbury's view when he argues that 'contempt for philosophers is the exclusion of everything good'.[38] More generally, contempt is not an attitude with which it is appropriate to become too comfortable. If one says of another that 'contempt is one of his readier emotions', for example, a certain condemnation, however mild, is generally assumed.[39]

It is perhaps difficult to take on a contemptuous attitude without making oneself contemptible. On occasion, to do one just is to do the other. To lie, for example, is often to treat another (the person lied to) with contempt and to make oneself contemptible thereby. The 1622 translation of Psalm 31 captures this symmetry neatly: 'Lying lippes ... which speak grievous things ... contemptuously against the righteous'.[40]

Lying is like self-contempt in this respect. In both cases, the subject becomes the object of contempt. The liar, by treating someone else as the object of contempt, often becomes himself an object of contempt. But this need not be self-conscious in the way required for self-contempt: he need not realize that his action makes him an object of contempt. Sir Philip Sidney was struck by the resulting thought: that a person has no special first-personal authority over what may be contemptible about them. That is why we need comedy in his view. A person may be blind to his own faults, but 'Nothing can more open his eyes, then to see his own actions contemptibly set forth'.[41]

We need not recognize we are contemptible until that fact is manifest in a way that anyone could appreciate. This is worth remarking since feeling contemptible turns also on recognition of what is not necessarily made manifest. It is close here to feeling ashamed, a fact on which the *Geneva Bible* (1557–60) draws in glossing Genesis 38.23. The margin alongside the phrase 'And Iudah said, Let her take it to her, least we bee shamed' contains the elucidation 'become a contempt'.[42]

13.

On occasion, contempt may be something it is not simply natural or excusable but *obligatory* to feel, given what integrity directs us to care about or endorse – obligatory in the sense that to fail to feel it would be a criterion of one's lack of integrity, rather than merely a symptom of its loss. The issues raised by this possibility return us to our starting point, for they fall squarely within the area which Cottingham's work prompts us to investigate: how contempt is related to integrity.

Sophocles' Ajax found himself obliged to regard the gods with contempt for the hand they played in his affairs. It is clear from what he says and does that 'I do not *want* to regard the gods in any other way, and *hence* I cannot but regard them with contempt' does not describe his situation. To suppose him incapable of doing what he did not want to do would wholly change the case, making him weak or feckless in ways in which he is not. It is also clear that he would not subscribe to the self-description: 'I am *unable* to regard the gods in any other way, and *hence* I cannot but regard them with contempt'. It changes the case totally to suppose that his will is just coming into line with his situation; that would make him submissive in ways in which he is evidently not. Rather, he meant something more like 'I neither want nor am able to regard the gods in any other way; I do not want to be able to regard them in any other way, nor to be able to want to regard them in any other way'.[43]

And if we look for an explanation, Sophocles encourages us to appeal to something further back. Given the significance Ajax attaches to various relationships, actions, ways of living, and other matters in ways that define his integrity, he neither wants nor is able to regard the gods in any other way. Responding in this way to the gods is not something we should describe as 'making his life worth living'; nor should we describe its absence as 'making his life *not* worth living'. These phrases imply that his life would be at least *possible* without this response. But this is precisely what he denies. This response is a condition of his being the agent he is; it would not be him if any other response were possible; that another response is possible in a person's life would be sufficient of itself to show that it is not *his* life.

The situation in which Ajax finds himself helps characterize contempt more closely, via its relations with integrity. It tells us something about possibility issues: that contempt and integrity are such that one can feel obliged to react with the former as an expression of the latter. It is not conclusive about value issues: for example, whether one *ought* to have the kind of character which would oblige one, in certain circumstances, to react with contempt as an expression of one's integrity.

There are certainly good reasons to be concerned about so strong a position. These reasons fall into three separate categories, depending on the direction from which they come. Since our investigations in this paper enable us to discriminate these reasons, I will conclude by sketching each category.

The first kind of reason comes from integrity itself. As we have seen, regarding or treating others with contempt is to risk making oneself contemptible. Making oneself contemptible is to lose one's integrity. Hence without due caution, discrimination, and self-control, it will be self-defeating out of *integrity* to regard or treat others with contempt: one stands to lose precisely that from which one acts.

The second kind of reason is roughly characterized as 'moral'. As we have seen, regarding or treating others with contempt involves the intention or desire to cause injury or pain to the object of one's contempt. Intending or desiring to cause injury or pain to others is usually morally impermissible. Hence one's reasons to act as integrity requires risk being declared illegitimate or rendered ineffectual by what morality requires, or vice versa. Without careful limitations on both sides, integrity will conflict with morality.

The third kind of reason is promoted by concerns of a more broadly ethical nature, such as those explored and exploited by virtue ethicists. From this perspective, it may seem that any local conflict between contempt and standard moral theorizing is vastly outweighed by the continuity of one with the other. It may seem, for instance, that contempt is a thoroughly moralized attitude and feeling that it is only possible from within a framework established by moral theorizing. It may even seem, conversely, that moral theory is unthinkable without contempt; that it is only by marshalling contempt for much of what it is to be human and what is the good for human beings that moral theories are able to constrict our view of these matters sufficiently to make their hold on us seem appropriate at all, let alone justified. Hence if integrity requires us to regard or treat others with contempt, and if doing so embeds us further within standard moral theorizing, integrity will conflict with the attempt to cultivate a broader ethics.

These issues are difficult. This is not the occasion to settle them. But I hope to have shown that, if we take integrity as seriously as John Cottingham has advised we should, they are pressing.[44]

Notes

1. Cottingham, 2005, p. 172. Of particular importance to the arguments of this paper are Cottingham's works cited in the bibliography.
2. Kolnai, 1998, p. 82.
3. Strawson, 1982, p. 64.
4. Cottingham, 2005, pp. vii–x; 3.
5. Aristotle (NE: 1124b, 1172a, 1179b), Hume, 1898, 2:1, and 1793, 2:2; Kant, 1797, 6:462–4. The exceptions in recent decades include Brandt, 1946; Solomon, 1993, Ch. 8; Kolnai, 1998 and 2004, pp. 81–4; Hill, 2000, Chs 3, 4; Mason, 2003. But even here the focus is rarely on contempt itself but either on what Kolnai calls 'modes of aversion' more generally (from whose 'standard' cases he excludes contempt), or on questions subsequent to an analysis of contempt, for example whether there are situations in which contempt might be morally permissible or even required. Mason's positive contribution, for example, consists of six conditions which contempt must satisfy to count as 'properly focused and morally justifiable'. But we are in no position to judge the success or otherwise of her endeavour if we are confused about what conditions something must satisfy just to count as contempt simpliciter. Generosity sometimes covers for the absence of necessary specifying work in this area. Thus Mason says, for example, 'I refer to

contempt as an attitude. One might just as easily refer to it as an emotion or feeling' (Mason, 2003, p. 239). Kolnai is only more emphatic when he says contempt is 'pronouncedly a judgement-feeling' (Kolnai, 2004, p. 82).

6. Other concepts produce sentences which call for similar distinctions; for example, 'Abelard is jealous' (see Goldie, 2000, pp. 13–14).
7. Oxford English Dictionary, 1971, p. 895.
8. We retain 'to despise', of course, and the explicit equation with contempt is old. In his translation of Ch. 1, verse 2, of the Book of Obadiah ('Behold, I will make you small among the nations. You will be greatly despised.'), John Wycliffe found it necessary to disguise his gloss as text: 'Thou art ful myche contemptible, or worthi to be dispised' (Oxford English Dictionary, p. 896). It may be that, at that time, contempt-root words stood in need of explication and that 'despise' was the readier to hand.
9. Eliot, 1876, IV, 33.
10. Used regularly and widely, early and late, both in this form (Terence, Lucretius, Sallust, Cicero, Horace) and in the variant *temnere* (Lucretius, Vergil, Horace, Tacitus), all in Lewis and Short, 1886, p. 445.
11. Simple verbal forms do occur in other languages, of course – for example, in German (*verachten*) and French (*mépriser*). But far from being counter-examples, they are further evidence of this explanation. Like 'to despise' in English, these forms preserve accuracy because they are stipulated to have just one of the several possible meanings given above: regarding someone with contempt. Thus when Kant wants to make sure we know his discussion of contempt is not restricted to the 'regarding with' cases, he specifically supplements his use of *verachten* with explicit appeal to the Latin *contemnere* (Kant, 1797, 6:463).
12. Kant, 1797, 6:579–80.
13. Kant, 1797, 6:463.
14. Sofocles, *Ajax*, line 1342, p. 64.
15. Sofocles, *Ajax*, lines 426–7, p. 32.
16. See Brandt, 1946; Hill, 2000, Chs 3 and 4; Mason, 2003.
17. Diderot's letter to Wilkes quoted in Rothschild, 2004, p. 37.
18. Shakespeare, 1606, Act I, scene vii.
19. Eagleton, 2004, pp. 117–9.
20. Shakespeare, 1608, Scene 16, line 67.
21. Shakespeare, 1599, Act 4, Scene 3.
22. It is sometimes suggested that philosophy has a *tendency* towards contempt; that it encourages and in certain polemical circumstances requires that attitude (this is one implication I take from Nozick's observations on philosophizing in the 'Introduction' to his 1981 work, pp. 4–8). The history of the word 'diatribe' reinforces this view: what once referred to the search for reasonable compromise through consensus achieved by even-handed comparison of different opinions (still the predominant meaning in the 16th century when Erasmus wrote *Diatribe on Free Will* of 1524, his appeal for reasonable humanist debate in the fraught years immediately following Luther's break with papal authority), has soured over the course of recent philosophy to mean a bitter invective in which the opponent is regarded, and often treated, with contempt.
23. Beckett, 1986, p. 116.
24. Wittgenstein, 1953, §47.

25. Kant, 1797, 6:463.
26. Kolnai, 1998, p. 82.
27. Mason, 2003, p. 246.
28. Cassian, *De Institutis Coenobiorum*, X, 1–2.
29. Milton, 1667: Book II, lines 1–505, pp. 30–44 and Book IX, lines 1119–89, pp. 238–9.
30. The passage occurs in his shortened 'literal' translation of Aristotle's *Rhetoric* (II. 2). Aristotle himself does not fall into this trap in the passage Hobbes is paraphrasing: 'you feel contempt for what you consider unimportant, and it is just such things that you slight' (1681, p. 2195). The point is that you may consider something unimportant without thinking it unimportant in relation to you.
31. 'Often' because, though withdrawal often does cause pain, and in treating someone with contempt one hopes and intends that it does, the experience of pain need not transform the sufferer; and if it does, that effect need not be intentional – perhaps one does not appreciate the transformative power of pain, or perhaps one treats it as a side effect merely, not part of one's reasons for withdrawing.
32. As Brandt does, 1946, p. 115.
33. Auden, 1991, p. 53.
34. Eliot, 1859, Ch. 1.
35. See Taylor, 1985, pp. 60–1 and Williams, 1993, Ch. 4; pp. 219–23.
36. Mason, 2003, p. 242.
37. Smith, 2004, p. 286.
38. John of Salisbury, 1990, p. 160. Can he really have imagined his philosopher audience needed reminding? His argument, however, is unequal to the conviction: 'If all good things are consequent upon wisdom, and philosophy is the study of wisdom, then surely contempt for philosophers is the exclusion of everything good'.
39. This is how Bernard Williams describes Nietzsche (2001, p. xiv) in a passage that illustrates how mild condemnation may be consistent with a certain admiration.
40. *Oxford English Dictionary*, p. 896.
41. Sidney, 1595, p. 230.
42. *Oxford English Dictionary*, p. 895.
43. Thus the condition of Sophocles' Ajax falls into that category which Harry Frankfurt has labelled 'volitional necessity' (1988, pp. 80–94) and Bernard Williams's 'moral incapacity' (1995, pp. 46–55).
44. For discussion of these issues, I am most grateful to Nafsika Athanassoulis, John Cottingham, Roger Crisp, Brad Hooker, John Hyman, Ellie Mason, Dale Miller, David Oderberg, Brett Price, Michael Rosen, Samantha Vice, Daniel Whiting, and audiences at Old Dominion, Oxford, Reading, and William and Mary.

Bibliography

Aristotle, *Nichomachean Ethics*, trans. Irwin T. (Indianapolis: Hackett, 1985)
Aristotle, *Rhetoric*, trans. Roberts W.R., in *The Complete Works of Aristotle*, II, Barnes J. (ed.) (New Jersey: Princeton University Press, 1984)

Auden W.H., *Collected Poems*, Mendelson E. (ed.) (London: Faber and Faber, 1991)

Beckett S., *The Complete Dramatic Works* (London: Faber and Faber, 1986)

Berkeley G., *Alciphron*, Berman D. (ed.) (London: Routledge, 1993)

Brandt R.B., 'Moral valuation', *Ethics*, 56 (1946) 106–21

Cassian J., *The Institutes*, Ramsey B. (ed.) (New Jersey: Paulist Press, 2000)

Cottingham J., *The Spiritual Dimension* (Cambridge: Cambridge University Press, 2005)

Cottingham J., *Philosophy and the Good Life* (Cambridge: Cambridge University Press, 1998)

Cottingham J., 'The ethical credentials of partiality', *Proceedings of the Aristotelian Society*, XCVIII (1997) 1–21

Cottingham J., 'Partiality and the virtues', in Crisp R. (ed.), *How Should One Live? Essays on the Philosophy of Virtue* (Oxford: Oxford University Press, 1996)

Cottingham J., 'The ethics of self-concern', *Ethics*, 101 (1991) 798–817

Cottingham J., 'Partiality, favouritism and morality', *Philosophical Quarterly*, 36 (1986) 357–73

Cottingham J., 'Ethics and impartiality', *Philosophical Studies*, 43 (1983) 83–9

Eagleton T., *After Theory* (London: Penguin, 2004)

Eliot G., *Daniel Deronda* [1876], Cave T. (ed.) (London: Penguin, 1995)

Eliot G., *Adam Bede* [1859], Gill S. (ed.) (London: Penguin, 1980)

Erasmus D., 'Diatribe on free will' [1524], in Winter E.F. (ed.), *Erasmus and Luther: Discourse on Free Will* (London: Continuum Ltd., 2005)

Frankfurt H., 'The importance of what we care about', in his *The Importance of What We Care About* (Cambridge: Cambridge University Press, 1988)

Goldie P., *The Emotions* (Oxford: Oxford University Press, 2000)

Hill T.E., *Respect, Pluralism and Justice* (Oxford: Oxford University Press, 2000)

Hobbes T., *Aristotle; Treatise on Rhetoric, literally translated from the Greek, with the Analysis by T Hobbes* [1681], Buckley T. (ed.) (London: Henry G. Bohn, 1850)

Hume D., *Enquiry Concerning the Principles of Morals* [1898], Nidditch P.H. (ed.) (Oxford: Oxford University Press, 1975)

Hume D., *A Treatise of Human Nature* [1793], Nidditch P.H. (Oxford: Oxford University Press, 1978)

John of Salisbury, *Policraticus* [1159], trans. and ed. Nederman C.J. (Cambridge: Cambridge University Press, 1990)

Kant I., *The Metaphysics of Morals*, in *Practical Reason* [1797], trans. Gregor M. (Cambridge: Cambridge University Press, 1991)

Kolnai A., 'Disgust', in *On Disgust*, Smith B. and Korsmeyer C. (eds) (Chicago: Open Court, 2004)

Kolnai A., 'The standard modes of aversion: fear, disgust and hatred', *Mind*, 107 (1998) 581–95. Reprinted in *On Disgust*, Smith B. and Korsmeyer C. (ed.) (Chicago: Open Court, 2004)

Lewis C.T. and Short C., *A Latin Dictionary* (Oxford: Oxford University Press, 1886)

Mason M., 'Contempt as a moral attitude', *Ethics*, 113 (2003) 234–72

Milton J., *Paradise Lost* [1667], Orgel S. and Goldberg J. (eds) (Oxford: Oxford University Press, 2004

Nozick R., *Philosophical Explanations* (Cambridge, Mass: Harvard University Press, 1981)

Oxford English Dictionary, Compact Edition, Simpson J. (chief editor) (Oxford: Oxford University Press, 1971)

Procopius, *The Secret History* (London: Penguin, 1981)

Rothschild E., 'Empire beware!' *The New York Review of Books*, 25 March 2004, p. 37

Shakespeare W., *King Lear* [1608], Wells S. (ed.) (Oxford: Oxford University Press, 2000)

Shakespeare W., *Macbeth* [1606], Brooke N. (Oxford: Oxford University Press, 1998)

Shakespeare W., *Henry V* [1599], Taylor G. (ed.) (Oxford: Oxford University Press, 1998)

Sidney, Sir Philip, 'The Defence of Poesy', in *Sir Philip Sidney: The Major Works* [1595] Duncan-Jones K. (ed.) (Oxford: Oxford University Press, 1989)

Smith M., *Ethics and the A priori* (Cambridge: Cambridge University Press, 2004)

Solomon R.C., *The Passions: Emotions and the Meaning of Life* (Indianapolis: Hackett, 1993)

Sophocles, *Ajax* [409 BC], trans. Watling E.F. (London: Penguin, 1953)

Strawson P., 'Freedom and resentment', in *Free Will*, Watson G. (ed.) (Oxford: Oxford University Press, 1982)

Taylor G., *Pride, Shame and Guilt* (Oxford: Oxford University Press, 1985)

Williams B., 'Introduction', in Nietzsche F., *The Gay Science*, Williams B. (ed.) (Cambridge: Cambridge University Press, 2001)

Williams B., 'Moral incapacity', in his *Making Sense of Humanity* (Cambridge: Cambridge University Press, 1995)

Williams B., *Shame and Necessity* (London: University of California Press, 1993)

Wittgenstein L., *Philosophical Investigations* [1953], trans. Anscombe G.E.M., (Oxford: Blackwell, 2001, 3rd edn)

3
Self-Love, Love of Neighbour, and Impartiality

David S. Oderberg

1. Introduction

In an important and widely discussed series of papers, John Cottingham has defended a 'partialist' ethic against supporters of 'impartialism'.[1] The main theme of these papers is that what have come to be called particularistic obligations and permissions based on special relationships are the ineradicable and justified core of morality. These special relationships are said to begin with one's relationship to oneself – self-love, or *philautia* to use the Aristotelian term employed by Cottingham.[2] They then radiate outwards, to family, friends, and other social and communal groupings such as associations of various kinds (professional, recreational, and the like), geographical and political communities (civic bodies, one's country), and ultimately to all of humanity.[3]

This basic structure of moral preferences is, in my view, fundamentally correct, at least insofar as relationships among humans are concerned.[4] It has been a signal contribution to ethics by Cottingham to have underlined its importance, sought to give it a theoretical justification, clarified common misconceptions concerning what the structure entails, and refuted some of the most important objections to it coming from the camp of those who, following the current terminology, support a broadly impartialistic ethic. The terminology of 'partialist' and 'impartialist' is itself somewhat misleading though (as others have pointed out[5]), and I hope to dispel some of the confusions in the following discussion. On the more substantive questions – the nature, scope, and justification of partialistic preferences – there are, side by side with Cottingham's many correct points, a number of crucial positions he espouses with which a partialist ought to disagree, and others where expansion and clarification are called for. I will explore this in what follows, though a more detailed account of the specific moral problems raised by various partialistic relationships will be for another occasion. The present discussion is intended as a contribution to what must be an ongoing debate among moral philosophers, one which Cottingham is to be commended for having stimulated; a debate which, in the age of 'globalization', is more needed than ever.

2. The basis of self-love

Why is it that morality provides – to some extent, and with caveats and exceptions – that a person may, and in some respects must, exercise a preference for himself over others, for his own activities, commitments, and projects over those of other people? Why, in general, must I be more concerned with my own situation in life than with my neighbour's?[6] Why should I be more worried about whether I am doing my job properly than about whether my neighbour is doing his? About whether I can pay my bills more than about my neighbour's financial situation? Whether I am providing for my own family more than whether my colleague is providing for his? Why should I spend far more time and effort developing my own character than fretting over whether the person over the road is developing hers, or whether her character is good or bad?

The sphere of self-preference involves both permissions and obligations. I am permitted to offer Fred across the road the chance to taste the latest red wine I have acquired for my cellar. If Fred knocks on my door, parched and begging for water, I am obliged in charity to give him something to drink. If Albert and Bill are sitting an exam, and both are tempted to cheat, Albert is not obliged for one second to worry about what Bill might do but is under a strict duty to talk himself out of cheating first (and vice versa). In this latter case self-obsession is a positive obligation. Is this primarily a matter of psychological reality? For Cottingham, it appears that it is. Discussing the impartialism of William Godwin, according to which an agent's preferences must be directed at those who 'will be most conducive to the general good',[7] he asks rhetorically whether 'such an ethical blueprint ... is psychologically possible'. Personal affections and ties are 'an unavoidable part of what it is to be a human being'.[8] Again, '[w]hat empirical evidence we have suggests that transcending the ties of partiality is an enormously difficult process'; and '[i]n short, if ethics is sensitive, as it surely must be, to facts about what most people are capable of, the ethics of impartality is, prima facie, in deep trouble.'[9] Many similar passages can be found throughout Cottingham's writings on the subject.

This is not the only way in which Cottingham justifies partialist morality, but it is the principal one. There are others, one based on a view of perspectives within which ethics can legitimately be done, and another which is metaphysical in character and appeals to a more robust view of human nature. They introduce an ambiguity and unclarity into his argument, and I will return to them in section 4. For the moment, and restricting the issue to self-preference – what Cottingham calls 'agent-related partialism' and 'self-directed partialism'[10] – the emphasis on what is psychologically possible or realistic leaves it open, as Cottingham himself realizes, that a person *might* be capable of surmounting what is 'deeply ingrained' and of achieving a life of 'sainthood'.[11] But ought not all of us aspire to sainthood? Even if we cannot achieve it, must we not admire it and encourage it in those who seem capable of achieving it? If so, how can it be that at the same time we should believe that 'some degree of self-preference is morally desirable', not merely permissible?[12] How can a course of action be both morally desirable and yet such that we admire those who renounce it?

The most that Cottingham offers to loosen this apparent tension is to say that although we do not need 'to disparage sainthood or deny its existence' in order to defend self-preference, we must acknowledge that 'for most people, for most of the time', the 'autocentric perspective is ... all but impossible to transcend'. For the impartialist to legislate such transcendence for the 'mass of mankind' is a 'blatant violation of the maxim that ought implies can'.[13] Yet this will not do: not only is it incoherent morally, but it is to misunderstand the very nature of sainthood. The incoherence lies in supposing that a common ethic of self-preference should be supplemented by a moral ideal of true impartiality whereby an agent works to 'free himself from the bonds of selfhood'.[14] How can morality consist of a set of norms for the mass of mankind yet be overlaid by an ideal that is completely *at odds* with what those norms require? It is to treat the saint not as a person who follows par excellence the precepts that govern all of us and which the vast bulk of us obey only imperfectly; it is to place the saint in a wholly different species of agent, as though she were not *one of us* – an exemplar for mankind. Hence we can, without appealing to any specific conception of sainthood bequeathed to us by religious tradition, see that there is an argument in favour of thinking of the saint in a certain way – one that preserves a kind of *continuity* between the norms governing the mass of mankind, given our nature, and those governing the saint. The norms are in fact the *same*, though the saint follows them par excellence.

Moreover, we can see from religious tradition itself that the saint is not a person who transcends the life of self-preference in favour of one fully devoted to serving an impersonal general good. He is precisely the opposite: the saint is a person who takes the care of his *own* soul so seriously that he reaches a level of moral perfection to which the rest of us should aspire yet which we rarely meet. And the way in which this care of self – a kind of total and unflinching self-preference – manifests itself is not in devotion to an impersonal good, but first in the cultivation of a character that guarantees the saint will reach ultimate happiness or beatitude, and secondly (something inextricably linked to the first) in a love for others – a care of their souls – that takes those others *one at a time*, as individuals, rooted in their particular circumstances, and situated in highly particular relations to the saint. That the saint may choose to do what he does in his own city or in the wilds of Borneo is of no great significance. He is no utility maximizer, seeking whatever is 'most conducive to the general good', but a person who seeks to lead other individuals, one soul at a time, to their ultimate happiness – in whatever particular circumstances he and they may find themselves. These may involve many prior obligations and commitments which the saint is still duty-bound to perform, and many special relationships from which he can escape only on pain of serious wrongdoing. If he has the latitude to choose Borneo over Bournemouth, and is inclined to do so, then so he may. But he is under no obligation, and *sees himself* as under no obligation, to make some sort of contribution to an illusory, impersonal greater good. Now it is true that I am speaking primarily of the Christian conception of sanctity – the tradition to which Cottingham pays most attention. There may be differing conceptions in other traditions, but at least where the major monotheistic religions are concerned, to the extent that the non-Christian traditions have a conception of sanctity, it is of a piece with the Christian one.[15]

At the level of what is psychologically possible for most of us, Cottingham's observations are true enough: the brute fact is that most of us are, and always have been, constitutionally unable to reach the moral heights of the saint. Yet it is still an ideal to which we must all aspire, and history shows that sainthood can emerge in the most unlikely of cases and situations. Yet whatever the psychological realities, the spectrum from sinner to saint never deviates from the path of self-preference or self-love. Only a full-blooded theory of the good can explain why.

So why should anyone love themselves in the first place? And why should they love anyone else? Remember that what we are concerned with is not self-love as 'rank egoism' or selfishness,[16] nor a love of others that might be called concupiscence – love of another for your own sake, that is, for whatever pleasure or usefulness they have for you. Our concern is with genuine benevolence or charity, whereby one wishes the good of a person for that person's own sake, because they are capable of being good and pursuing the good, and you want them to be and pursue the good, and to help them where possible. Now if a person (*A*) has this attitude of benevolence to another (*B*), then the relation of charity between them will be a kind of partnership or union. Person *B* wants to pursue the good and be good; person *A* wants this for *B* as well, and to help him. Yet *A* also (ex hypothesi) wants to be and pursue the good. But the relation he has to himself is evidently not one of partnership – it is one of identity. So the basic reason *A* has to want the good for *B*,[17] namely that there is a kind of union or partnership between them in the pursuit of the good, must, *logically*, be outweighed by the reason *A* has to want the good for himself, namely that he has a nearness to himself outstripping all others – for nothing is as close as identity. Another way of putting it is to say that the very reason a person has for loving another is at the same time the reason he has for loving himself more.[18] This structure of motivation applies to the saint no less than anyone else.[19]

Here is another way of thinking about the necessity of self-preference, closely related to the argument just given. Charity is more than *mere* benevolence. Wishes are admirable but cheap. True charity requires beneficence as well: as we all know, actions speak louder than words (and much louder than thoughts). So in order truly to love someone, a person needs at the very least to be disposed to act concretely towards the person loved, in a way intended and likely to protect and promote[20] that person's good. But it is only rational to act (or be disposed to act) in such a way to the extent that one has some amount of realistic *control* over whether the good of the person loved is protected and promoted. To be disposed to do good to a person and yet have no realistic prospect of making any difference to that person's good[21] is irrational; or if not irrational, then it is insincere or hypocritical – perhaps a kind of 'babbling', as Cottingham, echoing Aristotle's discussion of akrasia, puts it in respect of impartialists who perforce do not live up to the norms of their own position.[22] Yet we can see immediately that *whatever* control one may have over the good of another, one must have *more* over one's own good. Can we think of an even remotely plausible scenario where one has more control over the good of another than one has over one's own good? Moreover, what else is there to motivate the degree of love one has for a person other than that (a) they are a person (and so capable of being good and pursuing the good) and (b) one has some amount of control over the ways and extent to which that person is and pursues the good? It follows, then, since one necessarily has the most control over one's own good, that one *must*, on pain of irrationality, love oneself to a greater degree than one loves anyone else, however close they may be. Self-love, then, in its priority of degree over love of another is a *rational* obligation.[23]

3. 'Love thy neighbour as thyself'

It is impossible to consider love of neighbour without discussing the very context in which it is rooted, namely that of Christianity.[24] I make no apology for this, first because of the enormous influence the Christian precept of neighbour-love has had over the centuries on ethical debate in Western philosophy, and secondly because Cottingham himself gives it extensive attention in his papers on partiality. As to the first point, I note in particular the extent to which even the most secular or unbelieving of moral philosophers have developed their ideas – usually impartialistic – out of the Christian precept. Typically they seek a non-religious, wholly secular conception of neighbour-love sufficient to replace the religious doctrine for an age in which no religion, especially not Christianity, acts as a norm of behaviour for the majority of people.[25] As to the second point, I note the consistent antipathy Cottingham displays towards the Christian precept of neighbour-love. I want to focus on this latter issue, and will argue that it is born of a serious misunderstanding of what the precept amounts to. Whether Cottingham still holds to this (mis)interpretation is another matter. I will return to the first point later in this section.

What does the injunction to love thy neighbour amount to, on the standard interpretation given to it by theologians and Christian philosophers over the centuries? It is quite clear that my neighbour is any human being, without distinction.[26] It is simply in virtue of sharing a common nature than every one of us is bound to love every other; in theological terms, we are all made in the image of God. Yet this is only the starting point for moral reflection, not the terminus. First, we must note that the love of all human beings could not possibly involve a love of *unqualified* beneficence, since we cannot do good, or even be disposed to do good, to every human being simpliciter.[27] Cottingham is quite right about the necessarily limited resources we have for doing good to others, an obvious fact when considering friendship.[28]

Secondly, however, the same point about limited resources does not apply to the love of benevolence: it would be curious to argue that we are not psychologically capable of unqualifiedly *wanting* the good for every human being,[29] as though doing so would induce in us a kind of mental exhaustion. Yet wouldn't Cottingham's strictures against insincerity and babbling apply? No, because his criticism is directed against impartialists for whom universal love is a norm of *action*, not of attitude; as he says, 'there must be some connection between the holding of a moral principle and the *actions* of those who hold it',[30] where the context makes clear that the principle concerned is one of sacrificing my particular interests and relationships for the sake of global utility. His accusation hits the mark, but the precept of universal, unqualified benevolence is untouched.

Thirdly, given that beneficence cannot apply globally in an unqualified way, and given that the general precept of loving one's neighbour includes beneficence, it follows that to *that* extent love of neighbour cannot apply globally in an unqualified way. So to whom does it apply? Again, the standard – and quite plausible – view is that it applies to those in need, by a kind of moral law of gravitation (to put the point metaphorically but vividly). That is to say, the closer the relationship and the more severe the need, the greater the obligation of charity – but the idea needs unpacking. The obligation involves both action and attitude. Overlying the wholly general and equal benevolence for all human beings is an unequal benevolence based on the psychological reality of degrees of closeness and the constitutional limitations on a person's spreading their affections over every other person without distinction. Again, on this Cottingham is right. Moreover, it is not just a question of affection but of natural limitations on meaningful ties, whether it be to physical proximates, town, city, community, club, political organization, country, and so on. Psychological integrity demands that the dispositions to action on the part of an agent must bear some fairly close relation to the attitudes the agent has, or could realistically have, to the potential object of the action. We would think a man very odd who said to himself: 'I love all people equally. I love my wife too – she's a person, after all. But because she is my wife, my beneficence is primarily directed at her.'[31] Beneficence and benevolence cannot come apart altogether. A person wants to do well by a proximate precisely *because* he loves her in particular or has some other particular positive attitude or affection towards her, no matter how thin it might be.

In what way does the parable of the Good Samaritan[32] suggest anything different from what has just been outlined? None, as far as I can see. The Jew went down from Jerusalem to Jericho. Having been assaulted by robbers and left for dead, he was passed in the street by two of his own race – a Priest and a Levite – who ignored him. The Samaritan, however – not of his own race – 'came near him, and seeing him was moved with compassion' (my emphasis).[33] And Christ asks the lawyer (who posed the question 'who is my neighbour?') which of the three was the neighbour to the victim, to which the lawyer correctly replied, 'he who showed mercy to him'. The message is clear. The Priest and Levite were what we might call 'default proximates' by virtue of various communal ties – blood, racial, religious, country. The Samaritan was outside all of these, but he became a proximate as soon as he was, like the other two, physically close and in a position to help. The victim was in need, and the person who was not a default proximate was both willing and able to exercise beneficence. Note the use of words in the parable such as 'came near', 'seeing', 'moved': we are not concerned here with a person thinking the abstract and precious thought, 'whom might I help today?' but with someone who passively became a proximate through simply passing by, and then actively involved himself in the victim's plight. Needless to say, by calling the Samaritan the neighbour among the three, Christ was not implying that the other two were in *no* way neighbours; from the point of view of proximity, they were as much neighbours to the victim as the Samaritan. The true *neighbourliness*, however, was exercised by the latter.

So it is clear from the Parable of the Good Samaritan that loving one's neighbour, at least according to the Christian understanding, requires acting in particular circumstances towards particular people with whom one is in some relation of proximity. The proximity need have no passive element: the aid worker who *chooses* to travel to the wilds of Borneo to provide medical care for people she has never met, and never would have known anything about but for her choice, still exercises the virtue of neighbour-love, even though the proximity is self-imposed. (If doing this involved wrongful treatment of her own nearest and dearest, of course, she would *not* be exercising such a virtue, she would rather be doing good to some at the expense of others to whom she had a more serious obligation. So says the partialist, and I agree.) Moreover, the differential beneficence shown to others must, as I have argued, be grounded on differential benevolence; we can safely assume that the Samaritan, *moved* by the plight of the victim, felt a far more intense love and desire to help him than he felt for the Priest, the Levite, or anyone else who happened to be passing by at the time.

If differential benevolence and beneficence, then, are to co-exist with *equal* love for all human beings, since neighbour means 'every person without distinction', we have to say something like the following.

The injunction to 'love thy neighbour *as* thyself' (my emphasis) must – as far as the qualification 'as thyself' goes – refer only to *manner*, not to *measure*.[34] As far as benevolence goes, it must mean that we ought to want the same generic good for ourselves and for all of our fellow human beings without distinction or qualification. As far as beneficence goes, it must mean that we ought to have a *disposition* to do good to others that is qualitatively equal in respect of those others and equal to my disposition to do good to myself. But this disposition *must* be subject to qualification: that our general inclination to do good to ourselves and others in equal *manner* is also an inclination to do good in unequal *measure*, depending on which relations of proximity we are in with respect to other people, where the measure is also governed by the severity of the need of those who are our proximates. Further, that differential beneficence must be grounded (at least in usual cases) in a benevolence that is also unequal in intensity or measure. Finally, for reasons I have already given, the intensity or measure of benevolence and beneficence one has towards oneself will and must be greater than one has towards other people.[35]

Yet despite this fairly standard understanding of what the precept of neighbour-love amounts to, it is not the one Cottingham espouses, and throughout his writings on impartiality we find disparaging references to what he regards as a precept positively inimical to an agent's psychological and emotional integrity. Perhaps things go wrong at the very beginning, when Cottingham relies – unwisely – on the explicit link drawn by utilitarians such as Godwin and, latterly, Peter Singer, between the maxim of utility and the precept of loving one's neighbour as oneself.[36] It is simply incorrect, albeit rhetorically useful, for a utilitarian to equate any kind of principle of utility with the Christian precept of neighbour-love. The principle of utility is not even a legitimate development of the precept for a secular age; it is a *replacement* for it. If the interpretation of the precept I gave above is correct, then one can see on its face how loving thy neighbour as thyself has nothing to do with utilitarianism or any other kind of consequentialism.

Having accepted the exegetical move made by Godwin and his followers, however, Cottingham goes on to tell us: 'Even a little reflection on the precise implications of loving one's neighbour *as oneself* shows that it represents a grotesquely impracticable conception of morality', and he follows Mackie in calling it the 'ethics of fantasy'.[37] It is doubtful, he wonders, whether anyone who 'seriously attempted' to live by the precept 'could survive as a person, as a whole individual, at all'.[38] Such a person would 'risk ceasing to be a whole human being ... risk losing [their] human integrity and individuality'.[39] Again, not only is disparagement of self-preference in favour of the 'life of universal *agapē*' hypocritical, but 'taking seriously the injunction to love one's neighbour as oneself would be incompatible with an enormous range of ordinary, intuitively quite legitimate, human pursuits ... The contrast between Aristotelian *philia* (friend-love, personal love) and Christian *agapē* (neighbour-love, universal love) is instructive here'.[40] Cottingham tells us that '[t]he Christian injunction to love your neighbour ... as yourself seems to presuppose something impossible: that the sense of special concern which is the hallmark of genuine personal relationships could somehow retain its strength when indefinitely diluted to extend to all humans.'[41]

What does Cottingham recommend instead of Christian neighbour-love? He splits Aristotelian ethics off from its supposedly specious medieval development and commends to us a return to the healthy pagan virtues described by Aristotle. Hence in a section explicitly titled 'The Christian Tradition Versus Aristotle',[42] he takes 'duty to self' in Christian teaching to be 'very much at the bottom of the list, below duty to God and neighbour'.[43] Yet as we have seen, the position of self and neighbour is exactly reversed in the proper understanding of the precept: one is duty-bound to love, first God, then oneself as made in the image of God, then one's neighbour – for God's sake, as also made in the image of God and with whom one is partner in the task of obtaining happiness. (Why must one love one's neighbour for God's sake? Because if we rely on our neighbour-love's being motivated by something agreeable about our neighbour, our love will find itself somewhat faltering. Cottingham may show a touch of sympathy for Hume and the sentimentalist tradition in British ethics, but he also appreciates how little sentimentalism can gain for us when it comes to love of others.)

Instead we must, says Cottingham, 'move back to a pre-Christian perspective', replacing Christ's command to us to 'be perfect'[44] with the 'more down-to-earth slogan of the Aristotelians', which is 'nothing to excess'.[45] The Doctrine of the Mean is to replace the requirement to love one's neighbour, because to follow the latter – in particular as embodied in the Christian saint – is 'lacking in that balanced sense of moderate self-esteem that is necessary for a fulfilled human life'.[46] Yet as I observed earlier, in the same paper Cottingham asserts that adopting his Aristotelian, autocentric perspective does *not* entail disparaging sainthood! It seems that Cottingham does see a problem in the very idea of a person who is 'maximally altruistic, and who (as Jesus himself did) gives up everything for his fellow man'.[47]

Moreover, his reinterpretation of the precept of neighbour-love along pagan lines turns a norm of charity into a norm of justice. For having taken on a misinterpretation of the precept, he then proposes that we avoid its unwelcome implications by adopting a more moderate, partly negative maxim owing more to Polemarchus than to Jesus: 'help your friends, and do not harm your neighbours' is a 'promising first attempt at a minimal definition of morality', where 'neighbour' can be construed globally.[48] Remove the original misinterpretation and one hopes the motivation for taking on this far narrower precept would disappear; but not because Cottingham's pagan reinterpretation has much in common even with the *properly interpreted* Christian maxim. This is because the hallmark of differentiation between justice and charity is that the duties of justice are primarily negative (apart from the fulfilment of agreements, contracts, promises, and so on) and those of charity primarily positive. 'Do not harm your neighbours' is precisely a demand of justice, not of charity. It reminds one of the famous remarks of Lord Atkin in the celebrated negligence case of *Donoghue v. Stevenson*:

> The rule that you are to love your neighbour becomes in law, you must not injure your neighbour; and the lawyer's question, Who is my neighbour? receives a restricted reply. You must take reasonable care to avoid acts or omissions which you can reasonably foresee would be likely to injure your neighbour.[49]

Now Lord Atkin goes on to gloss 'neighbour' in a more restricted way than Cottingham, framing the issue in terms of reasonable foresight. Nevertheless, Cottingham's more global gloss cannot turn a precept of justice into one of charity. His neo-pagan maxim obliges nothing positive in respect of my neighbour – no benevolence, no beneficence (qualified or not), no general attitude of *friendliness* to those not in need, and no gratitude for the kindness of strangers (also a matter of charity, not justice).[50] How any kind of charity is supposed to fit in with, or justifiably be added to, this minimal negative precept is itself not clear. Nor is it easy to see what basis is left even for the special feelings and preferences I have for my *friends*: the justification I offered above, on the standard interpretation of 'love thy neighbour', is based on a recognition that general benevolence and beneficence still must vary by *degree* in proportion to relations of proximity. But if the general attitude and disposition of neighbour-love is removed, as it is from Cottingham's reinterpretation, then what *rational* ground is there even for *loving* my friends, let alone preferring them over strangers? It can't be that my friends are human beings just like me, since so are strangers, yet they are excluded by Cottingham from any duty of charity. Can it be simply that they are my friends? But this won't do, because the question will now be: *why* are they my friends? Is it pure sentiment? Is it that they give me pleasure or are useful? Neither of these, as we know from Aristotle, is a basis for true friendship. With a general duty of love for others removed from the obligations of charity, it is hard to see what is left. If I am not bound positively to love all my fellow human beings, then the very *reason* for loving my own friends seems to vanish in favour of pure sentimentalism, whose limits Cottingham himself recognizes.[51] Moreover, why should a person even love themselves? Because they like or 'feel good' about themselves? Yet we know how fickle such sentiments can be. It seems Cottingham's reinterpretation of the maxim of charity is self-defeating.

Since Cottingham misinterprets what love of neighbour amounts to in the Christian tradition, this undercuts the very ground in which he fastens the supposed 'unmistakable logical implication about the nature of virtue' in Christianity, namely that it can be expressed as a 'linear function'.[52] He has no warrant for asserting that according to Christian virtue theory (one part of its overall ethic), for any kind of virtuous conduct or emotion, the more of that conduct or emotion the better; and that as the agent ascends in goodness via increased virtuous action and feeling, so he commensurately leaves self-concern behind. For since, according to Christianity, the aim of every person is to achieve ultimate happiness (by saving their own soul), so the increase in virtue could not *possibly* entail the abandonment of self-concern. If what I said earlier about the perfect self-concern of the saint is correct, the exact opposite is true. Moreover, it is an oversimplification for Cottingham to contrast his Christian linear function with a parabolic function supposed to represent the Doctrine of the Mean in Aristotelian ethics.[53] It is not merely a question of how *Aristotle* viewed the doctrine, but of how one should *reasonably* view it. It could not possibly be, for one thing, that the apex of virtue is as Cottingham represents it, with excess and deficiency symmetrically mapped on either side, in what looks like equal measure. If we know anything about what Aristotle thought about ethics, we know he disparaged any such quasi-mathematical interpretation of virtue and vice,[54] and in this he is surely correct.

More importantly, though, to represent Christian virtue as a linear function leaves no room for any kind of vice of deficiency, and this too is wrong. Since everyone is bound to give preference to their own good – not their own material welfare, or their own possessions, or their own pleasure, but, in the fullest and most morally loaded sense of the term, their own *good* – a person who acts in such a way as intentionally or otherwise culpably to neglect their own good is guilty precisely of a vice of deficiency, indeed the ultimate in bad conduct. In ordinary circumstances, everyone is bound in charity to look after their own health and bodily well-being. If Joe were to decide one day simply to hand over all his food to his next-door neighbour, or to a stranger in the street, with the result that Joe simply faded away from starvation, then even if we could interpret this as sane behaviour, it would certainly be a vice of deficiency, tantamount to suicide. (Aristotle would probably regard it as an excess, but from the Christian viewpoint it is probably better to regard it as a deficiency with respect to care of one's own well-being.) What if Joe were an aid worker whose specific job it was to distribute food to the starving? Then it might be an obligation of his very state in life to hand over even his own food; at least it would be to carry out a counsel of perfection, as such behaviour is often called in Christian theology.[55] But even Joe in his special state of life, or others who are under obligations of charity that exceed those normally imposed on agents, can be guilty of excess and deficiency. Joe might have an excess of zeal that causes him to neglect other duties; he might despair of being able to help as many people as he would like – such would be a deficiency of hope and confidence in his own work. Whether one should take any specific example, so many of which are all too common even in the least religiously inclined of people, to be a species of excess or of deficiency would require too much analysis for the confines of this discussion. The point is that such falling away from virtue is as well known in the Christian tradition as it is in pagan, other theistic, and secular traditions.

So it could not possibly be that the sort of 'emptying out' of one's self for others of which the New Testament and the behaviour of the saints speak so eloquently (and of which behaviour the Passion of Christ is the exemplar) is to be modelled as a linear function where more is always better. It is not simply that at some point self-sacrifice in most situations is a counsel of perfection and not an obligation (which would suggest, if one were to persist, somewhat dangerously, with lines and graphs, an asymptotic tapering off rather than a straight line as depicted by Cottingham).[56] It is that the unconditional, absolute obligation of seeking one's own good imposes clear, impassable obstacles in the path of one who would sacrifice everything for another, no matter how near and no matter what the severity of need. So Aquinas states the common understanding of love of neighbour when he makes it clear that although a person should bear injuries for her friend's sake, she may *never* commit a sin in order to benefit her neighbour, even if it is to free her neighbour from sin.[57] To put the matter non-theologically, no one may do wrong to benefit their neighbour. Call it an excess of giving if you like, or a deficiency of self-concern, or (better) both; but such behaviour, on the standard Christian understanding of these things, is unqualifiedly wrong and vicious. No saint literally 'gives up all for others', as Cottingham describes it;[58] for no saint gives up her own soul for others. Certainly, 'to the Aristotelian way of thinking',[59] that is what saintly behaviour can look like, so Cottingham is right inasmuch as from the point of view of pagan virtue[60] such behaviour appears to lack 'that balanced sense of moderate self-esteem that is necessary for a fulfilled human life'.[61] But that does not show Christian ethics to have overthrown the Aristotelian perspective, as any glance at the shelves of commentary by theologians such as Aquinas on Aristotle's ethics testifies. Rather, Christian ethics built on Aristotelianism, jettisoning some parts and retaining others. There is no glib contrast to be had between a linear and a parabolic function. The model cannot be arithmetical, nor can it be simple. The Doctrine of the Mean most certainly survives in the Christian tradition, but how it is to be interpreted, and what its place is in the space of virtue theory, cannot be explored here.

4. The 'God's-eye point of view'

If it were merely a question of how properly to interpret the precept 'love thy neighbour as thyself', we would not get much beyond exegetical and theological niceties. These should be of interest to any ethicist, theistic or not, since secular ethics, as I have already intimated, defines itself either in opposition to or as a development of ethics as rooted in the Christian tradition.

The issues go beyond mere interpretation, however, and suggest a more worrying thread in Cottingham's writings on impartiality. This concerns the kind of *justification* available for partialistic relations, which in turn is connected to the metaphysical – or perhaps better in Cottingham's case, arguable lack of metaphysical – foundations of a morality that allows and obliges agents to engage in certain kinds of preferential treatment of themselves and others, at the same time as obliging them to espouse a universal benevolence, and a universal but qualified beneficence, towards all human beings without distinction.

Cottingham's considered, overall position seems to be that it is vain to hope for an objective, external justification for ethical partialism. Note that I do not say an 'impartial' justification, because although he opposes this as well, it is in fact a separate and less important issue, for all that the two tend to be conflated in his writings. We can dispense with the second in fairly short order. Cottingham's scepticism towards any impartialist justification of partialistic preference is in my view quite correct, at least if we confine ourselves to those interpretations of impartiality that are his main targets. There can be no justification in terms of impartiality understood as global utility.[62] For all Godwin's later backsliding over whether one should save one's wife (father, and so on) rather than the great Fénelon, he never gives up on the view that the *right* thing to do is to save the author of the immortal *Telemachus*, even if, on subsequent reflection, he seems to think that a person might not be *blamed* for saving his wife instead, and if, as some commentators have suggested, Godwin ultimately opts for a more 'sophisticated consequentialist' position or toys with a kind of rule utilitarianism.[63] Further, the attempt to construct a Kantian-style justification in terms of universalizability, formal consistency, the rational will, or autonomy, will yield something too thin and insubstantial to justify an autocentric perspective with its subtle panoply of complex, multidimensional personal relations.[64]

Where, for Cottingham, does this leave the prospects for justifying partial preferences? This brings me to his ostensible scepticism about any external or objective justification. He brings out his worries in several ways. One is to amplify what I have charged is his misinterpretation of the Christian precept of neighbour-love, by asserting that 'the Christian moralist aspires, in effect, to adopt the perspective of God himself', whereby 'any clinging to the remnants of self-love, however understandable and "natural", represents a kind of failure – a falling away from the highest duty of mankind.'[65] Yet he adduces no evidence of any such view on the part of philosophers and theologians who have interpreted the precept. It simply does not follow from the mandatory aspiration to perfection that one must adopt the 'God's-eye view' of things. On the contrary, since God is equally concerned with the salvation of all souls, whereas for the individual the salvation of his own soul must be his primary objective, for the reasons explained above, it cannot be that humans must adopt the perspective of God Himself, even on the false assumption that they *can*.

In addition, it might be that Cottingham implicitly equates the God's-eye perspective with a consequentialist one, and that this is why he rejects it. In other words, he might think that Christian morality requires adopting the God's-eye viewpoint, but since this viewpoint is consequentialist or maximizing, the follower of such morality is bound to an ultimately impartialist ethic, which is unacceptable. But even if this is what he has in mind, there is no reason to think, and every reason to deny, that any such viewpoint is what the follower of the precept 'love thy neighbour' is supposed to aspire to. The very idea that God is in some sense a maximizer, and that since the follower of Christian morality is bound to imitate God she is therefore obliged to be a conse quentialist, has too many non sequiturs and absurdities in it to list here. On the other hand, if Cottingham understands by the God's-eye point of view the transcendence of self and adoption of a vantage point from which the good of the individual agent's soul is but one among many, then this too is simply not part of what adherence to the precept of neighbour-love entails.

In short, the failure of a utility-based justification of partiality does not of itself militate against other kinds of objective, external justification. And it doubly muddies the waters for the partialist to tie Christian neighbour-love to the God's-eye point of view, and then to think of that point of view as incoherent or unacceptable for being consequentialist or otherwise inconsistent with partialistic preference. For it gives the false impression that any attempt, as it were, to step outside the framework of our special relationships in order to give them an objective foundation is ultimately self-defeating. I will now explore the issue of justification at greater length.

5. Inside-out ethics, levels of justification, and natural law

The principal way in which Cottingham broaches the issue of justification is by his repeated assertion that we can only build our ethics 'from the inside outwards'.[66] The phrase is somewhat obscure, but other statements give it some flesh: since we live, he thinks (at least when he wrote these words in 1997) in a 'post-Nietzschean cosmos, with no divine creator looking down on the planet ... there is a sense in which we need instead to create our own values, from our own resources'. This means that 'the search for detached sources of value is not just a *philosophical* mistake ... it is also a mistake which distorts our everyday understanding of what gives human life worth and meaning'. Rather, if we are to 'give richness and meaning to the short journey each of us has to undergo', we must see that 'we ourselves generate that worth and significance by the intensely personal commitments and preferential networks of mutual interdependence to which we wholeheartedly devote ourselves'.[67] Elsewhere, he says that 'each of us must construct the blueprint for fulfilment from the inside outwards, by using our reason to reflect on the best pattern for a worthwhile life';[68] and, on the Aristotelian autocentric view of human fulfilment, 'the working out of the activities that generate or constitute such fulfillment is taken to be a task which falls within the autonomous control of each individual human being'.[69]

There are some hints of what I submit to be the proper way of looking at these things in the above passages and their general context; taken as a whole, though, the picture they paint is worrying, and not just for a theist. For what they suggest is that the autocentric point of view can only be justified – if such would even be a justification – by an essentially subjective process of discernment with no underwriting by truths that transcend the perspective of the agent 'constructing the blueprint for fulfilment'. One does not have to be a partisan of global utility-style justifications of partiality, or of appeals to consistency, universalizability, and the like, to see that appealing to an 'inside-out' conception of the good life is insufficient for showing why a structure of partial preferences commends itself to *all* agents at all times and places, no matter what the contingencies of social setting, historical condition, or psychological and emotional disposition. Why is it that every person *must* strictly prefer their own good – not necessarily, to repeat, their own material welfare, or their own pleasure, or their own short-term interests – to that of anyone else, no matter how close or beloved? Why in some cases *may* they prefer the good of proximates to those of strangers, whereas in other cases they *must*? (I am not concerned with, or able to explore here, when the agent is permitted and when they are obligated; it is enough to note that there is such a distinction, as Cottingham and other partialists readily accept.) Why, if an agent is free to construct her own blueprint for a fulfilling life free of any 'impersonally defined rules of conduct',[70] is it *not* permissible for a person to prefer his proximates over strangers in any and every case – or even to commit what would otherwise be blatant wrongs in defence of the 'intensely personal commitments' he had constructed for himself, such as lie, cheat, steal, or simply run roughshod over strangers? If the autocentric perspective allows him to prefer himself over others, may he not do with others as he will, if it is in furtherance of his own personal projects?

I do not mean to suggest for a moment that Cottingham would allow any such conduct, or that he would see it as following from autocentricity. My concern is that it is just not clear why none of it follows, in the absence of a transcendent framework of principles that places inherent limits on the dimensions of self-love, love of proximates, and love of neighbour construed globally. The disquiet I have is not one that should be reserved for theists, but shared by any theorist who believes in a realist foundation for ethical attitudes and decision making. Will the principles we need involve 'impersonally defined rules of conduct'? Not if by 'impersonal' is meant that they make no reference to persons (as opposed to impersonal utility, formal consistency, or some such). They must make reference to persons, to agency, and to the good that objectively fulfils persons as agents. Alan Gewirth, for one, has sought to give a justification for partialistic preference in terms of a principle of universal human rights.[71] Since it is a human right voluntarily to form associations, whether family, community, nation, and so on, there is an impartial justification – in the sense of one applying equally to all agents irrespective of their particular circumstances – for being, at least to some extent, unimpeded in the exercise of preferences for those groupings and their members as against others. The justification, argues Gewirth, applies indirectly, in other words, not at the level of individual action, but at the level of rules and institutions that express the human right to form such associations. So, to use his example of a baseball game, the umpire can call a batter out and force him from the box against the batter's will without thereby violating his freedom, since the umpire's action is in accordance with rules justified by the universal right to free association; the batter 'has freely consented to play the game and to abide by its rules'.[72]

Although Gewirth's general approach to justifying partial preferences is admirable, it has serious problems that show it to be inadequate, one of the main ones being that many, perhaps most, of the associations and institutions within which partiality is either permissible or obligatory are not voluntary. More precisely, they are not voluntary in the sense required for his argument and certainly not for all of the agents who belong to them, yet whose practice of partiality with respect to them is every bit as justified as it is for those who do act freely in the required sense – say in constructing or maintaining the institution, entering into the relevant relationships, and so on. Gewirth recognizes the problem in respect of one's country: 'There is a crucially important respect in which one's country is not a voluntary association, adherence to whose rules is at the option of its members.'[73] He tries to solve the justification problem by appeal to the idea that the 'universalist principle' of human rights includes not just freedom of association, but 'equal protection of the freedom and basic well-being of all the inhabitants'[74] of a country, where he means 'freedom' in a broader sense than mere freedom of association. This in turn justifies a 'minimal state' that allows enforcement of the criminal law, and thereby infringement of freedoms at the individual level, without violation of rights – due to the justification of such infringements at the universal, impartial level.

By bringing in further kinds of justification, Gewirth shows that if partiality is to be justified in all its various manifestations, a number of principles need to do some work; justification cannot be reduced to a simple formula of voluntary association. This in itself does not undermine his project, but it fails on its own terms since although the protection one receives from the state might justify certain preferences one has for that state of which one is a member over others, how does it justify a member's preferences for *other members*, that is, for one's fellow countrymen? Is it that each of us receives protection from everyone else as well? This is a highly artificial generalization, realistic in times of war perhaps, but not in ordinary times. Moreover, exactly which protections justify which partialities? Is there a narrow *quid pro quo* of some sort, or a larger idea at work? What if the state protects some of my interests but not others: is my partiality to be circumscribed, and if so how?

Moreover, what about institutions such as the family? People voluntarily create families, but they are also born into them: no consent is had or possible. Gewirth does not extend his 'equal protection' justification to families, so what should be said of familial preferences when there is no question of voluntary association? Surely he cannot want to say that Fred is allowed partiality towards his son since he voluntarily produced him, but not towards his mother because he didn't ask to be born. The baseball game model might work well for clubs, start-up communes, and political parties, but it has nothing to say to any person who finds herself belonging to something not of her own making (at least partly). Yet if we do what Gewirth does not, and extend his equal protection idea to families, or perhaps to those familial relationships that are non-voluntary, we end up with absurdities: are we then to say that I am not even *permitted* to exercise partial preferences in favour of my second cousin twice removed, who lives on the other side of the country, because in no sense can I be construed to receive any protection from him or to share with him in any kind of mutually protective relationship? What if we cannot stand the sight of each other? Are we still forbidden to exercise any special preferences towards each other (for example, to bequeath everything I have to him because he is my sole surviving family member)? I doubt that Cottingham for one would countenance such a thought, nor should any defender of partiality. That my cousin is *my cousin* does matter, and can sometimes be enough for partiality towards him.

Must we, then, take Godwin's bait by affirming that there is after all some 'magic in the pronoun "my"'?[75] Not at all in the sense in which Godwin intends it, which is without any reference to the goods secured by the existence of families and other particular relationships – by which

I mean not any general utility, whether at the level of individual actions or at the level of rules and institutions, but the goods secured *for those who are in such relationships*. And this is where the other thread in Cottingham's discussion of ethical theory is relevant and important, albeit not disentangled by him from more subjectivist, anti-realist, Nietzschean thoughts. For Cottingham does in several places recognize that it is simply essential to human flourishing that there be families, friendships, and by extension communities and nations or other political associations devoted to the common good of their members. He accepts Aristotle's insistence that we must live 'according to nature', that is, according to what fulfils us in our entire human essence. He affirms that our 'ordinary and characteristic' dispositions of preference for self and proximates carry at least prima facie ethical weight sufficient to place the onus on the Godwinian impartialist to justify overturning 'our natural human sentiments and predispositions'.[76] He acknowledges that 'moral backing' is given to our familial preferences by 'the close emotional bonding which people develop towards their offspring and the role which such bonding plays in the fulfilment and happiness of those involved'; and more generally, that 'human beings, or at least most of them,[77] find it difficult to flourish unless they can integrate their lives into at least some network of partiality, some structure of mutual dependence and loyalty'. 'In order to live happy lives', Cottingham judges, 'human beings may require, beyond self-concern and family concern, wider partialist structures of interdependence'. Yet he finishes this last point by saying that the concerns had by people within those structures 'will not be limited to that which an impartial observer might assign on the basis of purely objective criteria'.[78]

Now if by 'purely objective criteria' Cottingham means simply utility, or some other impersonal standard of goodness that does not derive from the experience of those who stand within partialist structures, we can agree. But an account of flourishing in terms of what is good *for persons*, given their *natures* – an account founded on the facts of human existence, which as far as anyone can tell, and reason itself proposes, are not mere contingencies or empirical generalizations subject to falsification – is also objective, independent of subjectively constructed blueprints for living. Such blueprints are not the *source* of worth for partialist structures; rather, the structures and relationships of partiality are part of the fabric of human nature to which any worthwhile and reasonable blueprint for living must *answer*. Perhaps this is what Cottingham means when he says that structures of partiality 'seem to rest on an unassailable moral foundation in so far as any ethical blueprint which attempted to eliminate them from the world altogether would be self-defeating'.[79] If so, then post-Nietzschean thoughts can safely be set aside – in favour of a return to that robust ethic and metaphysic of natural law within which partiality and the objective good for man are most clearly and plausibly shown to cohere.

Notes

1. Cottingham, 1983; 1986; 1991; 1996; 1997–8. For some of the discussion, see Baron, 1991; Friedman, 1991; Jollimore, 2000; Etzioni, 2002.
2. Cottingham, 1983, p. 90, referring to the *Nicomachean Ethics*, Book 9, Ch. 8: 1168b.
3. In fact Cottingham does not mention all of these groupings, and there are others one could mention, but they fit into the overall structure he proposes. I leave aside for the moment the question, briefly tackled by Cottingham himself, as to how one may distinguish between legitimate and illegitimate preferences (questions of race, class, and gender being the most prominent).
4. As a theist, I hold that a human being's particularistic relationships begin with his relationship to God, on which the structure of all human relationships is based. This will not be an explicit theme of the present paper – much of what I will argue is at least not directly dependent on it – though it will inevitably play a part in my discussion of the proper interpretation of the Christian precept to love one's neighbour. Also, the term 'moral preference' and related terms must be understood correctly; it is far too easy for the opponent of partiality to load these terms with a meaning the supporter certainly does not give them. It is part of the aim of this paper to make the necessary clarifications, following Cottingham's instructive example.
5. Deigh, 1991.
6. I will say more about the meaning of 'neighbour' later, but for the present I use it to cover any other person *including* those closest to me.
7. Godwin, 1985/1798, Book II, Ch. II, p. 169. See pp. 168–77 for the infamous discussion of Archbishop Fénelon and the valet, in earlier editions the chambermaid.
8. Cottingham, 1983, p. 89 for both quotations.
9. Cottingham, 1991, p. 815 for both quotations.
10. Cottingham, 1986, p. 364–8. The difference between the two is that agent-related partialism concerns the 'general structure' of agency – the idea that 'in deciding whether to support X's goals or Y's goals, the fact that I am X may legitimately carry a certain degree of moral weight' (Cottingham, 1986, p. 364). Self-directed partialism, also called by Cottingham 'self-favouritism', involves the further thought that as far as the *content* of my commitments is concerned, 'I may assign special weight to my own private interests and satisfactions (as against those of others) simply because they are mine' (Cottingham, 1986, p. 366). He goes on to identify 'philophilic partialism' as a kind of self-directed altruism towards nearest and dearest, whereby I favour their welfare over that of non-proximates simply because the former are specially related to me (Cottingham, 1986, pp. 368–70).

11. Cottingham, 1991, p. 815.
12. Cottingham, 1991, p. 802.
13. Cottingham, 1991, pp. 815–16 for the three quotations.
14. Cottingham, 1991, p. 815, in reference to the Buddhist monk. Cottingham treats such a person and the Christian saint in the same way, as though all such persons aim at the same transcendence of self. It is true that this is what the Buddhist monk aims at, and to this extent he really does follow a pseudo-ideal at odds with anything grounded in the reality of human nature. The case of the saint is wholly different, a distinction Cottingham does not appear to acknowledge.
15. Here is a quotation from a work that explains the nature of Christian virtue, with obvious implications for the notion of sanctity: such virtue 'is an active reflection of the moral attributes of God, and a certain partaking, such as the creature can receive, of the virtue of God. Giving the soul an active resemblance to her Creator and a divine attraction to unite her spirit with Him, this virtue begins in faith and is perfected in charity [that is, love of God], and is the true nobility of the soul'; Ullathorne, 1882, p. 29. Such an explanation implicitly links virtue to concern for the state of one's soul, the objective being, of course, unity with God in beatitude. Love of others, for the sake of God, is built on this concern. And what is true of people in general will be true of the saint in the extreme. Consider also Proverbs 11:17, which says: 'A merciful man doth good *to his own soul*: but he that is cruel casteth off even his own kindred' (my emphasis). This is cited as encapsulating saintliness by the famous Jewish Talmudic scholar of the third century AD, Resh Lakish, in the Babylonian Talmud, *Ta'anit* 11:b. Indeed the Hebrew verb *gomél* suggests not just doing good to one's soul, but *perfecting* it.
16. Cottingham, 1983, p. 90; 1996, p. 65.
17. 'Basic' in the sense of the general reason that motivates love for all human beings, as opposed to more particular reasons having to do with one's attitude to this or that individual.
18. This argument is nothing more than an unpacking of the brief statement of the idea by St Thomas Aquinas in the *Summa Theologiae*, II.IIae, q. 26, a. 4, resp. (1916, vol. 9., pp. 336–7).
19. None of this is to imply that concern for one's own good, in some specific instance, may come apart from concern for another's good: one may lay down their life for their friend (John 15:13), where one gives up a mere bodily good of one's own for the sake of a friend's bodily or spiritual benefit. Or, conversely, one may prefer a specific good of one's own, say one's health, at the expense of doing for others what would otherwise damage one's physical well-being. But in all such cases one's actions must in some way redound to one's *overall* good. So one's good and that of others, although they may come apart in certain specific kinds of case, can never wholly come apart, and the fundamental basis and justification of neighbour-love is one's desire for one's own perfection.
20. And to enhance, stimulate, encourage, and so on for all the proper attitudes one may have, and actions one may take, towards a person's good.
21. Let us leave aside possible mismatch between the control one has and the control one *believes* one has. A person may believe they have control and not have it (or the converse), such that they will not be irrational if their belief

is reasonable, and so on. Spelling out these details is tangential to the main argument, and in fact irrelevant to one's own case, where it is certain that a person who believes they have no control over their own good is either irrational or in some other way malfunctioning cognitively.

22. Cottingham, 1983, p. 93.
23. Although Aquinas does not spell out an argument from control for the priority of self-love, it seems consistent with the argument he does give, and a natural corollary of it.
24. Other religions have versions of the same precept, of course, but I intend to restrict the discussion to the religion that places it at the heart of morality, in which it receives its fullest treatment, and that has had the greatest influence on Western civilization.
25. This was already becoming apparent in the time of Hume and Godwin. It is implicit in the latter's answer to Dr Samuel Parr's *Spital Sermon* condemning Godwinian impartialism. At one point in the reply, discussing the 'doctrine of universal philanthropy', Godwin reduces Christ merely to having the status of being 'among its most conspicuous advocates', as though Christianity were just another place in which the doctrine is to be found. Needless to say, since Godwin identifies universal philanthropy with the 'maxim of utility', Christ turns out to be just another utilitarian, albeit a 'conspicuous' one who made good use of parables. See Parr, 1828 and Godwin, 1968/1801. The relevant points in both are summarized in Singer, Cannold, and Kuhse, 1995.
26. For a representative sample of glosses on Luke 10:29–37 the Parable of the Good Samaritan, see Aquinas, *Catena* (1997, vol. 3, pp. 370–7), and also the *Glossa Ordinaria*. The interpretation of the man who fell among thieves as being, in a manner of speaking, Adam himself, representing all human beings since we share a common nature, was a universal teaching of the Fathers, held int. al. by SS Augustine, Chrysostom, Ambrose, Irenaeus, and Clement, and by Origen. A more recent, standard discussion of the subject, says: 'Our fellow man here [in the context of the obligation to love our neighbour] means absolutely every man without exception' (Higgins, 1992/1958, p. 333).
27. This is the case whatever the scope given to 'every'. If it has narrow scope (meaning something like 'being disposed to do good to every human being at the same time') it is obviously a disposition no sane person could have. But even if it has wide scope ('for every human being, being disposed to do good to that individual', with the implication that the disposition is to actions at different times) it is still not a realistic disposition to have, indeed arguably incoherent. What disposition do I have to do good right now to a Kalahari bushman? What disposition could I have? I could certainly put myself in a position of being so disposed, for example, by visiting the Kalahari, or finding out about aid projects to which I might contribute, and so on. But to do any of these things is precisely to put myself in a position of proximity (of whatever degree) to some individual, as a necessary precondition for my having any meaningful disposition to do good to them. Beneficence is always circumscribed in this way; benevolence is not. Note, however, a single exception to what I have just said, one of relevance only to theists. It is possible to be beneficent to all people at once simply by praying for them. Indeed, one should suppose it an obligation to pray for all people. This specific exception is recognized by Aquinas

(*Summa Theologiae* II.IIae, q. 31, a. 2, ad 1; 1916, p. 401), and is mentioned also in Scripture (1 Tim 2: 1–5). I am grateful to David Gallagher for bringing it to my attention.

28. See, for example, Cottingham, 1991, p. 800–1, echoing Aristotle's famous discussion of the limits of friendship in the *Nicomachean Ethics*, Book 8, Ch. 6: 1158a11.

29. Note – wanting the good for every person, not wanting to *do* good to every person.

30. Cottingham, 1983, p. 93.

31. Modulo other family relationships, etc.: we can easily make the thought more complex, but not more natural or admirable.

32. At this point I note that Cottingham, even though his interpretation of the parable is wrong, is however right to dismiss Marilyn Friedman's criticism of him on this score. Friedman claims he has two different interpretations of the scope of 'neighbour' in the parable – a 'narrow' one in 1983 and a more global one in 1991. She gives no textual evidence of the former, nor is there any, Cottingham makes it quite clear in his 1983 paper that he reads 'neighbour' in the global sense both as regards the impartialist thesis and as regards his own, more minimal reinterpretation of the precept of loving thy neighbour. So it is not at all clear how Friedman manages to detect an 'earlier reading' that has a 'rhetorical purpose' but is nevertheless a 'misinterpretation of Christian doctrine', albeit neither intentional nor unintentional (Friedman, 1991, p. 827, n. 26). Rather, since both Friedman and Cottingham construe 'love thy neighbour' globally without qualification, they both misinterpret the doctrine, as I will show. But whereas Cottingham is quite clear that his criticism is of impartialism as so understood, Friedman mistakenly thinks both she and Cottingham have in their sights only an especially narrow reading of 'neighbour' that takes no account of need, rather than any kind of impartiality thesis (p. 828). But Cottingham's criticisms of 'love thy neighbour' are consistently directed at its alleged impartialism, not at a supposed, objectionably narrow reading of the precept taken as a partialist injunction, and which reading is not to be found in his 1983 article. Friedman, then, mistakenly interprets both the precept and Cottingham.

33. 'ἦλθεν κατ' αὐτὸν καὶ ἰδὼν αὐτὸν ἐσπλαγχνίσθη' (Luke 10:33).

34. I use the term 'measure' to mean something like intensity, or strength of feeling and concern. Aquinas speaks of a 'more potent reason' (*potior ratio*), and also of 'quantity' of love (*quantitatem*): Aquinas, *Summa Theol.*, II.IIae, q. 26, a. 4, resp. and ad 1 (1916, pp. 336–7).

35. This, at least, is how I interpret *Summa Theologiae* II.IIae, q. 26, aa. 4, 6, as do writers who base their moral philosophy on the same foundation: see, for example, Higgins, 1992/1958, pp. 332–7; Glenn, 1930, pp. 183–9.

36. Cottingham, 1983, p. 86. On Godwin, see 1968/1801, pp. 332–3; on Singer, see 1993, p. 11, where he misinterprets the Christian precept of neighbour-love as meaning that one should 'give the same weight to the interests of others as one gives to one's own interests'.

37. Cottingham, 1983, p. 87; Mackie, 1977, pp. 129–34.

38. Cottingham, 1983, p. 87.

39. Cottingham, 1983, p. 88.

40. Cottingham, 1991, pp. 800–1.

41. Cottingham, 1991, p. 801.
42. Cottingham, 1991, pp. 808–13.
43. Cottingham, 1991, pp. 808–9. The only theological citation he gives for his understanding of this aspect of Christian teaching is, rather oddly, John Locke: p. 808, n. 36.
44. Matthew 5:48.
45. Cottingham, 1991, p. 809.
46. Cottingham, 1991, p. 811.
47. Cottingham, 1991, p. 810.
48. Cottingham, 1983, p. 98.
49. Donoghue v. Stevenson, [1932] A.C. 562, at 580.
50. This is because by rendering thanks to another I do not give him what is his (as when, say, I return borrowed property), but what is mine – my pleasure, my relief, and so on, at being helped.
51. Cottingham, 1991, pp. 806ff.
52. Cottingham, 1991, pp. 809–10.
53. Cottingham, 1991, p. 811.
54. Aristotle, *Nicomachean Ethics*, Book 2: 1106ff.
55. Aquinas, *Summa Theol.*, II.IIae, q. 26, a. 5, ad 3 (1916, p. 339), on the perfection of charity (*perfectio caritatis*).
56. In other words, if one insisted on looking at it quasi-mathematically, the existence of counsels of perfection (as opposed to strict obligations) would modify the linear function so that the straight line of obligation plotted with respect to conduct and goodness – the more the better – would taper off at the point at which more wasn't strictly better in the sense of being more fulfilment of duty. Rather, more self-sacrifice, say, would mean more goodness but increasing at a lesser rate. The graph would be saying, in effect: 'As you carry out your obligations of charity (for example), then the more you do so the more good you are without deviation or slow-down. But when you start doing things that are admirable but not obligatory – counsels of perfection – then yes, you do increase how good you are, but not *so* much. You're adding icing to the moral cake, but no more.' One can see how metaphorical this is all bound to become.
57. Aquinas, *Summa Theol.*, II.IIae, q. 26, a. 4, resp. and ad 2 (1916, pp. 336–7).
58. Cottingham, 1991, p. 811.
59. Cottingham, 1991, p. 811.
60. Not just Aristotelian. Also, Cottingham's parallel between Christian love and Platonic communal life among the guardians is tendentious (Cottingham, 1983, p. 90). Platonic thought had to undergo many mutations before it could resemble something to which Christian theologians were able to make appeal.
61. Cottingham, 1991, p. 811.
62. Cottingham, 1983; 1991, pp. 802–5; 1997–8, pp. 1–8.
63. For a very useful survey and interpretation of the development of Godwin's views, see Singer, Cannold, and Kuhse, 1995.
64. Cottingham, 1991, pp. 805–6.
65. Cottingham, 1991, p. 89.
66. Cottingham, 1997–8, p. 7; 1996, p. 75.
67. Cottingham, 1997–8, p. 7, for all of these quotations.
68. Cottingham, 1996, p. 75.

69. Cottingham, 1991, pp. 812–13.
70. Cottingham, 1997–8, p. 7. Cottingham uses the expression in the context of what makes human lives 'valuable', and I share his principal target, according to which I am permitted or obliged to save one life or another in a Godwin-style fire case according as the life to be saved contributes to social utility. But it seems he has something more radical in mind, speaking of the way in which 'we ourselves generate that worth and significance' by means of our personal commitments; and lest he be thought to be making a purely epistemological point about how we come to *know* what is valuable in our lives, he is explicit that '[h]ere, in a sense, epistemology and metaphysics coincide'.
71. Gewirth, 1988, pp. 283–302.
72. Gewirth, 1988, p. 293.
73. Gewirth, 1988, p. 299.
74. Gewirth, 1988, p. 299.
75. Godwin, 1985/1798, p. 170.
76. Cottingham, 1991, pp. 813–15.
77. The qualification, as far as I can see, is unwarranted. I do not think one will find a single person in history, no matter how reclusive, eremitical, withdrawn, or devoted to 'saving the world' (if that means anything) who has not either relied on some structure of particularistic relationships or suffered for the lack of it. Hence I think Cottingham is wrong to claim that 'clearly there have been human beings (hermits, wandering friars, and so on) who have managed to live without the ties of special affection' (Cottingham, 1986, p. 369). A cursory look at the lives of the Desert Fathers should put paid to the notion, let alone consideration of the special affection Christ Himself showed to the Apostles: 'You are the salt of the earth. But if the salt lose its savour, wherewith shall it be salted? It is good for nothing any more but to be cast out, and to be trodden on by men' (Matthew 5:13); and many passages in which His particular love for His disciples is manifest.
78. Cottingham, 1986, p. 372, for all of these quotations.
79. Cottingham, 1986, p. 370.

Bibliography

Aquinas T., *Catena Aurea* or *Commentary on the Four Gospels Collected Out of the Works of the Fathers* (Southampton: The Saint Austin Press, 1997)
Aquinas T., *Summa Theologiae*, in *The Summa Theologica of St. Thomas Aquinas*, trans. Fathers of the English Dominican Province (London: Burns Oates & Washburn, 1916; vol. 9)
Baron M., 'Impartiality and Friendship', *Ethics*, 101 (1991) 836–57
Cottingham J., 'The Ethical Credentials of Partiality', *Proceedings of the Aristotelian Society*, 98 (1997–8) 1–21
Cottingham J., 'Partiality and the Virtues', in Crisp R. (ed.), *How Should One Live? Essays on the Virtues* (Oxford: Clarendon Press, 1996)
Cottingham J., 'The Ethics of Self-Concern', *Ethics*, 101 (1991) 798–817
Cottingham J., 'Partiality, Favouritism and Morality', *The Philosophical Quarterly*, 36 (1986) 357–73
Cottingham J., 'Ethics and Impartiality', *Philosophical Studies*, 43 (1983) 83–99

Deigh J., 'Impartiality: a closing note', *Ethics*, 101 (1991) 858–64

Etzioni A., 'Are Particularistic Obligations Justified?', *The Review of Politics*, 64 (2002) 573–98

Friedman M., 'The Practice of Partiality', *Ethics*, 101 (1991) 818–35

Gewirth A., 'Ethical Universalism and Particularism', *The Journal of Philosophy* 85 (1988) 283–302

Glenn P.J., *Ethics* (St. Louis, Missouri: B. Herder Book Co., 1930)

Godwin W., *Thoughts Occasioned by the Perusal of Dr. Parr's Spital Sermon, Preached at Christ Church, April 15, 1800* [pub. 1801], in Marken J.W. and Pollin B.R. (eds), *Uncollected Writings (1785–1822) by William Godwin* (Gainesville, Florida: Scholar's Fascimiles and Reprints, 1968). Also available at http://dwardmac. pitzer.edu:16080/Anarchist_archives/godwin/thoughtsonpar.html (accessed 27.7.07)

Godwin W., *Enquiry Concerning Political Justice* [1798] (Harmondsworth: Penguin, 1985, 3rd edn)

Higgins T.J., S.J., *Man as Man: The Science and Art of Ethics* [1958] (Rockford, Illinois: Tan Books, 1992)

Jollimore T., 'Friendship without Partiality?', *Ratio*, 13 (2000) 69–82

Mackie J.L., *Ethics: Inventing Right and Wrong* (Harmondsworth: Penguin, 1977)

Parr S., 'A Spital Sermon, Preached at Christ Church upon Easter Tuesday, 15 April 1800; to Which are Added Notes', in Johnstone J. (ed.), *The Works of Samuel Parr*, vol. II, (London: Longman, Rees, Orme, Browne and Green, 1828)

Singer P., Cannold L., and Kuhse H., 'William Godwin and the Defence of Impartialist Ethics', *Utilitas*, 7 (1995) 67–86

Singer P., *Practical Ethics* (Cambridge: Cambridge University Press, 1993, 2nd edn)

Strabo, W., *Glossa Ordinaria* (c.9th), at http://vulsearch.sourceforge.net (accessed 27.7.07)

Ullathorne W. (Archbishop), *The Groundwork of the Christian Virtues* (London: Burns and Oates, 1882, 6th edn)

Part II The Emotions and the Good Life

4
Akrasia and the Emotions

Nafsika Athanassoulis

1.

John Cottingham's work in moral philosophy is far reaching and has been at the leading edge of some of the most exciting developments in recent research, such as the revival of interest in the concepts of 'character' and 'virtue', the debate between impartiality and partiality, and the role of the emotions in the good life. His most ambitious and innovative contribution to some of these questions is outlined in *Philosophy and the Good Life.* The book has two main aims, accomplished through an impressive overview of philosophical developments from the ancient Greeks to modern thinkers: the first is an attack on what Cottingham terms the ratiocentric view of ethics, the second a persuasive case that any plausible answer to what is the good life for humans must take into account the insights of psychoanalysis.

The root of ratiocentric ethics is, unsurprisingly, the Platonic confidence in the power of reason. Reason reigns supreme, with the emotions being subjugated to its rule. Cottingham takes us on a journey of the philosophical reliance on reason through history, which shows that this ratiocentric approach pervades the work of most writers. Even those who, like Aristotle, admit to a greater role for the emotions, allowing them to be guided and shaped by reason, are still tied into the Platonic model of human conduct. Even this Aristotelian picture is over-reliant on reason and therefore fails to capture our full humanity. A more realistic conception of humanity should be at the centre of any account of the good life, as opposed to a vain and counterproductive concentration on an ideal and trans-human conception of all-powerful reason.[1]

The second main argument in the book develops a view of the emotions such that only by accepting the insights of psychoanalysis can we really understand humanity in a way which contributes to the project of elucidating the good life for humans. The psychoanalytic insight, which brings crashing down the ratiocentric account of human nature, is that 'the influence exerted by unconscious phantasies and desires is such that the full significance of the materials over which reason solemnly deliberates is often not fully transparent to the agent herself'.[2] Reason can never be all powerful, whether one thinks its role is to subjugate, extirpate, or rationalize the emotions, because our very own desires, feelings and emotions are fundamentally outside of our understanding. Fundamentally the ratiocentric model is based on a vain conception of humans as 'masters of their own house', fully and consciously in control of their own selves. Psychoanalysis destroys this conception, showing how there can be substantial and influential parts of mental activity, which fall short of full, reflective awareness. In Cottingham's words psychoanalysis has effected an expulsion from paradise, but this paradise was illusory in the first instance.[3] Reason is not a supremely authoritative voice, and we should abandon this picture of human nature in favour of a more realistic account of the substantial, non-transparent and possibly unrestrained influences of the emotions.[4]

2.

Clearly the main objective of any attack on the ratiocentric conception of ethics is the Platonic account of an all-powerful reason, which harnesses and controls the emotions. As such, this Platonic account is the main target of Cottingham's dissatisfaction. However, in an impressively nuanced and far-reaching discussion Cottingham shows how the ethical views of many other philosophers are fundamentally flawed by adherence to this Platonic ideal. A sizable portion of this discussion concerns itself with Aristotle's views (mainly) on ethics. Cottingham rightly distinguishes the Aristotelian role for reason from the Platonic insistence that the good for man must consist in an exclusive concentration on rational activity. Aristotle's view is more like rational hegemonism, a view that allows room for both reason and the emotions, but which requires the latter to be guided, shaped and formed by the former. Although differing from Plato's view, Aristotle still maintains its basic tenets, a fact which becomes apparent in Book X of the *Nicomachean Ethics* when Aristotle returns to and praises the Platonic-style supremacy of contemplation. Aristotle's view is characterised by a naiveté regarding the transparency of the emotions and the possibility of bringing them under the control of reason, with a fundamental commitment to a Platonic-style approach to the centrality and importance of the role of reason.

Nowhere is this more evident than in Aristotle's account of *akrasia*. For Cottingham, Aristotle's classification of the four states of character as virtue, continence, incontinence and vice is simplistic, failing to capture the complexities of our emotional responses:[5]

> [f]rom our late twentieth-century perspective, we have (rightly) become suspicious of normative models which encourage the dangerous delusion that man can, with impunity, dominate and suppress the world around him – whether the external world of nature, or the complex inner world of the human psyche.[6]

Aristotle's explanation of how it is possible for an agent to do other than what he judges is best remains tied to the Platonic model, arguing that akratic behaviour is tied to a cognitive defect. This reluctance to free himself from the ratiocentric account of human nature, shows Aristotle's lack of a proper understanding of the significance and influence of the emotions. Fundamentally he fails to appreciate that reason's domain is not absolute and the influence of the unconscious means that significant elements of the agent's own psyche are not fully transparent even to him. The influence of the emotions is such that their full impact is not available to the deliberations of reason, is not transparent at the time of making decisions and may even not be revealed later on. This Aristotelian insistence on controlling what is potentially unknowable creates not just a false picture but threatens 'to cut us off from the roots of what makes us most endearingly vulnerable and most fully human'.[7]

It seems almost as if Cottingham is more concerned with making his case against Aristotle than Plato, as the Platonic view of the predominance of reason is easily discredited and fairly widely accepted as extreme, whereas the Aristotelian picture is more appealing as being more inclusive, plausible and realistic. However, this appeal is misguided and therefore potentially more distracting. By stepping down from the more extreme forms of ratiocentricity, Aristotle's position may appear a more plausible account of human nature, however it still retains its ties to the centrality of reason while at the same time failing to fully appreciate the unknowable nature of the emotions. This seems to make it a more significant target than the Platonic claim, and one that it is more important to defeat.

In this paper I wish to present an alternative account of *akrasia*; one which explains the Aristotelian attachment to a fundamental role for

reason in a non-corrosive manner and which allows for a more fundamental role for the emotions, which may be more compatible with
some of Cottingham's claims for them. In a sense, this is an interpretation of some Aristotelian ideas, which will attempt to present them as
more attuned to Cottingham's project. Cottingham does hint that a
radial reconstruction of Aristotle's ethics could develop a picture more
compatible with these modern insights that have led us to lose confidence in the power of reason.[8] It would be foolhardy to claim that I will
offer such a complete and comprehensively radical reconstruction, but
perhaps I can offer some hints as to how Aristotle may be interpreted in
such a direction. All questions of interpretation require precise attention to detail and exegetical analysis, even more so for a topic as complex and disputed as *akrasia*. To an extent I will try to refer to passages
in Aristotle's work which support the case I will construct, but I will also
rely on referring to the work of others who have constructed a better
case than I possibly could for the interpretation of particular points.

3.

Let us begin where Aristotle begins, with the Socratic claim that no one
acts knowingly contrary to what is best; they only do so through ignorance. This Socratic claim seems to be the pinnacle of the Platonic
reliance on reason and the importance of knowledge in an account of
the good life. Although Aristotle starts off his discussion of *akrasia* in
Book VII of the *Nicomachean Ethics* by accepting that such a claim is
manifestly contrary to plain evidence,[9] he does conclude his discussion
by accepting a modified version of it.[10] I will go on to consider
Aristotle's modifications to the claim and their significance, but before
doing so, it is important to consider the Socratic claim itself, and its
appeal. Cottingham's work has encouraged us to view the distorting and
unrealistic implications of this ratiocentric approach, but I think it is
important to begin by spelling out some of the reasons for its appeal in
this context.

Following a significant piece of work on weakness of will,[11] most commentators see the central problem here as being about a failure to con-
vert intention into action. This is explicitly not a particular problem
relevant to morality, but a general concern about cases where an agent
believes that something should be done (has the opportunity to do it)
and fails to do so. Although I am happy to accept that weakness of will
is a phenomenon wider than that present in moral cases, I think it is a
mistake to subsume the *moral* instances of *akrasia* under the general

cases of failures to turn intentions into actions. It is important to consider the moral case as a special case of weakness of will and why this is the case should become apparent if we consider the appeal of the Socratic dictum.

The specific case of weakness of will which has to do with moral *akrasia*, is concerned with cases where the agent knows what ought to be done, this is a moral 'ought', but does not do it. It is crucial to note here that the subject of the agent's knowledge is the moral good. The Socratic 'knows what is best' refers to wishes and choices that derive from conceptions of *eudaimonia*, so this is a moral conception of what is best or what is good.[12] What motivates the Socratic claim is that the agent's knowledge *is* of the moral good, for how can one know what one *ought* to do and still not do it? Morality exerts an attraction, such that it is difficult to conceive of the possibility of being receptive to this attraction and simply ignoring it.[13] Cases of weakness of will in general may be perplexing, but cases of *akrasia*, whose subject is moral knowledge, are particularly perplexing, and perplexing in a special way that has to do with the object of the agent's knowledge. The basic Socratic claim is that human beings always most desire and hence pursue what is best, these being moral concepts, understood by reference to *eudaimonia*. Knowing what is best morally and not pursuing it, therefore seems impossible because of this connection between evaluation and motivation, so the *akratic* must be ignorant.[14]

Now, let us consider this claim in Aristotelian terms and see whether there is any evidence for us to think that Aristotle would find it appealing. *Eudaimonia* is the end of human action, Aristotle tells us:

> that which is choosable for its own sake and never because of something else we call final without any qualification. Well, *eudaimonia* more than anything else is thought to be just such an end, because we always choose it for itself and never for any other reason ... A self-sufficient thing, then, we take to be one which by itself makes life desirable and in no way deficient; and we believe that *eudaimonia* is such a thing. What is more, we regard it as the most desirable of all things, not reckoned as one item among many; if it were so reckoned, *eudaimonia* would obviously be more desirable by the addition of even the least good, because the addition makes the sum of goods greater, and the greater of two goods is always more desirable. *Eudaimonia*, then is found to be something perfect and self-sufficient, being the end to which our actions are directed.[15]

Since practical wisdom is a correct conception of the end of human action, *eudaimonia*, how can the dictates of practical wisdom ever be ignored and not carried through into action? How can one know what practical wisdom requires and not be moved to do so? Surely the conclusions of all practical deliberation should in some way speak in favour of performing an action, but we can, in general, accept that things may go wrong between arriving at these conclusions and affecting them in practice. However, the conclusions of practical wisdom are the subject for the sake of which everything else is done and which is chosen, chosen for its own sake and chosen knowingly so that there should be no gap between deliberation and action. To use Wiggins' words: 'For a man to embrace a specific conception of eudaimonia just is for him to become susceptible to certain distinctive and *distinctively compelling* reasons for acting in certain sorts of ways'.[16]

The relevant state of character for understanding this point is virtue. In the case of virtue, deliberation flows smoothly into action, illustrating the full appeal of the noble and the good.[17] If the possibility of the incontinent agent is the one that poses all the problems, then the state of character of the virtuous agent should be easier to understand as this is the unproblematic case. The virtuous agent is characterised by a special sensitivity to relevant features of the situation, a perceptual capacity, which allows him to reliably 'see' what is required and, more importantly, combined with practical wisdom, why it is required of him. The very instance of perceiving these morally salient features incorporates a motivational element, since virtue is by its definition a purposive disposition, a tendency to respond to relevant circumstances with the right reason and the appropriate desire, which results in the right action. Indeed, that the situation requires the appropriate response (for example a situation which requires a kind response) is a full and adequate account of the agent's motivation to so act, and any other incentive to so act (for example to gain a personal advantage) actually disqualifies the agent from being virtuous. Indeed McDowell argues that the demands of virtue are not one of many reasons which must be set against each other, but rather the only salient aspects of the situation, and all other reasons as a result are silenced.[18]

This explains the appeal of the Socratic claim. Since the object of our concern is the noble and the good, any account of human action must incorporate the idea of the attractiveness of morality. Given that, it is indeed perplexing how one can know what one (morally) ought to do and still not do it.

4.

All this may explain Aristotle's attraction to the Socratic claim, but, of course, means that Aristotle (and indeed Socrates) now has a problem with explaining the possibility of *akrasia*. Aristotle frequently asserts that the virtuous, continent and incontinent agents all share in the right principle,[19] but if they all know and therefore all feel the attraction of morality, why do two of them, the virtuous and the continent, act and one does not, the incontinent? And, further, why does the continent agent only act after a struggle with contrary motivations? There are a limited number of possible answers to these questions. One, as we have seen, is to accept the Socratic conclusion that the incontinent must be acting in ignorance. This kind of answer requires full faith in the power of reason to control recalcitrant elements in the psychological make-up of human beings and is most vulnerable to the sorts of concerns Cottingham raises against the ratiocentric model.

Another suggestion is that the incontinent agent is somehow cognitively deficient. If affirmation of the practical syllogism must, of necessity, result in action, if an agent fails to display the action then he cannot be said to have knowledge.[20] However, such a view cannot be attributed to Aristotle as it is incompatible with many of his remarks on how the *akratic* shares in the right principle and the idea that *akrasia* (and continence) involves struggle.[21]

Yet another possibility is to see *akrasia* as a struggle between reason and emotion. Reason pulls in the direction of the good; emotions are wayward and derail the process that would have otherwise ended in action. The incontinent agent, in this picture, fully appreciates the demands of morality but is swayed by contrary desires to do otherwise. This explains continence as a similar case of struggle, but one that the agent wins over his emotions. This seems exactly like the sort of confrontational picture of reason set against the emotions that Cottingham cautions us against. However, we needn't worry as this picture makes little sense, given what we have said so far. Since morality exerts an attraction, in this account, cases of incontinence are cases where a competing motivational pull, that of desires, wins the day. For this to be possible we would have to assume that either the motivational pull of morality is weak or the desires are extremely strong. However, both these options are problematic. It is implausible to accept that morality exerts an attraction, but insist that it is a rather weak one. For how could recognition of the noble and the good be attractive but only mildly so, given that the object of the attraction is the noble and the good? On the other hand, we could accept that the attraction of morality is appropriately significant, but develop a picture of human nature as literally ravaged by contrary, extreme desires. However, even if such a picture were plausible in itself, it would then be difficult to explain continence and virtue. For if such desires are so overwhelmingly strong, how can the struggle ever be won (the continent agent) or the desires ever be extinguished (the virtuous agent)?

These thoughts seem to bring us back where we started, for if some people understand the demands of morality, but still do otherwise, we have to assume that this understanding is incomplete. However, we can explain this problem with the account of the *akratic* agent's knowledge without having to commit to a strict division between reason and the emotions. Indeed the picture of the *akratic* as lacking in the full and complete knowledge which characterises the virtuous agent, can only be understood if we abandon the confrontational model of reason and desires.

5.

Let us start by considering what happens in the, perhaps more straightforward, case of virtue. Aristotle warns us that, in moral matters, failure is possible in many ways, whereas success is only one.[22] It is easier to miss the target than hit it, but for our purposes it should be helpful to start with an account of virtue as there is only one way in which one is virtuous.

Virtue, then, is a purposive disposition concerned with choice. The virtuous agent is characterised by having the right reason, in accordance with the right desire, so that his practical deliberations flow smoothly into the right action. That virtue is a purposive disposition reveals a lot about the role of desires in the virtuous agent. We are *moved* with respect to our desires, but we are *disposed* in respect to the virtues.[23] This tells us something both about the nature of desires and the role they play in the character of the virtuous person. Desires are diverse, changing and can move us to act in many different ways, whereas dispositions are settled, entrenched and stable tendencies with respect to specific emotions. Thus, one can be moved at different times by different, transient and fleeting desires, and this is what desires do; that is, they move us. However, virtues involve stable, reliable dispositions with respect to appropriately trained and dependable desires. The virtuous agent is characterised by reliability; that is, he can be reliably expected to act

consistently in situations which require a virtuous response. He has settled dispositions with respect to the virtues, which means that he can
be counted upon to have the appropriate feelings as elicited by the
appropriate situations.

This does suggest a level of control over one's emotions and indeed the
Aristotelian picture of moral development points towards such a conclusion. For Aristotle moral development involves a long, time-consuming
and difficult process of sensitisation to moral requirements. Later, we
will go on to consider exactly what this process involves, but for now
we can accept that through a process of education, training, habituation
and realisation of the noble and the good, virtuous agents come to have
settled dispositions to behave in particular ways. They are no longer
moved by whatever desires they happen to have, in unrelated ways, but
are disposed to react in the right manner, towards the right people, with
the right emotions. The virtuous agent's emotions are not emotions he
happens to have, which happen to move him in different ways, but cultivated dispositions, chosen and developed because of the ways they
affect the agent's motivation. Thus dispositions are fixed, cultivated and
sensitised emotional tendencies to feel and act in appropriate ways, which
have been developed and promoted because of the sorts of tendencies
that they are. This is a picture of the emotions as settled dispositions,
working in accordance with reason and flowing smoothly into action.
We now need to say a bit more on how this is achieved and on exactly
what is the relationship between reason and the emotions.

Virtue is a purposive disposition concerned with choice and determined by the right reason (*orthos logos*). To say that someone is virtuous
is to say that they have a reliable sensitivity to the requirements of
virtue. A kind agent is a person who is moved to respond in kind ways
to situations that require a kind response. It is the situation itself which
generates the requirement for the virtuous response, and accounting for
why that is so can only be done by referring back to the particulars of
the situation. That is, if one were to ask why is a kind response the correct response in this instance, the only possible answer would have to
make reference to particular features of this situation that generate the
requirement for kindness; for example, he is in pain or she is hurt. It is
by giving an account of the situation one is faced with that we can
explain why the requirement for a virtuous response is generated, and
the virtuous person is the person who can perceive what these requirements are, how they are generated, and is able to respond to them
with the appropriate emotion. At the same time, specific virtues can
only be understood by reference to the situations which give rise to the

requirement for this appropriate response and therefore, *in light* of the appropriate response (the virtuous action). Earlier we explained the virtue of kindness in these terms, but see also, for example, Aristotle's account of 'favour'. Favour is defined both in terms of the benevolent feelings appropriate to it and the resulting action that has to do with rendering a service, a service to one who needs it; thus linking the kind of action that is appropriate with the particular circumstances that generate the need for a favour. The circumstances which explain the appropriateness of acting benevolently in rendering the favour are, as we would expect, varied: from a small favour in response to a moderate need through to a pressing or great need, or a favour difficult to achieve, or one which only one person can grant, or an agent who is the first person to do so, or who has done so to the highest degree.[34]

Crucial to this account is this perceptual capacity to 'see' morally salient features – this 'situational appreciation', to use Wiggins' term. The requirements of virtue cannot be fully captured in advance of coming across particular situations that generate them, nor can they be encapsulated in rigid or overriding rules. It is only when faced with the situation requiring the appropriate response that the virtuous agent can perceive what that appropriate response should be, and this is further supported by Aristotle's emphasis on education through habit, training and action. For it is only when we expose ourselves to appropriate situations and try to act in appropriate ways that we will come to see why they are appropriate and therefore why they are required. The process of moral education is exactly this process of exposure to the right response, so that we come to appreciate why particular reasons are special calls for action and should affect us in particular ways. Crucially, reason and emotion need to be working together, working in a particular way that implies co-operation rather than subjugation, in order for this capacity of situational appreciation to be exercised.

We now need to consider in more detail Aristotle's account of the emotions. It seems that, in general, there are competing accounts of the role of the emotions, particularly in relation to reason. In some of these accounts the emotions are presented as wild forces, outside the scope and control of reason, which must be eliminated and whose demands one must become entirely immune to. A slightly more useful role for the emotions has them as in principle contrary, but possibly open, to the direction of reason. Thus, the emotions should be controlled, limited, subjugated by reason. Yet a more co-operative picture sees the emotions as open to rational persuasion, amenable to training and development so that they can be useful allies to reason. Finally, another possibility is that the emotions are crucial parts of rational deliberation and the good life cannot be achieved without a full recognition of their importance and contribution. In general, Aristotelian commentators tend to emphasise his acceptance of the emotions as possible allies to reason, provided they are trained and habituated in appropriate ways and tend to present this as one of the advantages of his approach, often in opposition to rival methods of thinking. However, I suspect that an astute commentator could find textual evidence for almost all of the above positions on the emotions in Aristotle's work, and I think this is because it is a mistake to present his position on the emotions as unitary. Aristotle warns us not to expect precision from our subject matter, he warns us that we will need an acquaintance with psychology if we are to inquire into human goodness,[25] so why do we expect a single, neat and tidy answer to the question of the relation between reason and the emotions?

Let us distinguish between three kinds of desires (desires in general, *orexis*): emotions (*pathe*), appetites/sensual appetites (*epithumiai*) and rational wish (*boulesis*).[26] In the virtuous person emotion acts in accord with reason, motivating the agent towards the right action, while right action flows unimpeded from the agent's deliberation. By emotion here I mean the *pathe*. Aristotelian moral development involves a long process of habituation, education and training, through which the student of virtue moves from starting points, 'the that', to understanding 'the because'. This process of gradual development is neither exclusively cognitive nor exclusively emotional, but also, neither are these two separate dimensions which come together in virtue, but rather reason and the emotions are engaged in an entirely intertwined and interdependent process, each shaping the other's development.

This is an important point to make, as the relationship between reason and the emotions should not be characterised by a picture which presents one of these two elements as overpowering the other, or as having relative merits which must be preserved at the cost of the other approach, or as in any way as a rival, confrontational or antagonistic account where one element struggles to get the 'upper hand' over the other. Rather reason refines and influences our affective responses, while the emotions colour and shape our rational judgments. Coming to see the world is a matter of both emotions and reason. Our emotions colour how we perceive the world and, through moral imagination and empathy, allow us to make sense of what we perceive. The judgments we make are influenced by our emotional understanding and are shaped by the insights afforded to us by the emotions.[27] For example, the judgment that someone needs assistance is intimately tied with an emotional response to the perception of that person's pain; it is the feeling of sympathy at another person's suffering that generates the thought that assistance is required here. At the same time our emotions are influenced by our judgments. For example, the realisation that someone's suffering is the result of a well deserved, just punishment will put an end to any emotions of sympathy towards him. Reason will shape the type of emotional response based on the appropriateness of its judgments, for example, we are moved to pity when the misfortune suffered is undeserved, but rejoice at good fortune that is deserved.[28] This is an emotional response that is directly influenced by a judgment regarding the merit of the good fortune and one that can radically change in focus through a new understanding of what is happening in this particular case. Our emotional responses should be appropriate, that is they should be related in the appropriate way to the correct judgment of what it is we perceive.

It is through both reason and emotion that we view the world, understand what it is we are seeing, evaluate it and respond to it.[29] And it is through both reason and emotion that we move from mere beginnings, 'the that', beyond knowledge to full understanding, 'the because'. Coming to understand 'the because' is coming to fully appreciate why 'the that' was required in the first place, but this is not a different kind of knowledge, that is, one lower level, the other higher level, but a different kind of understanding of the same things, a full appreciation of the noble and the good, which includes an internalisation of the noble and the good. This is what is involved in saying that virtue involves choice, and choice of the good means choosing it knowingly and for its own sake.

For Aristotle reasoning and emotion combine to produce choice, the result of which is action.[30] So choice is neither exclusively reason, nor exclusively emotion, or the subjugation of emotion by reason; rather 'choice is either appetitive intellect (*orectikos nous*) or intellectual appetition (*orexis dianoitiki*); and man is a principle of this kind',[31] by which he means that man is a union of reason and emotion that causes action. It is interesting to note that Aristotle chooses to give us both formulations, both 'appetitive intellect' and 'intellectual appetite', in a sense refusing to give primacy to either reason or emotion. He also makes choice rather than action central in determining character, a point he will need to distinguish between the virtuous and the continent man later on.

Finally, one more relevant concept here is the idea of rational wish (*boulesis*). Practical reason (*nous*) alone is not sufficient for producing movement, but when action results from practical reason then this also involves rational wish. Rational wish is aimed at the good, for we do not wish for anything unless we think it is good,[32] and it is not connected to the seeking of pleasure and the avoidance of pain like all the other emotions. Since wish can be directed by reason, if we reason to the noble and the good, our rational wish will be aimed at the noble and the good, and it is characteristic of the man of virtue that his rational wish aims at the noble and the good.[33] Thus, whereas emotions may aim at all sorts of pleasures, wish is the rational longing for the noble and the good.

The virtuous man then perceives and judges everything correctly, having both the right reason and the right desire, his choice affirms the truth of what he has affectively deliberated about, becoming the standard of what is noble and good, which is exactly what his rational wish aims for.[34] His deliberation, wish and choice are expressions of his character, that is, they are, in different ways, intrinsically connected to the noble and the good and his virtue displays itself in his action which proceeds unimpeded from his character. As we would expect from our original discussion concerning the appeal of the moral good, we do not need to ask how motivation is possible given the agent's deliberation, choice and wish; rather motivation comes about through the agent's understanding of the noble and the good. Coming to understand the good is tantamount to coming to see, coming to be persuaded, and coming to be motivated to do the good, hence choosing the good. In this sense 'understanding' is a technical term, involving perception, appreciation, affirmation and motivation by the noble and the good.

6.

So much for what should be the unproblematic case of the virtuous agent, but given all this, how can we make sense of the *akratic*? Now it would be a mistake to think that all *akratic* behaviour is one unified phenomenon. Aristotle himself distinguishes a number of ways in which one can be *akratic* in Book VII of the *Nicomachean Ethics*.[35] I will concentrate on two interpretations of what might be occurring when agents act *akratically*, one has to do with the development in the relationship between reason and the emotions, the *pathe*, the other with the role of *epithumiai*.

We need to give an account of knowledge in the virtuous, continent and incontinent agents. For, the way we characterised *akrasia* at the beginning means that we still need to account for how it is possible for the *akratic* to have knowledge but to act against it, especially since the knowledge in question is knowledge of the noble and the good. The answer to this seems to be that Aristotle means more than one thing when he speaks of knowledge and admits to many distinctions to the idea. Book VII starts with the Socratic dictum to emphasise the attraction of morality, but this attraction is only effective on those on whom it is felt, that is, the virtuous agents. The incontinent agent possesses knowledge in the sense of knowing what is right, but not in the sense of being disposed to do what is right,[36] which gives a good indication of at least two ways in which one can have knowledge. What Aristotle means when he claims that the incontinent man knows what is right in the sense of actively contemplating it but only as a man who is asleep or drunk is said to know without exercising this knowledge,[37] is that the link between knowledge, understanding, choice and motivation is broken. This is mere knowledge, without the motivational appeal of the noble and the good, which comes through such knowledge, without the choice being made knowingly and for the sake of the chosen and without the rational wish aiming at that which the virtuous agent aims at.

Interestingly, this is also the difference between the continent agent and the virtuous agent, in that the continent also knows but is not disposed in the proper sense of the word. Proper dispositions result unhindered into action, whereas the continent action is the result of struggle. In this sense the continent cannot be said to be disposed to act in accordance with the right reason; rather, although he does act rightly, it is only as a result of winning the struggle. On another occasion, were he to lose the struggle, he would not perform the right act.

However, it is fair to ask a further question: why is it that the virtuous agent knows in the full sense of the word, whereas the others do not? In what respect is the knowledge of the continent and incontinent agents lacking? When we considered the virtuous agent we painted a picture of choice as the result of both reason and emotion, affecting each other and shaping the outcome of deliberations. Perhaps the fault of the continent and incontinent agents is insufficient moral maturity. That is, virtue is the end product of a long process of development, while continence and incontinence are earlier stages on this developmental road. For example, developing the emotional sensitivity required to bring salient moral features to the attention of reason in the proper manner is a difficult task, and immature agents are unlikely to have mastered it in its entirety. The incontinent agent's vision is obscured, like that of the drunk or the sleeping, because it has not been fully and properly developed. Like a student who merely parrots what he knows, the incontinent does not fully understand what he knows, and coming to understand requires both rational and emotional development. Hints of the proper understanding of this knowledge can come through (and surely this will be a gradual process, with set-backs, dependent on the circumstances one comes across, the temptations one is exposed to, the different ways in which the different aspects of one's natural tendencies develop, and so on) and these will be instances when continence wins the struggle. Thus, Aristotle can conclude: '... that the Socratic dictum "Nothing is mightier than wisdom", is right. But in that by "wisdom" he meant "knowledge", he was wrong; for wisdom is a form of goodness, and is not scientific knowledge but another kind of cognition'.[38] This wisdom (which we have termed 'understanding' and contrasted with knowledge) requires both rational and emotional judgment and, through choice, involves being motivated to pursue the noble and the good.

So much for the first interpretation of akratic action, which has to do with the development of the relationship between reason and emotion. Previously we mentioned *epithumiai* as a species of desire, and it is now time to return to this idea. We have said that emotions are intricately connected with reason, affecting judgments and being affected by them; however *epithumiai* are different. *Epithumiai* are an irrational species of desire having to do with natural desires, such as the desire for food, thirst, hunger, sexual pleasure and generally desires having to do with the senses.[39] Unlike rational desires (which include emotions and rational wish), which are open to rational conviction, that is, we can come to have them when convinced that something is pleasurable, one cannot be talked out of one's *epithumiai*. Rational desires are modified and may even come into existence or cease to exist based on the judgments of reason; for example you can convince a person not to act on his anger by pointing out how the object of his anger is undeserved. But one's *epithumiai* persist; for example, one remains hungry until one eats and before that he cannot be rationally talked out of his hunger, although they are amenable to reason in another sense; that is, one can be talked out of acting on their *epithumia*; for example, one can be persuaded not to eat even when hungry.[40]

Now most of these remarks on *epithumiai* occur in the *Rhetoric*, which does not touch on the topic of *akrasia*, but I think that they can help illuminate the discussion of *akrasia* in the *Nicomachean Ethics*; for it is the term '*epithumiai*' which is used when explaining how weakness of will is possible when appetite becomes the principle from which the *akratic* acts.[41] *Epithumetic* appetites are particularly strong, natural desires, which are not amenable to reason, exactly the sorts of things one would expect to be able to exert contrary influences. Appetites associated with our need for food, drink, sex, and all our senses are all good candidates for the kinds of desires that can subvert one's purpose and take over, resulting in *akratic* behaviour.[42] *Epithumetic* incontinence then is like an opportunistic infection, a strong, natural, irrational desire (*alogos orexis*) which waits its opportunity to manifest itself and take over, resulting in incontinent action. All *epithumia* needs is a mere hint of pleasure from the senses to rush off towards it.[43] It is important that what we have here is 'a mere hint from the senses' rather than a rational judgment, as *epithumiai* are not amenable to reason like other emotions. Consider how anger is compared to a hasty servant who hears the instruction of his master but in his hurry to carry it out hears half of it, or a guard dog who barks too quickly before he can ascertain whether the person at the door is a friend or foe.[44] Unlike anger which listens to reason but not always clearly, *epithumiai* are influenced not by judgement but by mere impression of the world, the impression of pleasure.

This accounts for why *akrasia* is a temporary condition, one that the agent can 'wake up' from or 'recover' from as in the case with drunkenness,[45] since when the pleasure ends the *epithumia* for it also comes to an end. If *epithumiai* are not amenable to reason, we cannot expect them to be habituated, trained or made to fit with the prescriptions of reason. Furthermore, given that *epithumiai* concerns themselves with fundamental desires, desires for food, drink, sex, and so on, it would also seem implausible to assume that they are eradicated in the virtuous man. Does that mean then that even the virtuous man is subject to the whimsical influence of the *epithumiai*? The answer here is that although we cannot control their existence or their aim, we can control whether they manifest themselves in action, an idea that corresponds to our understanding of what strength of will should be all about. The virtuous man has not eradicated his *epithumiai*, in the sense of not having any, but he can control whether they manifest themselves into action in accordance with the right principle.[46]

7.

We should now return to Cottingham's objection to the Aristotelian emphasis on the power of reason and ask, to what extent can we hold Aristotle to the charge of ratiocentricity? If we allow due weight to the influence and nature of *epithumiai*, as well as understanding the co-operative and mutually dependant relationship between reason and emotions, I think we will find that Cottingham's charge has less of an impact on Aristotle.

Epithumetic desires are by their nature strong and difficult to control, given that they are concerned with fundamental human drives. As such they play a crucial role in the phenomenon of weakness of will, subverting the dictates of reason. We have developed an account of *akrasia* such that it is these *epithumetic* desires for food, drink and sex that create the very problem of how an agent can know what is best and still not do it, allowing *epithumetic* desires to play a crucial role in our understanding of moral psychology. The ratiocentric model may be strong here and we may discern Platonic influences,[47] but this is only in respect to these particular kinds of desires, the *epithumiai*. At the same time, although there is a ratiocentric shape to this project of controlling these types of desires, it is important to note that Aristotle has a special place for them. He distinguishes these particularly strong desires for food, drink and sex and gives them a unique role in his account of the relationship between reason and desires. He also acknowledges that they can never be controlled as such, in that their existence cannot be affected by reason, the best we can hope for is for reason to determine whether we should act on them or not.

The interaction between reason and emotions, the *pathe*, entirely defies the conception of the ratiocentric model. Aristotle is not concerned to expunge these emotions, or to blindly subjugate them to the power of reason, rather he presents a co-operative and, more than this, interdependent picture of reason and emotion. Emotions shape the kinds of reasons that we have, while reasons change our emotions, both elements, emotions and reason, required for moral perception and choice and therefore for being properly motivated by an understanding of the noble and the good. The Aristotelian picture sees emotions play a full and equal part in what is required in coming to understand the noble and the good. At the same time, this account of the emotions does not share, in its entirety, the ratiocentric faith in the ultimate power of reason, as virtue can only be found at the end of a long and difficult road and may indeed be more of an ideal than an actuality.

This interpretation of *akrasia* is significant for two reasons. Firstly, it does away with the standard picture of the belief/desire model, a modern account of reason and desire that has come to dominate our interpretations of Aristotle. As we have seen the Aristotelian picture rejects this idea of two separate and rival forces, rather, integral to the notions of 'choice' and 'virtue' is an account of appetitive intellect or intellectual appetition. Secondly, it may well be that the account of virtue proper is an ideal, one which beings as vulnerable and fragile as we are can never achieve. This means that the good life is never fully under the control of reason, but Aristotle did not expect it to be nor does he see virtue as a struggle to bring about rational control. The good life is to be found at the interplay of reason and desire; it is fragile and susceptible to the vagaries that affect the inter-development of our affective and rational capacities.

We have, then, two interpretations of *akrasia*. The first has to do with *epithumiai*, appetitive desires associated with food, drink and sex, which are not amenable to reason in the sense of being able to be shaped by reason like *pathe*. The influence of these appetites can distort the dictates of reason so that they do not result in action, although it is possible to learn to control not so much the appetites themselves (that is, whether they are present) but rather whether they result in action. The second interpretation of *akrasia* has to do with the relationship between reason and emotions, the *pathe*, which can be habituated and educated to flow smoothly into the right action, but which is a long and arduous process, open to set-backs and struggle, a struggle which is exhibited in continence and incontinence.

Although we have not said much on this specifically we can conclude with some remarks on psychoanalysis and Aristotle. Clearly Aristotle has no account of the unconscious, but this does not necessarily mean that he should be read as assuming all desires to be immediately or easily fully transparent to reason. A certain kind of desire, *epithumiai*, plays a critical role and one of the main desires of this kind is the desire for sexual pleasure, which, contra Cottingham, allows Aristotle to be interpreted in a way that is more compatible with psychoanalytic accounts of the centrality of sexual desires in our psychological make-up. *Epithumiai* are deep, strong desires that are not under the control of reason and, although there is no explicit evidence of this thought in Aristotle's writings, we might plausibly assume that the thought that *epithumiai* could be entirely inaccessible to reason is not incompatible with what Aristotle does say about them. To further develop an Aristotelian metaphor, perhaps one's *epithumiai* are hidden from reason in the same way that one's full knowledge is hidden from a drunken man due to his drunkenness. There is something about these kinds of desires that makes them both inaccessible to reason and explains why they are inaccessible due to their very nature; they distort what reason can perceive, including their own presence.

Furthermore, the claim that the road to virtue is long, arduous, subject to set-backs and by no means certain, can be read to suggest that even *pathe* are, at times, more compatible with a psychoanalytic view of reason than Cottingham claims. If the emotions shape reason in as much as reason shapes emotions, then inappropriate emotions will cloud reason and may even cloud reason with respect to the true nature of these very emotions. The claim that there is such a thing as moral progress indicates that the agent can come to see through this 'cloud' to the noble and the good, but this is a difficult process and one which is not won by reason triumphing over the emotions.

8.

Cottingham's concern with the Aristotelian picture of the relationship between reason and desires seems to be three-fold. In the first instance Aristotle's view is characterised by a naiveté regarding the transparency of the emotions, which is demonstrably wrong in light of the psycho-analytic insights. Secondly, despite Aristotle's more compatible account of the relationship, his overall approach is one of optimism that the emotions can be brought under the control of reason. Finally, as a corollary of this optimism there is the thought that errant emotions can be rehabilitated, re-establishing the agent as 'master in his own house'. As we have seen Aristotle has, at least a partial, defence to these claims. Although clearly Aristotle does not recognise the full force of the uncon scious, his account of *epithumiai* as we have read it allows for strong and deeply routed emotions which can never come under the control of reason in terms of being extirpated. And even if the final picture of virtue is one of harmony, this is only achieved through a long and arduous process that betrays the fragility not only of reason but also of the emotions. For, the development from continence and incontinence to virtue requires true co-operation between the right reason and the right emotion, those aimed at the noble and the good, with cognitive judgments shaping emotional responses and emotions determining how we reason about the world. Finally, there is the question of the extent to which reason can master the affairs of the emotions. On this, I think there is even closer convergence between Cottingham's position and Aristotle's, although we do need to reconsider Cottingham's claim.

Cottingham's challenge to the dominance of reason makes use of the idea that human lives are subject to the vagaries of fortune. Psychoanalysis introduces fortune in our desires, which lead down avenues we can't foresee or control, at odds with the picture of all-powerful reason controlling the passions. The Freudian insight is that 'the area of 'fortune' – the recalcitrant residue over which rational choice has no control – extends inwards to the very core of our being. The complexities of the human psyche, the opaque and intensely problematic character of our deepest motivations, mean that the deeper significance of the very goods we strive for, the very plans we construct, is often obscured even from the strivers and constructors themselves'.[48] A linear picture of rational progression is rejected, replaced by a picture of past events being understood in the light of present revelations. Humans suffer from hubris, an arrogance of deliberative rationality, in believing that it is possible to have access to and evaluate all the relevant information when making a moral decision. This information only becomes available through genuine, deeper awareness and suffering which comes after the decision has been made.

The psychoanalytic insight is based on the importance of discovery. Motives, passions and influences operate at the time when we make our decisions, but they are hidden from us, unconscious. Psychoanalysis helps us to discover these hidden influences, as it involves '... a long process of recovery, rehabilitating those parts of the self which are initially submerged beneath the level of ordinary everyday awareness'[49] where '... the subject aims finally to unmask himself, to be at last faithful to the hidden truth of his desire, to recover the disassociated fragments of the self, and in so doing transform his self-understanding'.[50] The time dimension is important here since we are not restricted to the specific act in two ways: on the one hand many of our influences stem from our childhood and have their roots deeply in our past, on the other hand many of these influences are so deeply hidden that they can only be uncovered in the future. Thus, an overview of a whole life, as opposed to a 'slice' of time, is important.

However, both these points, the vagaries of fortune and the difficulties of discovering our own inner selves, form part of Aristotle's insight. Others have argued much more persuasively than I could here,[51] that the picture of human goodness Aristotle presents is fragile and vulnerable. This vulnerability stems precisely from the kinds of creatures human beings are and from the fragility of the project itself. Aristotle warns us that we will need to be exposed to the right influences at an early age, develop the right habits, be educated in the ways of virtue and count on a bit of luck for all this to go favorably before we have any chance of developing our reasoning and emotional responses in the right direction. Virtue requires the right emotions at the right time towards the right people for the right reason, but it is easy to miss and failure comes in many ways.[52] Although Aristotle talks about one way as the way of virtue, there are many ways in which things can go wrong and he frequently reminds us that it is not possible to specify all of them, and it is easy to make mistakes.[53] In the discussion of the mean Aristotle warns us that some extremes resemble the mean and may fool us, that we have a tendency to misperceive one extreme as opposed to the mean, that natural inclinations color how we view the extremes in relation to the mean, that we are likely to go wrong when judging pleasure and pain and that we must become self-aware, guarding against our own failings.[54] It is also interesting to note that as there are many ways of going wrong identifying them cannot be a matter for a rule to capture, but must rest with perception, a faculty which requires reason and emotion to co-operate. Aristotle also draws our attention to the possibility of holding out against strong emotion as long as we see it coming and have time to prepare for it,[55] leaving open the possibility that some emotions will 'creep up' on us unawares and their influence will not be accessible to reason.

Furthermore, Aristotle, probably more than any other philosopher, emphasizes how the moral project is a life-long process of maturity. Moral development is fundamentally affected by what happens to us as children, but this is not incompatible with the claim that moral development is not complete when we become adults. This life-long process surely requires awareness of our previous choices, how they affect our current states and a sense of self as developing and becoming more sensitive and aware both of the world around us and our own inner selves. Much of this forms part of the concept of 'character' as a 'work in progress'. Character development is an on going process, one which is influenced by what has gone before and how this is perceived by the agent, which requires gradual development and has no guarantee of success. Character evaluation and reflection is certainly something that we can only engage in if we consider the agent over time and have access to not just his actions and their consequences, but also what motivated these actions and the internal relationships between thinking and feeling about the noble and the good. If the psychoanalytic insight allows for the possibility of discovery and reflection on what one discovers, which can lead to change, then I think there is much in Aristotle that is compatible with this picture.[56]

Notes

1. Cottingham, 1998, p. 40.
2. Cottingham, 1998, p. 47.
3. Cottingham, 1998, p. 166.
4. I will return to this point at the end of this paper.
5. Cottingham, 1998, p. 52.
6. Cottingham, 1998, p. 44.
7. Cottingham, 1998, p. 51.

8. Cottingham, 1998, p. 26.
9. Aristotle, *NE*, 1145b 27.
10. Aristotle, *NE*, 1147b 15.
11. Davidson's work on weakness of will, mainly in Davidson, 1980.
12. As distinguished from a prudential conception or a comparison between alternatives, or other evaluative judgments not connected to moral evaluations.
13. It may be possible to fail to be receptive to this attraction of morality altogether and see no reason to act as it dictates, but this is a separate kind of issue. It is the knowledge of the moral good that is crucial here as this is tied to the claim that there will be attraction to the moral course of action. Once one is receptive to this attraction it is perplexing how one can, at the same time, ignore it.
14. Subsuming moral *akrasia* under the more general instance of weakness of will as a problem of intention can have peculiar consequences for one's reasoning. In his discussion of weakness of will Graham considers a pianist whose hands are recovering from injury, who rides her motorcycle despite her better judgment not to do so. He describes this decision as 'unfortunate', as it renders her deliberation irrelevant, but not unreasonable from an overall point of view. Such an account could not be used to explain moral *akrasia* as the thought that in being incontinent the agent's decision is merely unfortunate in making his deliberation irrelevant is peculiar to say the least, in that it ignores the appeal of the moral good. However we may end up making sense of the demands of morality, to describe a case of ignoring them as a case of unfortunate setting aside of one's deliberations is to miss the point. Graham, 1993, p. 119.
15. Aristotle, *NE*, 1097a 34ff.
16. Wiggins, 1980, p. 252.
17. I have tried to reserve the term "the noble and the good" for the good in the true and unqualified sense, while using the term "the good" for the good as it appears to each man.
18. For a detailed analysis on this, see McDowell, 1979. In general, similar views can be found in Santas, 1969; Wiggins, 1980; and Price, 2006.
19. For example, Aristotle, *NE*, 1147a 35–b 3.
20. Wiggins, 1980.
21. McDowell, 1996, makes a detailed case for this.
22. Aristotle, *NE*, 1106b 27–33.
23. Aristotle, *NE*, 1106a 4–6.
24. Aristotle, *Rhetoric* II, vii.
25. Aristotle, *NE*, 1102a 16–19.
26. So far I have used the terms 'emotions', 'desires' and 'passions' interchangeably, but in what follows I will use them specifically with reference to this distinction.
27. For example the characterization of emotions in Aristotle, *Rhetoric*, 1378a 20–3.
28. Aristotle, *Rhetoric*, 1386b 24–6.
29. For more detailed accounts, see Sherman, 1989; Leighton, 1996; and Nussbaum, 1990 and 1996.
30. Aristotle, *NE*, 1139a 32–3.
31. Aristotle, *NE*, 1139b 4–5 and for the general claim 1139a 32–3.
32. Aristotle, *Rhetoric*, 1369a 2.

33. Aristotle, *NE*, 1113a 21ff.
34. For example Arisotle, *NE*, 1113a 23ff.
35. Through out Book VII, for example the discussion of how different types of akratics respond differently to reformation, Aristotle, *NE*, 1152a 29–33.
36. Aristotle, *NE*, 1152a 6–7.
37. Aristotle, *NE*, 1152a 15ff. Note that Aristotle seems to be using the metaphor with drunkenness and sleep in more than one way, which can be confusing. In this passage, sleep or drunkenness is an analogy for a state in which there can be knowledge but it is not exercised. In the passage quoted below (1147b 7–10), the akratic with respect to *epithumiai* recovers from his *akrasia* by 'waking up' like the drunk or the sleeping.
38. Aristotle, *EE*, 1246b 34–7.
39. Aristotle, *Rhetoric*, 1370a 18ff.
40. These remarks are inspired by a detailed discussion of these topics by Leighton, 1996.
41. Aristotle, *NE*, 1111b 14–17 and various instance in Book VII, for example, 1147a 35–b 3.
42. Notice how Aristotle uses examples from the senses to illustrate his claim that desires can affect the practical syllogism and speak in terms of the desire carrying the body forward, *NE*, 1147a 24ff.
43. Aristotle, *NE*, 1149a 35.
44. Aristotle, *NE*, 1149a 25ff.
45. Aristotle, *NE*, 1147b 7–10.
46. Aristotle, *NE*, 1119b 15–19.
47. For example, Striker, 1996, p. 288, who analyses the Aristotelian account of *epithuniai* as being very close to the Platonic account of the relationship between reason and desire.
48. Cottingham, 1998, p. 134.
49. Cottingham, 1998, p. 140.
50. Cottingham, 1998, p. 141.
51. Most notably and eloquently Martha Nussbaum.
52. Aristotle, *NE*, 1106b 16ff.
53. For example, Aristotle, *NE*, Book II, ix.
54. Aristotle, *NE*, Book II, viii and ix.
55. *NE*, 1150b 19ff.
56. I am very grateful to Angus Dawson, Seiriol Morgan, Sam Vice, Tom Walker and Anthony Wrigley for comments on earlier drafts of this paper.

Bibliography

Aristotle, *Eudemian Ethics*, trans. Rackham H. (Cambridge, Massachusetts: Harvard University Press, 1996)

Aristotle, *The Art of Rhetoric*, trans. Freese J.H. (Cambridge, Massachusetts: Harvard University Press, 1994)

Aristotle, *Nicomachean Ethics*, trans. Thomson J.A.K. (London: Penguin Books, 1976)

Cooper J.M., 'An Aristotelian Theory of the Emotions', in Rorty A.O. (ed.), *Essays on Aristotle's Rhetoric* (Berkley, California: University of California Press, 1996)

Cottingham J., *Philosophy and the Good Life* (Cambridge: Cambridge University Press, 1998)

Davidson D., 'How is Weakness of Will Possible?', in *Essays on Actions and Events* (Oxford: Clarendon Press, 1980)

Graham G., *Philosophy of Mind: An Introduction* (Oxford: Blackwell, 1993)

Jackson F., 'Weakness of Will', *Mind*, XCIII (1984) 273–80

Leighton S.R., 'Aristotle and the Emotions', in Rorty A.O. (ed.), *Essays on Aristotle's Rhetoric* (Berkley, California: University of California Press, 1996)

McDowell J., 'Incontinence and Practical Wisdom in Aristotle', in Lovibond S. and Williams S.G. (eds), *Essays for David Wiggins: Identity, Truth and Value*, Aristotelian Society Series, 16 (1996)

McDowell J., 'Virtue and Reason', *The Monist*, 62 (1979) 331–50

Nussbaum M.C., 'Aristotle on Emotions and Rational Persuasion', in Rorty A.O. (ed.), *Essays on Aristotle's Rhetoric* (Berkley, California: University of California Press, 1996)

Nussbaum M.C., *Love's Knowledge* (Oxford: Oxford University Press, 1990)

Price A.W., 'Acrasia and Self-Control', in Kraut R. (ed.), *Blackwell Guide to Aristotle's Nicomachean Ethics* (Oxford: Blackwell, 2006)

Santas G., 'Aristotle on Practical Inference: The Explanation of Action and Akrasia', *Phronesis*, XIV:2 (1969) 162–89

Sherman N., 'Is the Ghost of Aristotle Haunting Freud's House?', *Proceedings of the Boston Area Colloquium in Ancient Philosophy*, 16 (2000) 63–81

Sherman N., *The Fabric of Character* (Oxford: Oxford University Press, 1989)

Stocker M., 'Aristotelian Akrasia and Psychoanalytic Regression', *Philosophy, Psychology and Psychoanalysis*, 4:3 (1997) 231–41

Striker G., 'Emotions in Context: Aristotle's Treatment of the Passions in the *Rhetoric* and His Moral Psychology', in Rorty A.O. (ed.), *Essays on Aristotle's Rhetoric* (Berkley, California: University of California Press, 1996)

Watson G., 'Skepticism About Weakness of Will', *Philosophical Review*, 86:3 (1977) 316–39

Wiggins D., 'Weakness of Will, Commensurability and the Objects of Deliberation and Desire', in Rorty A.O. (ed.), *Essays on Aristotle's Ethics* (Berkley, California: University of California Press, 1980)

Wilkerson T., 'Akrasia', *Ratio*, 7:2 (December 1994) 164–82

5
The Inner Life of the 'Dear Self'

Seiriol Morgan

1.

The last 30 years or so has been a period of considerable activity in the discipline of moral philosophy, as readers of this book will no doubt be aware. In my view the most important advance, and certainly one which stimulated much of the growth of interest in the subject, was the development of a variety of positions and arguments aimed at overthrowing what was seen by their proponents as the excessively rationalist orientation of Anglo-American moral philosophy as it had been practised hitherto. Attacking what they saw as the narrow, dry and rule-fetishistic focus of the deontology and consequentialism that dominated the subject at the time, both of which largely proceeded as if the permissibility or otherwise of actions was the only important or even legitimate question in ethics, these critics charged that moral philosophy had allowed itself to impoverish its own subject matter, by ignoring the emotions, qualities of character, and what makes a human life a good one, which were all once considered to be central concerns. Of course, the rise of contemporary virtue ethics was the most visible of these developments.

This period also largely coincides with that in which John Cottingham has been writing on the subject, to which he has made some seminal contributions. Cottingham was in the vanguard of the emerging critique of moral philosophy earlier in the twentieth century, focussing his efforts in particular on exposing the shortcomings of the widespread assumption that morality requires from each of us that we adopt maximally impartial perspectives upon the world and our actions within it when reasoning about what to do.[1] His distinctive claim was that not only did deontology and consequentialism ignore the question of the good life, but their joint insistence that the moral outlook must be a

111

maximally impartial one also ensured that the moral life and the good life could not coincide, since the moral life so conceived was deeply distorting of human flourishing. Human beings cannot reasonably be expected to take up the impartial perspective in their practical dealings with the world, because the value of life for us lies in various personal relationships and projects, which from that perspective can at best be of derivative importance. These observations led Cottingham to conclude that the conceptions of morality descended from the philosophies of Kant and Bentham were deeply flawed, and that the eudaimonist model of the ancients, in particular Aristotle's, was a much more fruitful one for ethical understanding.

In an important book published more recently, however, Cottingham has taken a substantial step towards a more radical critique of contemporary ethics.[2] This time his major influence is not Aristotle; indeed, the charge is one which now also cuts the ground from beneath the broadly Aristotelian position Cottingham himself once occupied. This time it is Freud, and in particular his understanding of human behaviour as in large part governed by the operation of unconscious forces opaque to reason, the nature and indeed even the existence of which we are frequently quite unaware. Cottingham has become convinced that the general picture of the human being advanced by Freud is in large measure an accurate one, and that this has profound implications for moral philosophy, implications that have been little appreciated by its practitioners up to now. Noting that the modern era has seen a profound loss of confidence that the good human life is one directed by reason,[3] Cottingham charges moral philosophy with having nevertheless blithely proceeded as if the last two centuries' developments in sceptical post-Kantian philosophy and psychoanalysis had never happened, largely just ignoring rather than engaging their profoundly subversive claims. Nor is there any possibility of overcoming the problem through a recovery of neglected older resources from the philosophical tradition itself, as was done when the first wave of critics looked back to Aristotle, since the ancient world was just as ignorant of the phenomena identified by Freud as Cottingham takes unreconstructed contemporary moral philosophers to be complacent about them.

Cottingham coins the term 'ratiocentrism' to denote the problematic set of assumptions he sets out to attack in the book. Although he focuses on the vulnerability of the eudaimonist approach to the Freudian critique, it is clear that all of the main currents in contemporary ethics are targeted by it; indeed, Cottingham thinks that ratiocentrism is the predominant outlook of the whole western moral philosophical tradition.

In a nutshell, ratiocentrism is the presumption that 'the rational ego is master in its own house',[4] and consequently that living a good life is a matter of the proper exercise of our rational powers. In Cottingham's opinion this presupposes that the psychological factors which govern an individual's actions are transparent to her conscious introspection. But on the contrary, the kind of self-knowledge that this requires is simply not available to us, as the Freudian critique has shown, and in carrying on with their projects as if it had not, contemporary moral philosophy is simply in denial about this:

> The old models of transparent rationality have been systematically eroded by the steady advance of psychoanalytic modes of understanding, to the point where the very idea of a rationally planned structure for the good life begins to look like a piece of naïve self-deception ... For those who have begun to come to terms with the implications of this loss of confidence, it must be something of a mystery that so many moral philosophers continue to write as though the mind were a transparent goldfish bowl, populated by clearly identifiable items called our 'beliefs and desires', in such a way that we only have to focus carefully on the relevant items, presented unproblematically to consciousness, in order to set about drawing up a rational plan for action ... Yet if it is the case that the very structure of the beliefs and desires on which we act can be subject to serious distortion of a kind which is often not accessible to us as we plan and deliberate, if our very grasp of what we truly want can be subject to a pervasive and potentially crippling opacity, then we need to rethink the optimistic vision of a rationally planned and organized life ...[5]

Let me say at the outset that I have considerable sympathy with Cottingham's concerns. Though I would once have identified myself as a defender of a broadly Aristotelian virtue ethics, it now seems to me that eudaimonist ethics has been too naïve in its optimistic assessment of our rational powers, and correspondingly too complacent about the darker side of human nature, in particular our capacity for wilful evil. Aristotle himself seems a good case in point, since his accounts of wrongdoing almost always have the bad person pursuing some kind of generally acknowledged good in circumstances in which this happens to infringe the rightful claims of others, as for example with the vice of *pleonexia*. Whilst clearly a great deal and probably the bulk of wrongdoing is of this nature, Aristotle rarely seems to sense that often what motivates human beings' vicious behaviour towards one another is the desire to have more than others, or that others should suffer, *as such*. For another, the tone of the *Nicomachean Ethics* suggests that Aristotle envisages that acquiring and exercising virtue will be a smooth and relatively uncomplicated process, at least for those who have received the right kind of upbringing, and are not such that their nature makes them natural slaves. But this very substantially downplays the conflicts that occur periodically in the lives of most people, and not just the bad or weak. And because of his very considerable influence upon the project, contemporary eudaimonist ethics is in danger of inheriting Aristotle's overconfidence without really noticing it.

Nevertheless, it seems to me that the way that Cottingham characterises the history of moral philosophy is too one sided, and this causes him to miss the way that similar (if less sophisticated) thoughts to those he endorses play a central role in some moral philosophies that seem to him to be paradigm examples of ratiocentrism. In my view, although Cottingham is clearly correct to say that the ratiocentric paradigm has been dominant in moral philosophy for the bulk of its history, there is a recognisable counter-tradition that can be identified, which has also exerted a significant if frequently unacknowledged influence on some of the moral systems and theories familiar to us. Instead of emphasising the power and authority of reason, and identifying the 'true self' with our rational faculties, this counter-tradition emphasises the will. For this reason, and for want of a ready-made expression, I'll refer to the outlook as 'voluntarism'.

The term 'will' is one of the least clear notions in philosophy, having been used in numerous senses, ranging from the mere power of voluntary action, through incompatibilist libertarian freedom, to the wilder metaphysically loaded conceptions of the will (or 'Will') as ubiquitous natural striving force in Schopenhauer and Nietzsche. So whilst the notion of 'ratiocentrism' is immediately intelligible, it is rather harder to say concisely what all of the proponents of the 'voluntarist' outlook share. But the basic contrast is this: whereas ratiocentric outlooks take the power of reason for granted in the genesis of our actions, and consequently must ascribe any failure to pursue the good as lying either in ignorance or else in a failure by the agent to properly use her core powers, voluntarists think that pursuit of the good involves more than properly grasping what it actually is. One must also commit oneself to it, and do so at least potentially in the face of a temptation to reject it, which lies at the core of the self. So not only knowing what to do but also having the will to do it is essential to being a good agent.

Although he was not the first to use the term *voluntas*, which appears in the Roman Stoics, the first genuine voluntarist in the philosophical tradition was Augustine, whose moral psychology effects a radical break with the view of the soul as capable of self-government through the self-sufficient use of reason. Instead, his work emphasises the impotence of reason to effect a change in the course of a human life when the will to do so is absent. The crucial question to ask about any man, in Augustine's view, is the nature of his deepest commitment, whether it is to his own gratification and power, or to the good works that God calls him to. 'For we are justified in calling a man good not because he merely knows what is good, but because he loves the Good'.[6] Orientation then, rather than understanding, is the central notion in ethics for Augustine. It is for this reason that he is widely credited with the discovery – or invention, depending on your point of view – of the will. But although this fact is generally insufficiently appreciated, Kant was also profoundly influenced by this tradition, and adopted much of its outlook in his moral philosophy. In doing so, he incorporated into it an appreciation of just the kinds of problems for moral philosophy that Cottingham's book highlights. Or so I will argue. I will not of course be claiming that Kant was some kind of proto-Freudian, as though he had an unarticulated grasp of psychoanalytic concepts such as repression, the unconscious, sublimation and so on, since he clearly didn't. But he did have an acute appreciation, nevertheless, of the way that reason is divided against itself, and of the difficulty this raises for moral agency. My claim will be that a number of features of Kant's supposedly ratiocentric ethics take the form that they do because he saw the need to address concerns analogous to those Cottingham raises, including some of those elements which have been found most objectionable by critics from Cottingham's old camp.

2.

Kant's own scepticism about the powers of practical reason is most clearly on display in *Religion within the Boundaries of Mere Reason*, in which he argues that a 'propensity to evil' is possessed by members of the human species universally.[7] We are, he claims, all 'radically evil', a term which in this context is not used, as it sometimes is, to mean out and out devilishness, something which Kant explicitly refuses to ascribe to any of us.[8] Rather, he means that we are evil 'at root'; that is, wickedness emerges from a primordial part of our nature, and is not a contingent characteristic acquired in the course of life. This propensity is impossible to eradicate, so its effects will be present in the actions of every human being throughout her life, even the best of us.[9] The most that we can do against the evil within us is to continually combat it, and the most we can achieve in this ongoing struggle is a slow progression from the bad towards the better, so that we commit less egregious breaches of duty, resist more by way of temptation, act more frequently in pursuit of the good ends we have adopted, and so on, without ever reaching a moral condition with which we can be satisfied.[10] So at least by the time he wrote the *Religion*, Kant had come to see rational self-possession as beyond us.

Nevertheless, it must be admitted that the *Religion* has long been viewed as an aberrant text in the Kantian corpus. Its publication was notoriously greeted with dismay by many of Kant's erstwhile admirers, who saw it is as a retreat from Enlightenment back towards religious superstition and misanthropy. And the book was basically ignored or treated as a historical curiosity by the bulk of writers on Kant's ethics throughout the last century, who seem to have found its claims impossible to square with the explicit commitments of the central ethical texts, never mind their spirit. So an initial scepticism that the received view of Kant's ethics as a paradigm of ratiocentrism can be convincingly undermined by appealing to what he says in the *Religion* is perfectly warranted. On the contrary; integral elements of Kant's system could have been designed with Cottingham's definition in mind. Or so one might think.

For one thing, it is quite clear that Kant thinks that standards of conduct are governed by reason alone,[11] and that to the extent that we allow 'empirical' considerations to enter our thought about value we completely undermine it.[12] For another, the enemy of morality from his earliest ethical works onwards is said to be self-love, which is the propensity to act to make our own happiness the supreme consideration in our practical reasoning.[13] The *Groundwork* makes clear that this is not only morally bad, but deeply irrational, since the categorical imperative has unconditional authority over our choices. This is because the pursuit of unfettered self-love involves the embrace of a material practical principle, throwing us into heteronomy, whilst the 'proper self' can only intelligibly choose a principle which preserves and expresses its autonomy.[14] Since the categorical imperative is the only principle that preserves autonomy, according to Kant, we all have reason to govern our behaviour by moral considerations.

To be heteronomous is to be a cause which has its source in something outside itself;[15] a heteronomous principle is thus one through which an agent allows his actions to be caused by forces 'alien' to himself.[16] Crucially, on Kant's view this includes the inclinations, since as a product of sensibility they are caused to exist in us by the material laws of the phenomenal world. The primary reason we have the inclinations we do is that they are thrown up by our animal bodies, prompting us to attend to its needs and pleasures; the basic incentives of sensibility are then stimulated and shaped by imagination and the forces of social interaction.[17] In none of this do we enjoy significant agency. But the 'real' self is transcendentally free; or at least, we must take it to be in our practical deliberations.[18] Indeed, spontaneity is all it is. So, if we embrace maxims of self-love when they conflict with morality, we are spurning what we most essentially are, because in choosing to act on inclination we choose to allow the causal forces of the world to be the determinants of what we do. Thus we make it the case that we might as well not have had wills at all, by behaving exactly as we would if we had not. Since such a choice is unintelligible, Kant thinks, we are rationally obliged to embrace the categorical imperative instead.

In this central argument, Kant seems to offer us a straightfoward reworking within his own intellectual context of the old Platonic position on reason and the desires. Just as for Plato, the reason we are said to have for avoiding bad action is that acting in this way allows reason to be dragged around by appetite, which is to unintelligibly renounce what we most essentially are. So Kant's basic picture of our moral situation looks like ratiocentrism pure and simple; a core rational self menaced by external forces, but secure to the extent that it makes proper use of its self-sufficient power to control them. And there is no hint here of the voluntarist suggestion that essential selfhood is somehow implicated in the wellsprings of wrongdoing. Or so someone sceptical of my thesis will be inclined to argue.

This understanding of what Kant is up to obviously gets a lot right. But it is not subtle enough, and does not grasp the whole of Kant's thinking on the matter, at least as it develops through the 1780s. In fact, the position defended in the *Religion* is the logical development of the account of agency and obligation presented in the *Groundwork*. This is because the *Religion* provides an implicit answer to a question which is ducked in the earlier work, the question of how the agent might come to act upon counter-moral inclination at all. The issue is this: A non-negotiable point about morality for Kant is that for an action to be appropriately subject to moral assessment the agent must be responsible for it, and for him to be responsible for it he must have freely chosen it. Since our inclinations are at least primarily the product of the operations of causes within the phenomenal world, then on Kant's view responsible action cannot have simple inclination as its driving force. In order for action upon desire to be action we can be responsible for, the agent must have freely made a choice to take the existence of the desire as sufficient reason to act to satisfy it. In Kant's terms, he must have incorporated the incentive into his maxim.[19]

But the question now arises as to what could motivate the agent to do so, when an inclination runs counter to duty. Kant insists that there cannot be a genuinely motiveless choice;[20] all intentional action must be action upon at least some putative reason or other. So every action must present itself to the agent as having at least something going for it. What is it in this case? Now, this might very well seem like a bizarre question, and an illegitimate demand for more in the way of an answer than is necessary. Surely, one might respond, the thing that the action has going for it is that the agent wants to achieve the end it is aimed at. But this would be to fail to grasp how Kant conceives of the agent. As the *Groundwork* argument for the authority of morality shows, what Kant thinks we most fundamentally are is our noumenal selves, whose essence is spontaneity; basically, freely operating rationality, or reason-responsive freedom. Insofar as this relates to our choices rather than our beliefs it is practical reason, which Kant equates[21] with 'the will', a term which he frequently uses in reified fashion as if speaking of some discrete faculty of the mind,[22] but by which he simply means the self considered in its free and rational aspects. It is this part of the self that makes the choice about whether to act upon sensible incentives or not; and in doing so it cannot be pushed about by the inclinations, on pain of losing the responsibility that Kant insists is essential to all genuine agency. The choice must be entirely its own.

So the appeal to the fact that the end of an action is desired misses the point, since the question is, what is it that leads the will to take desire-satisfaction as a reason for action when such action conflicts with the categorical imperative? We need an answer not from the perspective of sensibility, but from that of the will alone. And it seems impossible to provide one. As we saw, the interest of spontaneous agency lies only in autonomy, so only freedom is normative for it. Since an immoral choice undermines autonomy, it runs entirely counter to the interest of the will. So it is quite mysterious how the will could ever be motivated to make it. Preferring the worse to the better is one thing, but given its interests it seems on the face of it entirely unintelligible how it could see the choice in question as having anything going for it at all.

This question receives no answer in the *Groundwork*, nor the second *Critique*. But at some point prior to writing the *Religion*, Kant came to see both that some account of how immoral inclination gets its motivational grip on the will was essential to his system, and that any such account must appeal to something about the will's own nature, some factor through which the will allows cajoling inclination to appeal to it. Since the will's nature is pure spontaneity, only considerations of pure reason and freedom can be normative for it. But it can't be anything to do with our rational faculties considered *per se*, since pure reason simply pronounces that to act contrary to the categorical imperative is the wrong thing to do. Nor can it be at root a failure in their operation. Kant explicitly denies that reason can go wrong in informing us of our duties,[23] but in any case if 'immoral' action resulted from a breakdown of reason it would not be immoral, because to that extent we would cease to be rational agents, and so could not be responsible for it.

Instead, we must look for the factor in spontaneity as such, since it is intelligible that the agent might go wrong in pursuing freedom, whereas it is not in the case of rationality. As the *Groundwork* argument for the authority of morality shows, freedom is normative for the will. It is because the categorical imperative is the principle that expresses the agent's freedom that pure practical reason has an 'interest' in it, and so can act upon it.[24] So similarly, we can understand how the will can find the principle of self-love motivating, if we can provide an account of how it can present to itself its actions in pursuing inclination irrespective of duty as expressing freedom, even though in fact they do the reverse. This is possible when we reflect that the ability to exercise the power of choice (*Willkür*) in pursuit of personal ends is a basic element of freedom. This seems intuitive enough: if I wish to φ, and some factor prevents me from φ-ing when otherwise I would have chosen to do so, to that extent I have become unfree. Kant calls this aspect of freedom 'outer freedom', and agrees that it can be limited by the actions of others,[25] and extended when those infringing choices are hindered.[26] On these grounds, one might be tempted to go on to conclude that, the more one gets to do whatever one feels like doing, the freer one is. And this is indeed the logic of outer freedom. But importantly, only choices that remain within the bounds of legality, that is, actions which are in accordance with moral duty, can genuinely secure freedom for the agent on Kant's account of it. To attempt to extend one's freedom by refusing to acknowledge limits on one's own outer freedom, by permitting oneself to act immorally, is a self-defeating endeavour. This is because any extension of the sphere of personal choice beyond the constraints of the moral law will entail the sacrifice of the 'inner freedom' of autonomy, which is of course more fundamental than any particular exercise of the power of choice.

Nevertheless, despite its ultimately inscrutable irrationality, the only way in which the will can motivate itself to abandon its real interests, and throw itself into heteronomy in pursuit of immoral inclination, is through the wishful embrace of this conception of liberty as extended into license, since only freedom can be a motive for it, inner freedom clearly precludes immorality, and no other conception is available. So an essential element of wrongdoing on the Kantian picture is the direct collusion of the wrongdoer's rational powers in the act, by way of a fantasy of achieving personal freedom through the rejection of all constraints on agency. Since any human being is capable of immoral action at any time,[27] all of us must have – or perhaps more accurately, *be* – wills that offer themselves this temptation. It turns out then that the picture of the human agent presupposed by the *Groundwork* is one in which an ineliminable licentious urge to treat our own outer freedom as sufficient ground for action lurks deep in the heart of each of us, as a corollary of our rational powers. It was precisely because he eventually came to appreciate this that Kant saw the need to write the *Religion*.[28]

3.

Kant thinks that the radical evil at the heart of the human will manifests itself in numerous ways in our moral agency and experience. When properly described, even a partial inventory of these will take us a long way towards rebutting the accusation of ratiocentrism levelled against Kant. For instance: one of the main charges Cottingham advances as part of his case is Kant's insistence that all human beings know the law. In his view, this ascribes far too much power to reason, and ignores the way that the subterranean elements of the self shape the contours of our supposedly purely rational perspectives upon the world.[29] And there is no doubt at all that Kant does assert this. Indeed he is clear that grasping the content of the law is easy for every person;[30] this is unsurprising, since the will of every moral agent legislates the law for himself. For Kant, it is this universally inescapable self-legislation which gives the moral law its authority over each one of us, and makes us all accountable.[31] But this is not at all the same thing as Kant thinking that all of our actions are performed with full conscious awareness of their accordance with duty or otherwise; that is, with unadulterated moral clarity. In fact Kant does not think this, for at least two reasons.

First, there is a difference between legislating the law in abstract form and applying that legislation in the concrete and messy situations that life throws at us. It is the former about which knowledge is universally complete and inescapable. Kant's view is that no one calmly reflecting on general principles of rightness and wrongness in the abstract can arrive at an incorrect answer as to the moral status of any of them. But he was also insisting as early as the first *Critique* that principles need to be tailored in their application and, anticipating famous arguments of Wittgenstein, that there could be no further rule ensuring success in this endeavour; instead we must rely on judgement.[32] So whilst everyone is in no doubt that one should not be wilfully cruel, what exactly constitutes cruelty to a particular person at some particular time can seem to the agent open to question. Is this mockery bullying, or is it simply toughening the lad up, and preparing him psychologically for the rigours he'll face later? Does this demand constitute more than my fair share, or is it a reasonable one for someone in my special position,[33] for example, someone who's had to put up with the kind of day I've just had? And so on.

This gap between principle and application is what allows Kant to square his uncompromising insistence that everyone is clear what they ought to do, and the more complex moral psychology that he develops in the later work, and which is also visible in the background of the earlier texts. If Kant thought that conscience made everyone fully face the true moral status of each and every act he performs then there would indeed be no room at all for the notion of inner forces and longings undermining the ability of a person to properly grasp her evaluative situation, one that Cottingham thinks is an essential part of any viable theory of human agency. But he does not insist on this. Nevertheless, there is certainly a sense in which the wrongdoer always knows that what she is doing is bad;[34] if there were not, and she were genuinely ignorant of how to apply a rule, she could not be faulted for failing to do so correctly, and so could not be in this respect a wrongdoer. This brings us to the second reason, which is the ongoing activity of self-deception.

Nowhere does Kant provide a systematic analysis of his views on self-deception and its place in his moral psychology. But he was well aware of the way that the character of the will shapes the overall personality of the agent over time, and the effect that this can have on moral perception. In large part this involves the modification of sensibility's appetitive and affective elements, since, while Kant holds these to be external to the core self, and their nature to be determined by causal forces, it appears that he thinks that one of the forces in question can be the will's own activity. The will can generate desire by using its powers of imagination to represent situations which appeal to appetite, by suggesting how it might be gratified in new and enticing ways. And it can inflame it by directing its thinking in particular directions, by entertaining ongoing thoughts of the lack of the thing the desire is for and the pleasures that would result from its satisfaction, for instance, or obsessing about how this could be achieved:

> But reason soon began to stir, and sought, by means of comparing foods with what some sense other than those to which the instinct was tied – the sense of sight perhaps – presented to it as similar to those foods, so as to extend the knowledge of the sources of nourishment beyond the limits of instinct. If only this attempt had not contradicted nature, it could, with luck, have turned out well enough, even though instinct did not advise it. However, it is characteristic of reason that it will with the aid of the imagination cook up desires for things for which there is not only no natural urge, but even an urge to avoid ...[35]

This moulding of sensibility can have good results; indeed, the possession of appropriately tutored affections and inclinations is one way that Kant conceives of virtue.[36] But frequently it is very much for the worse, he thinks, as his discussion of two important phenomena, 'unsociable sociability' and 'the passions', indicate. Unsociable sociability results from the tension between two inescapable elements of human nature: our need to be in the company of others, since we cannot effectively fulfil our needs or achieve our desires outside of society, and our perverse yearning for unfettered freedom of the will.[37] We have no choice but to be social, but put any number of individuals with the latter characteristic together and it is inevitable that those wills will find themselves continually coming into conflict. Thus the human being must inevitably experience the social condition as both a benefit it would be unthinkable to abandon and an ongoing burden. The obvious response to this is for the will to chafe under its restriction, and correspondingly set itself the task of reducing it, by dominating and manipulating the wills of others. This can be done by the straightforward acquisition of power, or more indirectly via the acquisition of status, since an individual can more effectively bring about his purposes when his desires and opinions are correspondingly held by others to be more important and worthy than those of individuals lower down the hierarchy. As a result human beings have a habit of developing projects with the fundamental aim of expanding the arena of the will's self-assertion, and in some people such projects can become the central concerns of their lives. It should be no surprise that such people routinely direct their thinking towards the domination and defeat of others, and that their sensible characters are shaped accordingly, so that these individuals' most pressing desires and most intense pleasures become associated with achieving and maintaining such perceived superiority.

These inclinations Kant calls 'passions'. Along with the affects, which are episodic upsurges of emotion which saturate the consciousness of their subject, passions are particularly dangerous qualities of sensibility, ones we need to be without in order to be successfully self-governing.[38] In each case the problem is that the experience of the sensible quality makes it difficult for the subject to properly use her reason, hence drawing us away from the moral thinking through which we can see what we actually ought to do. Affect does this by overwhelming a person with so much emotion that he is temporarily prevented from thinking straight. Kant's example is of a rich man erupting into rage and distress when his servant breaks a valuable goblet.[39] If only he could calmly consider how little the goblet represented of his wealth overall, he could get the incident into perspective. But the torrent of sensibility that washes over him when he sees it smash fully transfixes his attention, and until it subsides he will go on thinking that this is disaster unparalleled. Passions are calm by contrast, and consistent with cool and measured reflection, because, unlike affects, passions are inclinations, desires that have become habitual.[40] Kant presents us with various other metaphors which are supposed to illustrate this difference, of which the most illuminating is that affect 'works like water that breaks through a dam; passion, like a river that digs itself deeper and deeper into its bed'.[41] So uncontrolled anger is an affect, but its close relation hatred is a passion, since the first is a state one is in only from time to time, even for those prone to it, whereas the second is a settled disposition with respect to another person, one which permanently alters its possessor's mental landscape.[42] But note that passion's compatibility with the use of reason in no way makes the pursuit of their ends any more rational than those of affect. Quite the contrary; that it is 'inclination that prevents reason from comparing it with the sum of all inclinations in respect to a certain choice' is one of the defining characteristics of passions.[43] Kant is explicit that possession of a passion enslaves its possessor to it, and that no one who understood their nature could want to have one.[44] Rather, what is happening is that reason's powers are being harnessed to passion's agenda, as reason itself is being subverted. And this is only possible because it is the self-assertive tendency of the will itself, the 'malice which lurks behind reason', which underlies the phenomenon.[45]

This is made clear by Kant's extended discussion in the *Anthropology*, in which the passions are described as follows: All the passions are inclinations to subordinate the wills of others to our own. Kant mentions hatred, the desire for vengeance, and the 'manias' for honour, power and acquisition as examples.[46] So they are always inclinations directed at other people; they are never for objects, except indirectly.[47] Similarly, passions are inclinations that no animal can possess; only human beings have passions. This is because passions presuppose maxims, and hence a process of reason, even though they prevent 'sensibly practical' reason moving from the general to the particular.[48] Once developed, passions are extremely hard to shift, because the passionate person does not wish to be free of them – 'passion is an illness that abhors all medicine ... an enchantment that also refuses recuperation'.[49] Passion takes pleasure in surrendering freedom and self-control. But this surrender necessarily brings suffering with it, because reason never ceases to call us to inner freedom,[50] with which passion is unavoidably in conflict. Nor can passion ever really be satisfied; although it can be sated, it always returns. Finally, although passion conflicts with freedom, the idea of freedom is an essential component of their generation – '[Reason] alone establishes the concept of freedom ... with which passion comes into collision ... [Passions] aspire to the idea of a faculty connected with freedom'.[51] This is another reason why no animals but only humans can possess them.

On the face of it Kant's concept of a passion may seem problematic, since various of his claims about them appear to be in tension. In particular, passion's intimate connection with rationality, and its subsequent subversion of it, may seem to pull in opposite directions, as do his claims about our wilful embrace of them, and the universal aversion to them. But focussing on radical evil clears any mysteries up. Passions as Kant characterises them are exactly the kind of inclinations that one would expect a radically evil being to develop, granted his views about the way a free and rational being can shape its own appetites. The radically evil will has a yearning for the maximal possible extension of its freedom of choice, the unlimited indulgence of its whims. Since the only concrete whims it can have are in the form of its desires, the licentious element of the self is pulled towards prioritising self-love, and those whose wilful commitment is to license systematically take getting what they want to be of fundamental importance. But of course other people inevitably stand in the way of the satisfaction of many of our desires, so many will consequently be thwarted. Naturally, this is likely to loom large in the consciousness of the licentious individual, and it is entirely to be expected that her imagination should turn to representing situations in which such obstacles are overcome as desirable. Such situations would include the power to compel others to do as one demands, or the money to traduce them, the crushing of the will of someone who has infringed on one's own, and so on. But of course desires such as these are central examples of passions.

Radical evil is also the hermeneutic key which allows us to understand all the other claims Kant makes on the matter. Why are the passions directed only by men towards men? Only human beings can possess them because unlike animals we possess the kind of will and cognitive powers required to shape sensibility into these particular formations. Only other humans can be the object of them because only other people have wills, so only other people can be experienced as offering resistance to our own wills; and it is only this active resistance that affronts one's own desire for freedom, in such a manner that the willful individual will be motivated to set his imagination searching for ways in which he can take pleasure in overcoming it. No one really hates or resents animals, or inanimate objects (except by anthropomorphising them, as perhaps Ahab did). It is the choice that another makes to oppose us that sparks the will to defeat it, without which there would be no passions. Why are they hard to break free from? Why can't the will just choose to ignore them like any normal desire? The answer is not that they have some kind of special alluring quality for a will poised between good and evil. The passions hold us in a particular grip because their existence presupposes that the will is already colluding in evil, since only a will determined upon its own power could generate inclinations like these. So what the will needs to combat is not mere temptation by appetite, but its own attraction to evil as well; thus a complete reversal of its own moral orientation will be required to make any proper progress in defeating them, a much more radical proposition.[52] Meanwhile, the passions will constantly be occupying the individual's thoughts with their dark aims and obsessions, preventing her from adopting the broader perspective from which their bankruptcy would become visible, cajoling her to expend her rational powers in what is in fact reason's own dissipation. Finally, how can the passions arise from freedom, and require the idea of freedom, and yet in fact function to enslave their possessor? The reason is that they are generated in sensibility in those persons who have embraced the erroneous conception of freedom as license. Without that rudimentary understanding of freedom there could be no passions,

since passions are qualities which imitate the idea of the faculty of freedom. But just because the idea that freedom as such is outer freedom is
an erroneous one, those who pursue freedom in this manner fail to
achieve the genuine freedom that comes with moral commitment
and action. Those in whom the passions are well developed inevitably
possess the kind of will which has rejected the attempt to acquire it,
and their presence makes a change of heart all the more difficult.

Such a psychological profile represents the human being at his worst,
and it by no means describes the moral condition of everyone. But in
the account of the passionate person, which Kant provides, we can see
that, like Cottingham, he thinks that reason is entirely vulnerable to
being crippled by the darker elements of the psyche; and also, crucially
in this context, that the root of all this trouble is not some mere extra-
neous element that can be simply dominated or domesticated or extirpated by appropriate use of the rational powers of the core self, but is
the deviant activity of spontaneous reason itself. And since the propensity to evil is universal, every one of us will be subject to some degree to
the self-assertive drive, and its corresponding appetites and blindnesses.
Radical evil is never overcome, even in those who have turned their orientation away from self-love, and embraced morality as their fundamental maxim. Whatever our moral histories and habits, whatever the
extent of our sympathies and docility of our desires, and whether or not
we are committed to the categorical imperative as our fundamental
principle of action – something about which in any case no one can be
sure[53] – any one of us might at any time find our inner attraction to evil
welling up despite ourselves, and casting some dark and self-centred
course of action in a seductive light. Or more likely, and more troubling,
we may suddenly come to dimly understand of some project we are
engaged in, that this has been true of it all along.

4.

By now it should be clear why I take Kant to have at least one foot in
the voluntarist camp, and his thinking about wilfulness and implicitly
self-deception to provide at least a partial anticipation of the kind of
post-Freudian concerns that Cottingham raises. Admittedly, there is no
indication that Kant ever ascribed any serious role to childhood events
and insecurities in producing akratic or otherwise counter-moral motivation. There are some tantalising suggestions of ideas along Freudian
lines; for instance, the section of the *Anthropology* entitled 'On the representations that we have without being conscious of them', where he

discusses the 'obscure' representations, of which we can only be indirectly conscious.[54] In a dramatic break with earlier thinkers like Locke, who held the contents of the mind to be essentially available to direct introspection, Kant states that the bulk of our representations are obscure. So he holds that in fact most of our mental activity goes on beneath the surface of consciousness. He also claims that we can be active in forcing uncomfortable thoughts into obscurity, and, interestingly, that this is what we characteristically do with respect to our sexual urges.[55] But it would be quite wrong to try to turn Kant into some kind of proto-Freudian, as I said earlier. Nevertheless, he is certainly not an unreconstructed ratiocentrist either. Just as Cottingham does, if for somewhat different reasons, he takes moral agency to be continually under threat from forces which are both mysterious from the point of view of conscious reason, and particularly hard to subject to conscious control, because they have their root in just the same inner part of the psyche.

For this reason I want to suggest that there are remarkable congruities between the Kantian picture of the moral situation of the human agent, and Freud's account of the human animal. This is something that can easily be obscured by differences of emphasis in the accounts of the two philosophers, and also by the importantly different way they conceive of their projects. At a relatively superficial level, the particular vocabularies that each uses to articulate his position carry rather different connotations and associations. For one thing, Kant's language is that of evil, stressing personal responsibility for the wrongs we do, and correspondingly guilt for our transgressions. Despite its very different intellectual roots, there are clear echoes of the Christian doctrine of original sin here. There is nothing like this in Freud, whose language at least presents itself as that of the morally disinterested scientist, non-judgementally identifying and classifying the human organism's psychological pathologies, with purely the aim of relieving the suffering they cause in mind. So Kant's *Religion* project can give the impression of being intimately bound up with an excessively moralising agenda, something with which Kant is often popularly associated anyway, in stark contrast to Freud's ostensibly more humane emphasis on helping people without making them feel guilty, by treating their troubles not as failures, but as sicknesses that have happened to them.

I think this would be overblown however. When Kant says that evil is at the root of wrongdoing he simply means that it must involve a choice in wilful opposition to the moral law; he is not suggesting that every minor moral transgression should be viewed with the seriousness that the major moral wrongs picked out by the colloquial use of the term deserve. And the existential impact of a doctrine such as Kant's cuts both ways in fact. On the one hand, it requires that everyone think of themselves as flawed and failing, and quite rules out anything like moral self-satisfaction. On the other, in arguing that the evil urges to which we are subject are ultimately ineliminable, and that even the best of us will periodically fail to resist them, he allows us to occupy a standpoint upon our actual transgressions which is somewhat comforting. Kant's view is that for every particular immoral action one performs, one was free not to do it, and so one is morally responsible for it and carries the appropriate corresponding guilt. But granted the inner bent of our nature, and the way it continually skews our reflection towards self-centred ends as well as the sheer number of daily opportunities we have to go wrong, for every agent it is inevitable that there will be ongoing transgressions, even if each particular one could itself have been avoided. So whilst insisting that accepting appropriate guilt for our bad actions is rationally mandated, this sense of wrongdoing's general inevitability allows us to avoid being crushed by it. Consequently Kant explicitly condemns moral despair, and the self-hatred that comes with taking oneself to be morally worthless.[56] All this strikes me as exactly the right way one should relate to one's own wrongdoing.

But this issue about language also reflects a more substantial difference, which in turn raises a problem to which I think Cottingham devotes too little attention. As I mentioned above, they take themselves to be engaged in doing quite different things. Kant's project is supposed to be one in moral philosophy, that is, a practical one conducted within the first- and second-personal perspectives. He aims to present to each agent an account of her practical situation, identifying what morality demands from her and providing a compelling argument for the practical authority of those claims, *for her* as deliberator. Freud's by contrast is supposed to be a piece of empirical science, conducted from the third-person point of view, albeit with the aim in mind of achieving results that are first-personally desirable. What Freud was trying to provide his readers was a therapeutic methodology to be used *by* analysts *on* patients, in order to effect their release from pathological symptoms. His implied audience is the analyst as personally disengaged student of human nature, presented with objects of investigation in the form of particular human subjects, which of course he gets to observe from a vantage point outside the flow of the life in question. The situation Freud envisages is one where a person finds that he has locked himself into a pattern of behaviour that is in some way bad, from which he seems unable to escape, and that he does not understand his behaviour as a result. He goes to the analyst, whose job it is to produce the narrative which makes clear what it is the individual has in fact been pursuing and why he is attracted to it. This new self-understanding is supposed to provide the analysand with renewed powers of agency; but he only achieves this as a result of being given the self-interpretation by someone who is not subject to the passions that drive him. For this reason it is not possible to read Freud's texts as directly offering to individuals the same kind of personal practical guidance as Kant's do.

So, granted then that Freud was not trying to provide us with a moral philosophy, we need to go beyond what he actually gives us in order to apply his insights within it. The central questions of moral philosophy are practical ones, about what to do, what type of life to pursue and so on; they are questions that actual agents can put to themselves at particular times during their lives, in an attempt to make better rather than worse choices. After Freud, we should now accept that human agents are subject to powerful urges from the unconscious, which can colour damaging courses of action in a rosy hue and indeed make them seem dazzlingly attractive; what's more, our evaluative sensibility can be skewed and distorted by subterranean forces as well. How should this affect our conception of the situation the agent deliberating practically finds himself in? Obviously the considerations adduced by Freud introduce the worry for the deliberator that at any particular moment of choice he doesn't really want what he thinks he wants, and that his perceptions of value might be illusory projections of some deep inner yearning quite alien his conscious goals. But, *ex hypothesi*, these are not things he can discover through any ordinary process of self-reflection, because these motives swamp the rational powers of someone in their grip. So what is he to do?

Here neither Freud nor Cottingham provide us with enough help. Consider for instance Cottingham's illuminating example of Cecil.[57] Cecil is the erstwhile family man who suddenly leaves his wife and family for a younger, brasher woman, telling friends and colleagues that he has found love, and having broken free of stifling convention, is embarking on a new life of joyful spontaneity. Naturally, the affair doesn't last. Within months the new couple have begun to bore and irritate each other, and Cecil increasingly comes to find his new partner to be shallow and uninteresting in comparison with his wife. They split up. Cecil tries to go back to his family, but is refused. He is devastated and sinks into depression as he realises he has traded the most valuable things in his life for a mirage.

The example is supposed to show the poverty of standard ratiocentric accounts of akrasia, which have to locate the source of moral weakness in some failure to properly exercise rationality in the face of appetite. As Cecil reflects on his behaviour after the event, he finds it an utter mystery to him. He is no mere philanderer who has been caught out; he sincerely thought that he was beginning his life anew, this time to live fully authentically. But now he cannot see how he found any of his lover's characteristics attractive at all, let alone how he thought he could spend his life with her. So his was not a case of weakness in the face of the desirable, or the overvaluation of present gratification. It was the turning against him of his evaluative sensitivity itself. What Cecil didn't and couldn't at that time understand is that the whole episode resulted from a deep-seated need for a vicarious provision of the maternal affection denied him in childhood. In possessing characteristics similar to his mother, and yet appearing to bestow affection on him through flirtation, Cecil's lover made an electric connection with his unconscious longing, and so became 'irresistibly' attractive.

Cottingham's whole focus is about what someone like Cecil could do *after* unfortunate life events such as these; his view is that moral progress and an increase in self-control is possible, but only by eschewing the ratiocentric assumption that reason is the captain of the soul, and accepting that rationality cannot provide us with the power to occupy some uncontaminated Archimedean point from which these perceptions can be securely evaluated, since reason is as caught up in the stream of the unconscious as everything else. It is only through coming to grasp what these forces are that we can escape from being their playthings. But of course this will be difficult, since they are not like ordinary appetites, whose ends and power to tempt we well understand. Rather, both their sources and their real aims are in the main opaque to us. Consequently, only the deep and unfamiliar self-knowledge that psychoanalysis provides can give us the ability to identify the effects of such forces in our outlook and motivation, and give us some measure of agency with respect to them.

These are certainly important observations. It seems quite clear that such forces exist, and frequently drive human behaviour. Most of us will have encountered people, for example, whose lives consist in an ongoing series of relationships with 'the same' unsuitable partner, never succeeding in breaking free of the pattern, with the problem being that they find it hard to direct their behaviour rationally because they do not understand what is driving their attraction. Similarly, Cecil's is a tragic yearning, for if not actually logically self-defeating it will almost inevitably be so practically, since any woman possessing those self-centred characteristics that would make her suitable as a maternal stand-in for Cecil would for that very reason be unlikely to make him a suitable long-term partner. Sufficient self-knowledge to avoid falling into these traps would make an enormous difference to such people's lives; indeed, all the difference between happiness and misery.

But we can also consider the example from the perspective of the deliberating Cecil, considering whether to leave his wife, or Cecil reflecting later about his deliberations at the time. One thing one might feel like claiming about the period of choice is that in fact there wasn't really any choice; granted the psychological hook-up between his long-repressed longings and the other woman's fatally attractive persona, she was literally irresistibly attractive, and there was no chance of him doing anything but leave his wife. But whatever an outsider looking in might conclude, this self-understanding doesn't seem available to Cecil, because it is incompatible with his no-doubt crushing sense of guilt. He does not and cannot view the destruction of his relationships as something that just happened to his life, with its coming about through his behaviour incidental. He will feel nothing like he might if, say, his wife had some kind of personality change after an accident, which then caused the relationship to break down. It is not the world's fault, it is his alone. So his self-understanding can only be of him having brought the result upon himself, through personal weakness and failure.

What Cecil's sense of guilt will lie in is his acceptance that, despite the acknowledged maelstrom of sentiment that assailed him, he could and should have resisted the course of action that at the time seemed so attractive. The reason he must take himself to have been able to have done so is that he can identify the resource which he could have made use of, which is precisely his knowledge of right and wrong. Indeed, this was the only resource available to him to avoid disaster, since the whole problem was the untrustworthiness of his affective nature, as his desires and emotions were pushing him in the wrong direction. Whatever the strange and heady excitement the new woman sparked in him, he was not literally swept off his feet; he could still have concentrated on those features of his situation which told against his course of action, in an attempt to steady himself, and do the right thing. He could and should have thought about the respect he owed to his wife after years of partnership, the value of loyalty, the effect of his actions on his children, and so on. These are the factors that could have provided him with a source of motivation to counter the disastrous temptation he actually succumbed to.

The psychoanalytic clarification of the nature of an agent's self-destructive motives after the event is no use to the agent trying not to go wrong in the first place. Nor will it be able to do much to promise to assuage future guilt for the actions she must perform now. Even if it can identify the motives which clouded a judgement, the agent must still see it as *her judgement* insofar as she views herself as an agent, one she made badly. And as Kant pointed out, we cannot but regard our own actions under the Idea of freedom.[58] The quotation from Kierkegaard, that life can only be understood backwards, but must be lived forwards, is clearly relevant here.[59] But from the Kantian point of view, it is too pessimistic. It is only with hindsight that we can have the distance to get a properly dispassionate grasp on the events of our lives, admittedly. But that doesn't mean that we understand nothing of our lives while in the midst of living them, or we would not be agents at all. Rather, although we do understand most of what we are doing in the process of doing it, we don't understand everything about our motives and behaviour, and we can never be certain that our self-conceptions accurately reflect the way we really are. This means that living a good human life can be a very difficult business, and very few lives proceed in a manner with which their owners are fully happy, with their lives and with themselves; indeed, those who take themselves to be happy are frequently the most confused of all. So the Kantian picture of the human condition is a tragic one in many ways. The human self is split against itself, subject to two fundamental sources of normativity which are in substantial tension with one another. When they conflict, the freedom of moral agency always trumps happiness; but the claims of happiness don't disappear, and inclination will not cease to torment us if we do the right thing. If we do the wrong thing, we cannot escape guilt and self-loathing.[60] Even if we commit ourselves to the moral life, we will inevitably fail to live up to it, because we can never fully control our own inner attraction to wickedness. In sum: we are most unlikely ever to be really happy, we are never fully in possession or control of ourselves, and ultimately we are bound to fail to preserve our dignity to at least some degree. But this is no reason for us not to strive to do the best we can; indeed, this is all we can do in the position we find ourselves in.

In my view various elements of Kant's practical philosophy have the character they do because Kant understands this to be the situation of the agent, and failure to grasp this has frequently resulted in their being misconstrued. In particular, this is the background against which Kant's account of virtue must be understood. Kant talks about virtue in a number of different senses, but the central conception of virtue in Kantian ethics is of virtue as strength, *fortitudo moralis.*[61] According to Kant, 'unholy' frail beings such as ourselves require not only autonomy in order to fulfil the requirements of duty, but also autocracy, the capacity to master unruly inclinations when they rebel against the categorical imperative.[62] Whilst our consciousness of the moral law informs us of our ability to comply with any duty just because it is our duty,[63] to actually do so requires effort if it conflicts with inclination, in proportion to the inclination's strength,[64] an effort which the individual will find difficult to produce unless her commitment to moral principle is firm and resolute.[65] Virtue is the *developed* capacity to exercise the will to face down the inclinations, a capacity acquired through contemplation of the dignity of morally worthy actions, and the repeated exercise of the will in carrying them out.[66] Kant variously refers to this as 'moral strength of a *human being's* will in fulfilling his *duty*',[67] 'the strength of a human being's maxims in fulfilling his duty',[68] and 'self-constraint in accordance with a principle of inner freedom'.[69] Thus what distinguishes the virtuous person is that he rules himself and is his own master, rather than allowing inclination to get the better of him; in particular, he is wise to the dangers of affect and passion.[70] In so doing he secures his own inner freedom, and exemplifies a noble character.[71]

Once again this is an element of Kant's moral theory which has been roundly condemned, usually by critics of an Aristotelian or Humean stripe, who have standardly presented it as taking the form that it does because of Kant's all-encompassing contempt for sensibility. One can easily see how a connection might be thought to exist between Kant's notorious remarks in the *Groundwork* about the worthlessness of acting upon even warm-hearted sentiment,[72] and the claim that virtue is the moral strength to resist the temptation to act in pursuit of self-love. And it is certainly true that Kant is suspicious of the inclinations, which he holds to lack sufficient constancy to reliably lead us to do the right thing. Even in those whose emotions have been cultivated to emphasise benevolence and sympathy, these temperaments cannot be relied upon, partly because they can fix upon undeserving objects[73] and partly because habits become ingrained within familiar contexts, and it is hard to predict a person's reaction when she is placed outside of them.[74] Or so Kant thinks. Much ink could be spilled over this issue, and it does seem to me that Kant is too pessimistic about our ability to control our emotions, missing as he does most of the intelligence that can exist within them. But I'll put this to one side, because actually the central problem in Kant's view is not inclination, but radical evil.

As a quality of the will, Kantian virtue is something that we can only ascribe to people from the first-personal and interpersonal points of view. It is invisible when we take up the third-personal perspective of the scientific observer of people. It is therefore basically a quality of the way that, within self-consciousness, under the Idea of freedom, we actively approach our own agency. It is a habit of thought insofar as thinking relates to action. Or perhaps better, a continuous conscious reiteration to oneself of one's resolve to act according to moral principle (since Kant associates habits with mindless mechanical repetition[75]). The virtuous person is someone who is always ready to face down temptations to act in ways that flout the moral law, and resist the impulse to self-assertion that can bubble up at any time. Similarly the acquisition of the kinds of self-knowledge that are useful for resisting our propensity to evil is a difficult matter, requiring considerable effort on the part of individuals, since genuinely confronting one's own faults is a painful occasion for self-contempt. Much easier to allow our attention to drift away from our real motives and what we are really doing, and let an indulgent and self-protective complacency about our actual moral worth become the default quotidian attitude to one's own behaviour, one in which we have persuaded ourselves that there is little bad in us that needs resisting. This is why Kant insists that self-knowledge has to be at the heart of virtue.[76] It is because of the radical evil he takes to lurk at the core of each of us that Kant insists that the Aristotelian model of the virtuous person as able to have full confidence in her own motivational response to the world is an unattainable illusion, and a dangerous one at that; whilst he does admittedly have considerably less confidence than Aristotelians in the susceptibility of the desires and emotions to being shaped in desirable ways, for Kant, even were one *per impossibile* to acquire an entirely benign set of inclinations, radical evil would in any case soon start to distort them again. And in this sceptical assessment of Aristotelian ratiocentric self-confidence, Freud and Cottingham surely ought to agree with him, even if their characterisation of the reasons will differ somewhat.

Cottingham himself briefly considers a 'resistance model' along Kantian lines, but rejects it for two reasons.[77] First, he thinks it underestimates the power of unconscious motivation, so that a policy of resisting it can only be a self-deceptive pretence. Second, he thinks that such an approach is quite incompatible with the aspiration to achieve *eudaimonia*. The Kantian response is this. To the first point, as I've been stressing, it is no part of the position to insist that we can be entirely successful in resisting our subterranean urges, and policing ourselves for self-deception, and desire-skewed value judgements. Quite the contrary; we certainly won't. But this doesn't mean we never will be, and the better we are at this kind of thing, the less we will go wrong. In any case, what else are we to do? To the second, the best response may be to bite the bullet. One of the central reasons Kant adduces for rejecting happiness as the primary goal of human action is its nebulous and uncertain nature.[78] Spending one's life trying to pursue happiness is a quixotic project, he thinks, since for any particular person what it might turn out to be may be very much at odds with his own conception of it, and so the person chasing happiness has little guarantee that he is not pursuing a mirage. There is considerably less ambiguity about what duty requires – indeed, none in the abstract – so the person who prioritises duty has his practical reasoning much more solidly grounded. The discoveries of psychoanalysis appear to strongly reinforce this impression about happiness, and indeed, offer further grounds for it. And once we abandon Aristotle's confidence that the non-rational parts of the psyche are amenable to reason, and so can be shaped so that they don't conflict with reason's ends and values, ought we not to abandon also the eudaimonist hope of achieving the harmonious inner unity they urge us to aim at, or at least revise the priority we ascribe to it? After all, why should we think that the kinds of things wanted by the unconscious are compatible with what we value from the rational point of view? Cecil's were not, for instance. If something like the Kantian division of the person is true – and for Freud, this should surely be at least contingently true for many people – then we need to ask which part to prioritise, should they come into conflict. And it seems to me that we should prioritise the – hopefully moral – values we endorse within rational, reflective self-consciousness, because we identify with these, whereas with the 'values' of the unconscious we characteristically do not. This will involve trying to resist the demands of the unconscious when they conflict with our values, with the only resources we have, which are just those Kant identified for opposing radical evil. Doing so will certainly have a cost, quite possibly a very high one. But it will also provide us with a personal dignity like that Kant ascribed to the moral person,[79] which can provide us with an uplifting if challenging way of thinking about ourselves, one which partially compensates for the loss of the eudaimonist fantasy.

So, to conclude: we are now presented with an interesting and perhaps rather ironic situation with regard to how we should understand virtue. Kant's account of virtue has long been criticised by those of the Aristotelian camp, with which Cottingham has been something of a fellow traveller at least. But if my reading of Kant is correct then the account takes the form it does precisely because Kant anticipated Freud in dismissing ratiocentric overconfidence, such as that on display in Aristotle's ethics. And a further irony, perhaps, is that one effect of the Freudian considerations Cottingham raises might be to push us towards a more sceptical attitude to the eudaimonist goal in ethics *per se*, a goal Cottingham appears to want to hang onto, despite his attack on the psychological naivety of the actual eudaimonisms currently on offer. Showing us how to live the good life is still what he takes the business of moral philosophy to be, even if we now see that this will be much harder than was once thought. But granted our frequently dark and alien inner natures, a worthier project might instead prioritise the pursuit of as much precarious moral dignity as reason can achieve, since we can no longer be confident that the two can be reconciled.[80]

Notes

1. See especially Cottingham 1983 and 1991.
2. Cottingham, 1998.
3. Cottingham, 1998, pp. 2, 104–112.
4. Cottingham, 1998, p. 28.
5. Cottingham, 1998, pp. 27–8.
6. Augustine, 1475, p. 462.
7. Kant, 1793, 6:29.
8. Kant, 1793, 6:35.
9. Kant, 1793, 6:37.
10. Kant, 1793, 6:48.
11. For example, Kant, 1785, 4:404.
12. Kant, 1785, 4:426.
13. Kant, 1785, 4:407.
14. Kant, 1785, 4:457.
15. Kant, 1785, 4:441.
16. Kant, 1785, 4:446.
17. Kant, 1786, 8:111–8.
18. Kant, 1785, 4:448.
19. Kant, 1793, 6:24.
20. For example, Kant, 1785, 4:460n.
21. Kant, 1785, 4:412.
22. For example, Kant, 1788, 5:20.
23. Kant, 1785, 4:404.
24. Kant, 1785, 4:448–53.
25. Kant, 1797, 6:237.
26. Kant, 1797, 6:231.
27. For example, Kant, 1788, 5:32.
28. See Morgan, 2005 for a lengthier account of these issues.
29. Cottingham, 1998, pp. 138–9.

30. Kant, 1785, 4:403.
31. Kant, 1785, 4:431.
32. Kant, 1787, A133/B172.
33. Kant, 1785, 4:424.
34. Kant, 1785, 4:424.
35. Kant, 1786, 8:111–2.
36. Kant, 1797, 6:456–7.
37. Kant, 1784, 8:20.
38. Kant, 1797, 6:408.
39. Kant, 1798, 7:254.
40. Kant, 1798, 7:251.
41. Kant, 1798, 7:252.
42. Kant, 1798, 7:252.
43. Kant, 1798, 7:265.
44. Kant, 1798, 7:253.
45. Kant, 1793, 6:57.
46. Kant, 1798, 7:252; 270–4.
47. Kant, 1798, 7:268.
48. Kant, 1798, 7:266.
49. Kant, 1798, 7:265–6.
50. Kant, 1798, 7:267.
51. Kant, 1798, 7:269–70.
52. Kant, 1793, 6:47.
53. Kant, 1785, 4:407.
54. Kant, 1798, 7:135.
55. Kant, 1798, 7:136.
56. Kant, 1797, 6:441.
57. Cottingham, 1998, p. 153.
58. Kant, 1785, 4:452.
59. Cottingham, 1998, p. 50.
60. For example, Kant, 1797, 6:438.
61. Kant, 1797, 6:380.
62. Kant, 1797, 6:383.
63. Kant, 1797, 6:397.
64. Kant, 1797, 6:394.
65. Kant, 1797, 6:390.
66. Kant, 1797, 6:397.
67. Kant, 1797, 6:405, Kant's emphasis.
68. Kant, 1797, 6:394.
69. Kant, 1797, 6:394.
70. Kant, 1797, 6:408.
71. Kant, 1797, 6:407.
72. Kant, 1785, 4:398.
73. Kant, 1788, 5:118.
74. Kant, 1797, 6:383–4; 1798, 7:121.
75. Kant, 1797, 6:407.
76. Kant, 1797, 6:441; cf. 405.
77. For example, Cottingham, 1998, p. 149.
78. Kant, 1785, 4:418.

79. Kant, 1785, 4:435.
80. I'm grateful to the Philosophy Department at the University of Bristol and to the Arts and Humanities Research Council, for jointly funding a period of research leave during which I worked on this article. Some of this material was presented to the Philosophy Department at the University of Cork, and I'm grateful to the participants at that event for useful comments, and especially to Joseph Biehl. I'd also like to thank the editors of this volume for very helpful advice.

Bibliography

Augustine, *The City of God* [1475], trans. Henry Bettenson (London: Penguin, 1972)

Cottingham J., *Philosophy and the Good Life* (London: Routledge, 1998)

Cottingham J., 'The Ethics of Self-Concern', *Ethics*, 101 (1991) 798–817

Cottingham J., 'Ethics and Impartiality', *Philosophical Studies*, 43 (1983) 83–99

Kant I., *Anthropology from a Pragmatic Point of View* [1798], trans. Louden R. (Cambridge: Cambridge University Press, 2006)

Kant I., *The Metaphysics of Morals* [1797], trans. Gregor M. (Cambridge: Cambridge University Press, 1996)

Kant I., *Religion within the Boundaries of Mere Reason* [1793], trans. di Giovanni G. (Cambridge: Cambridge University Press, 1998)

Kant I., *Critique of Practical Reason* [1788], trans. Gregor M. (Cambridge: Cambridge University Press, 1997)

Kant I., *Critique of Pure Reason* [1787], trans. Guyer P. and Wood A. W. (Cambridge: Cambridge University Press, 1998)

Kant I., *Speculative Beginning of Human History* [1786], trans. Humphrey T., in *Perpetual Peace and Other Essays* (Indianapolis: Hackett, 1983)

Kant I., *Groundwork of the Metaphysics of Morals* [1785], trans. Gregor M. (Cambridge: Cambridge University Press, 1997)

Kant I., *Idea for a Universal History with a Cosmopolitan Intent* [1784], trans. Humphrey T., in *Perpetual Peace and Other Essays* (Indianapolis: Hackett, 1983)

Morgan, Seiriol. 'The Missing Formal Proof of Humanity's Radical Evil in Kant's *Religion*', *Philosophical Review*, 114 (2005) 63–114

6
What Reason Can't Do

Michael Lacewing

> given the extent to which Freudian ideas have by now
> permeated our ways of thinking about human conduct,
> there is surely something remarkable about the almost
> wholesale disregard of those ideas by contemporary
> practitioners of philosophical ethics ... so many con-
> temporary moral philosophers ... [are] still writing ...
> as if humans were transparently self-aware creatures,
> and the task of ethics were simply that of intellectually
> analysing the structure of our goals, and rationally
> working out the best way to implement them.[1]

The aim of this paper is to analyse the central argument of Cottingham's
Philosophy and the Good Life, and to strengthen and develop it against
misinterpretation and objection. Cottingham's argument is an objection to 'ratiocentrism', the view that the good life can be understood in
terms of and attained by reason and strength of will. The objection
begins from a proper understanding of akrasia, or weakness of will, but
its focus, and the focus of this paper, is the relation between reason and
the passions in the good life. Akrasia serves to illustrate ratiocentrism's
misunderstanding of this relation and of the nature of the passions
themselves.

In the first section, I outline and clarify the objection. In the second
section, I present and provisionally elaborate on Cottingham's diagnosis of what a corrected understanding of the passions makes necessary
for the good life, viz. the rediscovery and reclamation of the source of
our passions, our childhood past. In the third section, I discuss whether
ratiocentrism could accept and absorb the critique as developed so far.
Cottingham is aware that his claim, with its emphasis on self-*knowledge*,

could be reinterpreted by ratiocentrism as no more than the need for reason to work with a different source of information regarding the passions in order to master them.[2] I briefly present three further objections to show why this is a mistake. In the fourth section, I argue that Cottingham's diagnosis is not quite right, and I seek to emphasise aspects of self-discovery that I believe Cottingham overlooks or underplays. What is needed is a set of interrelated dispositions, viz. acceptance, vulnerability, courage, and compassion; these can be inculcated and sustained by the journey Cottingham defends, but it is the dispositions, rather than the journey, that are properly considered a necessary part of the good life.

Some readers may wonder whether the view I defend is an alternative to or a form of virtue ethics. Virtue ethics has tended to prioritise the passions more than other normative theories, and all the more so in recent years, and this paper supports that trend. However, I would question the extent to which virtue ethicists have taken on board the argument against reason that follows, as sympathetic as they may be to the theory of the passions it defends. For example, one question raised by the critique concerns the internal structure of a virtue and its relation to rational insight. The argument suggests traits other than reason play an equally important role here. Insofar as virtue ethics retains the goal of a life planned and unified by reason, the argument forms an objection: the foundation must be broader. This said, my main concern is with what is necessary for ethical practice. I do not have space to discuss the implications for how philosophical theory should change or proceed in order to take account of what follows.

1. 'A rationally articulated plan'

In this section, I aim to clarify what it is that ratiocentric ethics claims which Cottingham rejects. I first introduce ratiocentrism and the objection from akrasia. In the next sub-section, I look at the models of ratiocentrism from the ancient Greeks and discuss Cottingham's claim that the passions are 'opaque' to reason. In the third, we look at developments from Descartes, and in the last, restate the objection.

The central claim of ratiocentrism is that the good life can be understood in terms of and attained by reason and strength of will. As a product of reason, philosophy has its role to play in developing an understanding of being human, one that can serve in attaining the good life. The aim, as Cottingham quotes from John Kekes is 'increasing our control by developing a reasonable conception of a good life, and bringing our actions in conformity with it'.[3] The ancient Greek ideal, that '[s]trength-ened by the instilling of the right habits, and guided by a rational vision of the good life',[4] we shall attain the good life, is still with us.

It is not my concern to run through the (important) differences between the classical Greek, Medieval, early modern, and contemporary accounts of how the rational plan for a good life is to be formed, what it recommends, and how it is to guide us, as the heart of Cottingham's critique targets a claim much deeper than the level at which these models disagree. Indeed, it takes in any ethical theory, whether consequentialist, deontological, or virtue based, that has as its foundation the possibility of reason discovering what the good life might consist in, and then securing such a life for us. No matter whether such theories are taken with a cognitivist metaethics, in which reason discovers what is objectively good, or a non-cognitivist metaethics, in which the good is a projection of our desires and attitudes, and reason merely discovers and organizes these responses into a life that can be lived. The problem with ratiocentric ethics is that, in the light of findings by psychoanalysis, 'the very idea of a rationally planned structure for the good life begins to look like a piece of naïve self-deception'.[5]

There are three fundamental obstacles to the rational plan for the good life: a lack of knowledge, a lack of control, and fortune. The third is not my concern here, for it is on the questions of knowledge and control that Cottingham focuses.[6] And in the end he illuminates the commitments of ratiocentric theories by the way they diagnose and respond to akrasia.[7] Akrasia, of course, is doing what you believe is not what is best. In all cases of akrasia, arguably, there is an equivalent structure at the level of motivation: feeling or desiring what you believe it is not best (for example, not appropriate) to feel or desire. This extension is important, as the ratiocentric models Cottingham discusses all understand the good life not just in terms of what one does, but what one feels as well. To certain deontological or consequentialist models, this may only be of instrumental concern, that is, it is only actions that matter ethically, and so desires and emotions are important only as motivation to actions. But whether one is concerned with emotions and desires (henceforth 'passions') intrinsically or only instrumentally, the question still arises of how to deal with akratic motivation, if not to correct or prevent it entirely, then at least to prevent it from giving rise to akratic action. Furthermore, akrasia cannot be dismissed as a peripheral issue in ethics: it is central to an understanding of the good life, for 'as long as there is a psychic split between what I feel like doing and what I am morally called to do ... then there will be an unresolved tension at the heart of my moral nature'.[8]

Ratiocentric ethics mistakenly claims that akrasia can be both under-stood and corrected by reason, and not just in theory, but in the actual, particular case. Understanding why this is a mistake leads to the objec-tion that reason cannot have the knowledge and control necessary for forming and implementing a plan of the good life.

What 'reason' is I shall leave implicit. It is clear enough that 'reason' as understood by the philosophers Cottingham discusses – Plato, Aristotle, the Stoics, and Descartes – is attributed a knowledge and control he argues it cannot have. Whether such knowledge and control could be gained by reason understood differently, I discuss in Section 3.

***

Socrates famously claims that 'No one willingly pursues the bad, or what he thinks bad'.[9] If I appear to act against what is best, this is a result of ignorance – in fact, I have done what I thought best in some sense. I may not have considered carefully what is best, and this may be a result of my passions in some way. But while passions may influence my beliefs about what is best, the force of reason, in the form of these beliefs, is so strong that I cannot act against it. Aristotle, eventually, similarly concludes that full and active knowledge of what is best is not present. If it were, he agrees with Socrates that it could not be 'dragged around' by the passions. We always do as reason indicates; but in coming to its conclusion, reason can be lead astray or 'clouded' by the passions.

What is to be done? A first solution is that if the balance of forces could be brought to favour reason, the good life could be secured. But the ability of passions to 'cloud' reason is not, or not just, about force, argues Cottingham; rather, reason, in its deliberations about the good, does not fully understand the passions and the vision of the good they present. As a result, it does not understand the *source* of their motivat-ing force. Without knowing where the passions get their strength from, reason will struggle to best them.

If force won't work, a second solution, then, is for reason to understand the passions: If akrasia is a *cognitive* defect, it can be corrected by reason. In commenting on the Epicurean version of *therapeia*, Cottingham notes that 'the kind of 'confrontation' [of the passions by reason] envisaged is taken to operate largely at the level of relatively transparent cognitive and emotional self-awareness ... [and] aimed ... at exposing them to the intellect as inherently confused and confusing'.[10] This comment indi-cates that ratiocentrism's commitment to the transparency of the pas-sions to reason is not a commitment that reason can *make sense* of the passions, but rather it can *either* do this, laying out the vision of the good they present for rational evaluation, *or* it can expose them as essentially confused, and so to be rejected.

But the passions are *opaque* to reason, Cottingham argues, in a way that falsifies both options. What is this 'opacity'? When we respond emotionally, we seek to understand ourselves; above all, to understand the vision of the world the emotion presents. To what are we responding, and how is that object presented? What are the reasons for the response? What explains the emotion's intensity, or its being precipitated now rather than on another, similar occasion? And so on. We look for a 'sufficient explanation', either showing how our response and the way in which it represents the world is appropriate, timely, proportionate, and so on; or explaining why it was inappropriate or disproportionate, for example, as a result of a particular bad mood, or a sequence of events that finally proved too much to bear. With our desires, we seek to identify the good they seek and the reasons for thinking it is good. We may seek to explain an inappropriate desire on the basis of confused thinking about what satisfaction its fulfilment would actually bring us. Now if we were able, simply upon self-reflection, to provide such a sufficient explanation that correctly identified the meaning of the passion the passions would be transparent. The claim that they are opaque is the claim that what explains a passion – its object, content, intensity, cause, timing, or vision of the good – is not always available in this way.

Furthermore, we believe, often rightly, that if we understand why we react as we do, this gives us some control over the passion. Our passions clearly respond to reasons; a reasoned account of the object and reasons for the passion should therefore alter it if necessary. But because passions are opaque, they are also recalcitrant. Ratiocentrism misunderstands and misdiagnoses the opacity and recalcitrance of passions, and this misunderstanding leads ratiocentrism to falsely maintain that the passions can be brought into line, by reason, with a plan for the good life that reason has devised or discovered.

As yet, we have had no argument to support the claim that passions are opaque. Cottingham will argue that the opacity stems from *unconscious influence*, deriving from the past, on our passions. To deny that there is such unconscious influence is now, I believe, to fly in the face of a huge amount of evidence, and Cottingham's claim is equally defended by many other philosophers of emotion.[11] So I shall not seek to defend the claim at any length, though I expand on it at the beginning of Section 2.

Cottingham takes akrasia to illustrate the opacity and recalcitrance of the passions starkly. But there is no reason, I believe, to think that passions are easily divided into the 'akratic' and the 'non-akratic' in nature.[12] All passions are open to unconscious influence. The passions that motivate akratic action do not derive their content or motivational force from a unique source, untapped by other passions. And the same passion can lead to akratic action, or not, in different circumstances. What makes the difference is the modulation of the passion in relation to the agent's conception of the good. So if the passions are opaque to reason in cases of akrasia, this tells us something about the nature of the passions *per se*. Opacity is always a potential threat to rational control: 'if our very grasp of what we truly want can be subject to a pervasive and potentially crippling opacity, then we need to rethink the optimistic vision of a rationally planned and organized life'.[13]

***

The possibility that ratiocentrism may yet accommodate the opacity of the passions arises in Cottingham's discussion of Descartes. Descartes recognises the opacity of the passions, and accounts for it in terms of their physiological nature and in terms of our past psychological history, including the pre-rational experiences of early childhood (here treading the stomping-ground of psychoanalysis). This understanding enables a more subtle and ameliorative approach to recalcitrant passions, viz. 'to use the resources of science and experience to understand what has caused things to go awry, and then to attempt to reprogram our responses so that the direction in which we are led by the passions corresponds to what our reason perceives as the best option'.[14] But whether this is really possible (through the activities of reason alone) seems to be a matter on which Descartes equivocated. At times, he is optimistic, and rejects the Stoic recommendation of *apatheia*, arguing that 'persons whom the passions can move most deeply are capable of enjoying the sweetest pleasure of this life'.[15] At other times, the opacity of the passions leads him to emphasise their *alteration* less and the *purity and strength of the will* more: 'Nothing truly belongs to us but the freedom to dispose our volitions',[16] and praise and blame should rest only on using this freedom well, that is, the resolution 'never to lack the will to undertake and carry out what we judge to be best'.[17] From this, a person 'will receive ... a satisfaction that has such power to make him happy that the most violent assaults of the passions will never have sufficient power to disturb the tranquillity of his soul'.[18]

Perhaps the most charitable way of reading these apparent equivocations is as a 'belt-and-braces' approach: using reason, change what you can; but what you can't change, protect yourself from – by cultivating purity and strength of will. Descartes holds fast to the idea that the conscientious exercise of the will, guided by reason, is all that is needed to secure the good life. But, Cottingham argues, this glosses over those very insights into the opacity of the passions that Descartes disclosed. First, and perhaps most importantly, the unconscious influences at work in recalcitrant passion, influences that may lead to 'violent assaults of the passions', work equally effectively by distorting 'the calm deliberations of reason about how best we should live'[19] (this is further discussed in Section 2). Second, such attempts to control, rather than resolve, one's passions create psychic pressures that can lead to catastrophic results. Cottingham notes that Aristotle's prescriptions for the good life strikingly contrast with the Greek tragedians', and of course Freud's, recognition of the force passions retain, even (or perhaps especially) when repressed.[20] Third, even supposing such control were possible, in light of Descartes' comment that the passions can yield 'the sweetest pleasure of this life', we should doubt whether it would result in the good life after all.

***

Let us take stock. First, Cottingham claims that the opacity of the passions to reason, and not just in the case of akrasia, means that reason lacks the knowledge that is needed for a rationally ordered and planned life. This ignorance is compounded by the fact that reason has historically misunderstood the passions, focusing on the issue of their force, rather than their source and meaning. Second, just as passions are opaque, so they are also recalcitrant. Attempts to control them by force, without understanding, either do not succeed – witness akratic passions and actions – or insofar as they do, they create a psychic pressure that is not properly considered part of the good life.

What is missing is knowledge of the true meaning or content of our passions. Ratiocentrism always presupposes 'that the end is clearly in sight, and that what has to be done is to arrange the pieces in the appropriate way ... what the psychoanalytic approach implies ... is that our innermost nature, and hence the structure of any possible recipe for its fulfilment, is *not* clearly in sight'.[21] Hence we face an over-arching practical problem, that 'Unless and until the past is reclaimed, unless we can come to appreciate the significance of our past, and the role it plays in shaping our emotional lives, then the very idea of an ordered plan for the good life will have to be put on hold'.[22]

Cottingham does not reject outright the claim that some form of cognitive defect *is* involved in akrasia;[23] there is something unknown, viz. the unconscious influence that is present and how it informs the conception of the options between which the agent is deliberating. But, finally, this is *not* knowledge reason gains later by the methods of confronting the passions discussed above. To gain this knowledge requires a different approach from any countenanced in ratiocentrism.[24]

It is worth noting that Cottingham does not seek to dismiss or replace reason.[25] Furthermore, he argues that psychoanalysis holds out 'the possibility that after acknowledging its lack of total mastery, our conscious power of understanding can eventually get to grips with those buried images, drives and fears'.[26] We may therefore ask, Is Cottingham's objection to ratiocentrism an objection to the *project* of bringing one's passions under the control of reason or just to how the project has been *conceived*? If we accept the criticisms he has made, and understand that we must reconsider the relationship between reason and the passions, must we 'merely' widen our view of how the good life is to be achieved; or are there further implications of his critique?

The remainder of the paper will be concerned with these questions. In Section 3, I discuss whether ratiocentrism can be updated to accommodate the fact of unconscious influence. In Section 4, I shall conclude by arguing that Cottingham has *not gone far enough* in displacing reason in his model of self-understanding. To begin with, though, in the next section, I lay out the basics of a psychoanalytic approach to the question of the passions.

2. Psychoanalytic ethics

We should begin by refocusing our target. For many philosophers may object that ethics is not predominantly concerned with the niceties of our emotions, but with our public actions. Cottingham grants that both the plan and execution of our lives in this sphere can be brought under reason,[27] but argues that the 'intensely private sphere of close personal relations ..., for most of us, forms the very core of a worthwhile life'.[28] And so it is with this arena that he is concerned. Even here, what is good – in general – is clear; we may relate personal goods to a good life. But 'These are relations involving uncertainty, vulnerability, deep physical and psychological needs ... [And so] what is not similarly accessible [to reason] is ... the power and resonance which informs each of the relevant relationships is a uniquely particular way, at the deepest level of our pre-rational drives and feelings'.[29]

As I noted in Section 1, I believe there is overwhelming evidence that our passions are subject to unconscious influence, deriving from our past. Because the influence is unconscious, the passions are opaque to conscious reflection, and because it derives from the past, we need to engage with our pasts in order to discover their meaning and significance. As Cottingham notes, despite philosophical reservations regarding psychoanalysis, this claim should not be controversial after reflection on the nature of our emotions. Ratiocentrism has had a tendency to understand emotions as easily identifiable elements within a static timeframe; we feel them, and can identify just what they are from that. But this view, challenged by a number of recent philosophers of emotion, fails to integrate the long psychic history which our emotions have, and which gives them their meaning, their power, and their resonance:

> Bringing to the surface the precise nature of our feelings, is not a matter of identifying simple items ... swimming around the transparent tank of consciousness ... our awareness of our emotional states, and of the nature of the objects to which they are directed, can frequently be distorted by all kinds of dark projections and shadows from the past.[30]

With its focus on the theory of reasons, and the equation of the right to that which we have conclusive reason to do, contemporary ethical theory does not address either the extensive influence our passions have on our judgments of what the best reasons are nor the inability of such judgments to integrate with our motivations. The psychology is complex: pride, vanity, self-importance, fear, embarrassment, self-defensiveness, envy, greed, self-absorption, and fantasies of power all play a role.[31] I would argue, without seeking to reduce these different motivations, that at the heart of the matter lies psychic pain. Psychoanalysis argues that we have a constant tendency in the face of painful emotions and experiences to unconsciously pervert our experience of reality by imagining it to be different.

There are many reasons why our passions can be painful. They can cause us anxiety, horror, guilt, shame, even terror. We can feel this way just about having them; or about not being able to control them; or about the prospect, or its absence, of what would satisfy our desires or arouse our emotions occurring in reality. I can be ashamed of my envy; I can be anxious that I can't control feelings of anger; I can be terrified that my love will make me dependent. Psychoanalysis argues that our minds have an in-built tendency to keep such painful mental states and what becomes associated with them out of consciousness. We turn them away. The many ways in which we do this are 'defence mechanisms'.[32]

Defence mechanisms utilize mental processes that, using the imagination, operate 'on mental content that represents the cause of anxiety in such a way as to reduce or eliminate anxiety'[33] or the other painful feelings just mentioned.[34] This barring of certain states from consciousness affects what we understand of ourselves, of others, of the situations in which we find ourselves, in other words, the world as we experience it,[35] and therefore, of course, of our reasons.[36]

As our emotions are not isolated events, these distortions are not 'one-offs', but, as Jonathan Lear argues, form an entire world-view:

> A patient of mine inhabited a disappointing world. Although she was quite successful at work, had friends, and so on, there was no success in the social world that would not be interpreted by her under an aura of disappointment. If she got a raise at work, it was because the boss was shamed into it – he really wanted to give someone else in the office a raise, but he felt he had to give her one to appear fair. If she was invited out for a date, the person had already tried to go out with others and had failed. If someone congratulated her on some accomplishment, they were just being polite. And so on. From a distance it is clear to us, as it was not clear to her, how active she was in understanding her world in ways that were bound to disappoint. And, of course, much of the analysis was spent working through these repetitive attempts at disappointment.[37]

In the light of all this, we see that neither the resolve to weigh up reasons better nor to act more consistently on the reasons we perceive is sufficient to overcome the difficulty the opacity of our passions presents to a ratiocentric vision of living the good life. We must engage with the influences of the past that has formed our passions and continues to inform their meaning.

This, Cottingham argues, is the project of psychoanalysis. But the point of the appeal to psychoanalysis is not to argue that everyone should enter analysis if they wish to attain a good life; the point is to uncover the nature of the psyche, that is, what is involved in being human. And the psyche is such that self-knowledge, knowledge of the meaning of one's passions, involves the recovery of the roots of our passions in childhood phantasies and a recognition of our emotional vulnerability.[38]

3. Reason's return?

I asked, at the end of Section 1, whether Cottingham's objection to ratiocentrism is an objection to the project of bringing one's passions under the control of reason or just to how the project has been conceived. Must we abandon ratiocentrism? Is what is needed for the recovery of the past, for us to come to know the meaning and significance of our passions and their roots in our childhood experiences, outside the power of reason? And in any case, once the knowledge has been gained, however it is to be gained, can't reason then form and enact a plan for the good life? In other words, could not the process of self-discovery, and the use of the knowledge it delivers, be interpreted rationalistically: 'This is perhaps how Freud, in many ways, after all, still the rationalist, sometimes saw it: "where Id was, there shall Ego be"'.[39]

This line of thought does indeed receive some support from Freud's understanding of the psychoanalytic aim, in which rational control is repeatedly mentioned. For example, 'We try to restore the ego, to free it from its restrictions, and to give it back the command over the id which it has lost';[40] 'The method by which we strengthen the weakened ego has as a starting-point an extending of its self-knowledge ... The loss of such knowledge signifies for the ego a surrender of power and influence';[41] 'whether [this] results in the ego accepting, after a fresh examination, an instinctual demand hitherto rejected, or whether it dismisses it once more, this time for good [is indifferent]. In either case ... the compass of the ego has been extended'.[42]

Furthermore, as Martha Nussbaum argues, the emphasis on the *meaning* of our passions provides grounds for thinking that they are amenable to reason – which would not be true if, as some ratiocentric theories had it, they were meaningless and so needed to be controlled by force. If we can make the cognitive content of the emotion available to the subject, then because reason extends 'all the way down into the personality', this offers the hope of a transformation in thought and feeling.[43] In Richard Sorabji's book-length treatment on the nature and possibility of a *cognitive* therapy of the emotions, he notes that modern cognitive therapy has had much more success with certain conditions than others. He records that rather than abandon the cognitive approach, David Clark, one of the leading researchers into cognitive therapy in the UK, suggested in discussion that the judgments involved are numerous and unconscious, and so difficult to identify. 'In time, however, all emotions will turn out to consist of judgements and all will be amenable to cognitive therapy'.[44] Clark's model here is to identify the 'cognitive abnormality' in the disorder, explain what keeps it from 'self-correcting', and develop 'specialized cognitive treatments' to 'reverse … the maintaining factors'.[45]

From the very first, however, psychoanalysts have been at pains to emphasise that whatever occurs in psychoanalysis, it is *not* a matter of the patient grasping *intellectually* the 'missing knowledge'. An intellectual approach, if this suggests detached self-scrutiny, is mistaken; what needs to be known – *how* it needs to be known – cannot be known this way. The passions are better understood by 'listening to the signals from within'.[46] Lear relays

> the old joke about the analyst who at the end of the first hour says, 'Your case is easy: you want to kill your mother and have your father to yourself. That will be $50,000, and we don't need to meet again.' The joke works because intuitively we assume what the analyst says may be true, but precisely because it is true the form of the utterance is utterly inappropriate … the mere assertion of content could never convey the truth of what is being asserted.[47]

Even were the patient to become convinced, by sound reasoning, of the truth of the claim, it would not be what she needed to know. Coming to understand the meaning of one's passions through an understanding of past unconscious influences, then, is not a matter of forming a *belief* on good grounds. The model of uncovering the mistaken judgment that underpins the akratic or recalcitrant passion is too simplistic, even when it is allowed that the mistaken judgment derives from childhood. As Freud notes,[48] the 'knowledge' lacks any connection with the unconscious passions involved and how they have affected her adult thoughts and feelings. It has as much effect on the person 'as a distribution of menus in a time of famine has upon hunger'.[49] So it would be a mistake to use such a model to support reason's claim to uncover the meanings of our passions.

A second reason for caution stems from the nature of the content of emotions, perhaps especially in the context of tracing this content to one's childhood. In standard cognitive therapeutic models, the emotion is grounded on (or is, in some versions) a judgment. But the nature of thought in emotion may not be so easily assimilated to propositional judgment. (Nussbaum is sensitive to this, Clark less so.) As Lear argues, passions – or at least those passions sufficiently deep to disturb our view of the world – are better understood as an orientation towards the whole world, rather than a 'mistaken judgment' occurring within it.[50] The disappointment (or what lay under the disappointment) of his patient gives a certain *structure* to her view of the world, rather than appearing as something *within* the world (as she experienced it). The disappointment governs the *possibilities* available to her, possibilities of interpretation, feeling, and response. When she comes to understand her activity in making the world disappointing, 'This is a moment in which the world itself shifts: there is, as it were, a possibility for new possibilities'.[51] Analysis consisted in changing her view of the world.[52]

There are models of emotion that attempt to capture this understanding of the nature of the intentional content of emotion in terms of 'construal' or 'seeing-as', constructing an analogy between the intentional content of emotion and that of perceptual states. The best developed of these models[53] steer away from reducing such content to that which could be captured by a judgment. The recovery of past meaning, then, involves a transformation in the subject's view of the world. While in *some* ways this is similar to correcting a mistaken judgment, neither the process nor the result is truly akin to it.[54]

A third reason for caution stems from the process of making sense of the past, of discovering and reclaiming the childhood sources of emotion. For it is unclear to what extent the intentional content, the meaning, of such emotions (or judgments) is 'given', as if waiting, fully formed in the unconscious, to come to light. Again, from the beginning, psychoanalysts have argued that a somewhat complex process of meaning-*making* regarding the past occurs throughout life, and throughout the process of recovering meaning. Past events are constantly reinterpreted and re-evaluated, both consciously and unconsciously, in the light of present experience.[55] An important part of this process is the clarification of what was *not* understood at the time – whether an event, a relationship, or a wish – although it was experienced as obscurely significant. The model of an unconscious *judgment* to be 'reversed' fits ill here. The unconscious meaning or source of the passion must first *become* something with which thought can work, something that can be articulated and evaluated.

The process by which the meaning of past influences on present passions and choices is recovered must be sensitive to this process of reconstruction. The meaning we presently make of the past is not isolated from the meaning we make of the present. However, the meaning we make of the present is under the influence of the past. Lear argues that we constantly give meaning to 'our world'. Unless I am psychotic, then 'my world' is pretty much 'the world', but I interpret and experience it (particularly the social world) idiosyncratically, consciously and unconsciously forming associations to and finding significance in a unique slice of the quotidian – a cup, a book, a glance, a pang of hunger; all this gives life so much of its flavour. And so we repeat the point made above, that 'rediscovery' of the past involves a transformation of the subject's view of the world. Psychoanalysis undertakes an investigation into the past *through* the meanings a subject makes of the present (as in the case of the woman's world of disappointment). The process seeks to transform the activity of making meaning from one of distortion, of present and past, into one of insight.[56]

4. Beyond reason

In Section 2, I argued for an understanding of the passions that made clear our need to engage with unconscious influences deriving from the past. In Section 3, I argued that an updated form of ratiocentrism cannot do this adequately; its models of knowledge and discovery are not appropriate to the project. What is it, then, that is needed?

Cottingham puts the point like this:

> Full self-awareness must involve more than widening the scope of deliberative reason; it requires a new kind of understanding, one mediated not by the grasp of the controlling intellect, but by a responsiveness to the rhythms of the whole self ... Unless we regain some sense of attunement with that totality, of which our intellectualizing is only the thinnest of surfaces, we will be clinging to the most pitiful illusion.[57]

The ideas of 'responsiveness' and 'attunement' need to be unpacked, and my aim in what follows is to make clear how the transformation of which Cottingham talks should be understood. One concern I have is that Cottingham can sometimes emphasise the acquisition of knowledge at the expense of the other elements I suggest are needed; so I intend to explain the transformation in terms that make transparent the inability of reason to enact it.

The case against ratiocentrism can be stated thus: gaining knowledge of the meanings of one's passions and choices is not knowledge one can acquire *without changing as a person*. The change that is required cannot be performed by either intellectual insight or strength of will, traditionally the two powers at reason's disposal. Instead, the transformation requires

a) recovering and accepting, as parts of oneself, those parts of oneself that have been rejected;
b) accepting one's vulnerability – both one's vulnerability in childhood and one's vulnerability now to the effects of childhood; this involves a form of relinquishing control, not just initially, but permanently, to achieve the 'responsiveness' Cottingham mentions. Because vulnerability is always potentially painful, and the parts of the self that were rejected were so because of the pain they cause or threaten to cause, accepting one's vulnerability involves the courage to endure psychic pain;
c) compassion for oneself, which enables the above.

'Recovery', 'vulnerability', and 'acceptance' are all, to some extent, terms of art. The ideas of recovery and vulnerability are Cottingham's; the elaboration on these, and the ideas of acceptance, courage, and compassion are mine.

I find that I cannot fully separate these three conditions in discussion; an analysis of each involves the others. Precisely what is meant by recovery, vulnerability, and acceptance will therefore perhaps not become clear until the end of the discussion of compassion. But let us start with recovery.

a. Recovery: vulnerability

Recovery is not discovery. Certainly, discovery is part of the process, but it is only a beginning. When Cottingham talks of the need to return to the past in response to the opacity of our passions, he repeatedly speaks of the need to 'recover', 'rehabilitate', and 'reclaim' it, and he notes this is not 'bland acceptance', that is, the type of acceptance involved in believing a fact, nor, as we have seen, a matter of information.[58]

The image suggested by a ratiocentric interpretation of the process of clarifying the opacity of the passions is that of the self identified with that which comes to know, and which essentially remains unchanged by the knowledge until it decides what to do with it. This is fundamentally mistaken. For until the past is reclaimed, the 'self' is incomplete. What represents itself as the self – in Freudian terms, the ego – cannot be taken as *the* voice of the person. The occurrence of 'akratic' passions is demonstration of this. As Lear puts it, his psyche is split into parts that are themselves at war with each other ... from an ego position, he may tell us who he thinks he really is; from a superego position, he may tell us what he'd like to be; and when he acts out he may express all sorts of id-like wishes that come from deep within him.[59]

Ratiocentrism's identification of the self with reason in the conflict with akratic passions leaves the passions 'alien' to the self, a sense reinforced by their opacity to reason. This only exacerbates the division.

The idea of recovery involves a different model of the self, of its relationship to itself and its 'parts', what it claims as its own. In recovery, parts of the self that have been disowned come to be integrated into the self. But putting the matter thus – in terms of a reflexive relationship – is perhaps misleading, for it suggests, as it has been suggested by, a self alienated from itself, and so needing some kind of relationship to itself. What is at issue is how the self *is*, whether it is able to be itself fully, through the full extent of its emotional experience.[60] My aim is to describe the traits of a self that enable it to achieve this. Recovery, then, is a process of self-transformation.

A first step in the process of reclaiming parts of oneself, which Cottingham takes from Jung, 'is an acknowledgement of precisely the fallibility, vulnerability and dependence that is an integral part of the strange openness we experience in our emotional lives ... It is only by giving up, in the first instance, our pretensions to rational control that we open the way for deeper, transformed, self-understanding'.[61] If this were the first step on the path back towards control, ratiocentrism could countenance it. But the sense of vulnerability deepens in the realisation that it is inescapable, a realisation that comes with the understanding of the passions, and their roots in one's childhood past, that Cottingham has been arguing for throughout. This realisation comes together with, and is a product of, the experience of how one's past continues to influence one's present understanding of oneself, one's passions, and the outlook on the world they embody.

I use the word 'experience' here for two reasons. First, Freud remarks that in the absence of actually *experiencing* this influence, it is extremely difficult to believe its extent and force.[62] Believing the psychoanalytic model of the mind to be true is an entirely different matter from experiencing oneself as an example of it. (Again, this is not to say that such experience is only possible in psychoanalysis, though of course, that curious human relationship is set up as it is precisely to enable such an experience to take place.) However, second, the analogy of Section 3 between the passions and perception suggests and supports the claim that the model for knowledge of one's passions should be perceptual experience rather than judgment. And perceptual experience has two key features of relevance to understanding 'vulnerability': first, it is 'passive' (in contrast to 'active' judgment) and 'open' (to the world); second, the knowledge gained is knowledge by acquaintance, not by description. These analogies should not be taken too far (for example, that introspection is an 'inner eye'), but both may illuminate the way in which a purely cognitive model of self-knowledge is inadequate to the process of understanding one's passions. To judge that one has such-and-such an emotion is not yet to experience that emotion. We can still make any number of accurate judgments about the world around ourselves with our eyes closed, or indeed, from books; but they are no substitute for experience. It is in the experience of the emotion – for unconscious emotions, very often, at first through an experience of its effects on other emotions, thoughts, understandings one has – that its content, its significance, its place in one's psychic life, is appreciated. Furthermore, the influence of the past never ceases, even when it has be reclaimed, after which one is able to appreciate and moderate it, not eradicate it. And so openness to one's emotional life, a willingness to at least tolerate and admit into thought whatever it is one feels, is necessary for self-knowledge to continue.

It is more enlightening to talk of recovering parts of oneself than of recovering passions, for it is rarely, if ever, that the influence of the past is transmitted through one desire or emotion. It is, rather, a (sub-)structure of passions, a way of seeing the world, with which we lose touch. For example, a fear of failure can lead to a refusal to take responsibility, which can lead to anger at others for not picking up responsibility. Behind the fear of failure, and equally responsible for the anger, could be anger at one's parents for repeatedly pushing one to the point of failure in the quest for 'achievement'. And so on. This part of ourselves, Freud says, 'must no longer seem contemptible, but must become ... a piece of his personality, which has solid ground for its existence'.[63]

b. Recovery: acceptance, courage, and compassion

The process by which the self-recovery occurs, and the dispositional state that results, I call 'acceptance'. This is not, of course, what Cottingham terms 'bland acceptance', the formation of a belief about a passion on the model of information. Nor is it a matter of taking an approving moral stance towards oneself. At its core is the willingness to tolerate, in experience, whatever one feels, without attempting to control or deny one's feelings.

Defence mechanisms are means by which we control passions or parts of ourselves that threaten psychological pain. This exercise of control – through repression, projection, or other means – creates a distance between the self as it understands and presents itself and those passions. One way of understanding the work of acceptance is in terms of taking 'ownership' of disowned parts of the self. That such psychological states and structures are genuinely part of one's psychology can be difficult to see or accept; the case of the disappointed woman exemplifies how we may seek to find in the world the sources of an emotion that in fact arises within us. Part of owning disowned parts of oneself, then, is a matter of withdrawing such projections. Developing acceptance involves undoing defence mechanisms.

This is not, however, a simple task. Defence mechanisms are maintained by the pain threatened by the disowned part of the self, were it to be incorporated into the self. If we return for a moment to akrasia, akratic passions are not ones we are comfortable with, and the parts of the self they express are ones we find most difficult to contemplate. We may, for instance, find it quite inconceivable that we could ever want *this* or feel *this* way; it seems so childish or unreasonable. This pain is unavoidable in the process of acceptance, although the setting of psychoanalysis attempts to mitigate it and make it bearable. Acceptance involves vulnerability and the willingness to tolerate pain.

Acknowledging the existence of a passion one feels is a first step ('discovery'), but still perfectly compatible with refusing to grant it, as Freud says, 'a solid ground for its existence'. What is missing in such acknowledgement is the sense that the passion is an aspect of *oneself*. Defence mechanisms are usually reinforced by a false and idealized sense of oneself; the parts of oneself defended against, even after their existence is acknowledged, are not yet one's own in the same way in which one identifies with other traits with which one is content. The pain caused lies not, or not only, in the disowned part of the self; it lies also in the gap between that part and one's self-image. Lear speaks of the gap between 'aspiration' and 'pretence'.[64] On the one hand, our passions aspire to expression and fulfilment; on the other hand, we can aspire to virtuous ideals beyond our present means, or even beyond human means. When these conflict, we pretend, on the one hand, that our passions do not exist, or that they are adequately fulfilled, or that they are no part of our 'true self'; on the other hand, we pretend that we meet the ideals we hold for ourselves, or that we can, that they are reasonable. But these ideals can themselves be defensive reactions to our passions.[65] Accepting our passions means bridging the gap between aspiration and pretence, not only between ego and id but also between ego and superego. It may not be just that which maintains the 'akratic' passion that needs recovering, but that which maintains the (false) ideal against which it offends; passions play their part on both sides of the akratic conflict. The sense of the self, that is, the sense of what is the self, has been limited by their defensive rejection. So a further aspect of owning the full extent of oneself is the move from a narcissistic relationship to oneself to a deeper understanding of what it means to be merely human. Once again, this is not a mere intellectual acknowledgement, but a structural change in the self.[66]

One could speak here of a 'change in attitude' of the self towards those parts that have been disowned. And I think this is right, except for the reservation I mentioned above: that the attitude of acceptance that replaces that of alienation and rejection returns the self to itself. The result of acceptance, then, is perhaps better described as the self *being* itself fully.

This model is, of course, not the way it seems when one is confronted with a passion that seems dubious when judged in terms of one's ideals for oneself. It is easy to feel that the passion – merely as a passion, quite independent of the acts it seeks to motivate – is to be morally disapproved of. How, then, can it be 'accepted'? This suggests moral complacency.

The objection is severally confused. First, it confuses acceptance with a kind of moral approval. But acceptance is, indeed must be, morally neutral, and moral judgments have no place in acceptance. This may only inflame the charge: acceptance refuses to condemn what should be condemned. But second, it is arguable that the mere occurrence of passions, in absence from any action upon them, is not a matter of moral judgment;[67] accepting a passion is not equivalent to refusing to condemn acting upon it. Third, we must, in any case, understand the passion before we rightly judge its moral credentials; and the argument is that acceptance is necessary for understanding, and so unavoidable. Fourth, and most importantly, the objection substitutes for self-understanding the attempt at self-improvement: 'The passion is not worthy; therefore I must not feel it'. Richard Wollheim notes:

> [the terminology of transparency] suggests that the process whereby I try to find out what I have desired, or what I have felt, *up until the present moment*, should, even as it starts up, substitute for itself the inquiry about which are the desires, which the emotions, with which I can live. That is premature. We cannot dispose of ourselves so speedily.

... The moral is this: if we try to change ourselves before we have come to recognize ourselves, learned to know ourselves, there is a clear danger. It is that we shall put one form of self-ignorance behind us only to embrace another.[68]

Acceptance does involve self-change; but this does not occur through the will to change in particular directions, according to pre-held ideals.

It is worth discussing further the role of the will in acceptance, not least because it contrasts strongly with the role of the will envisioned by ratiocentrism. Freud argued that the work of uncovering the sources of our passions was relatively easy compared to the work of overcoming our resistance to accepting them, resistance premised on the avoidance of psychic pain.[69] Facing up to pain calls for courage, which is often understood as steeling one's will. But it is paradoxical to think of someone 'steeling' themselves to be vulnerable, to tolerate whatever emotional experience arises. There is a *relinquishing* of the will here; and the will demonstrates itself (for the project of self-knowledge is still willed) by not asserting itself. The courage of vulnerability is the courage of letting go, of allowing oneself to feel that which is painful. This contrasts with courage in the face of physical pain, which does involve steeling oneself; what the two forms have in common is that both enable one to continue functioning despite the pain, to not give up on one's end. In the case of deepening self-knowledge, this is to not give up on letting go of attempts to control one's experience of one's emotion.

This process does not leave the self unchanged, but 'enlarged', where that enlargement is not first of all to be understood in terms of reason's control, but in the sense of that with which the self is prepared to fully identify. This willingness must come prior to any attempts to exercise control over the reclaimed parts of the self for them to be recovered at all. But there is a second transformation that this first enacts: the passions that seemed so intolerable themselves change, becoming less threatening, more amenable to influence and compromise, as they become integrated.

There are two further difficulties in attempting to involve the will further in the development of acceptance. First, Freud speaks of re-educating the ego 'to overcome its inclination towards attempts at flight and to tolerate an approach to what is repressed'.[70] Our will, then, is predisposed from familiarity to move in a certain way when painful emotions threaten to arise. Hence its active involvement, beyond the commitment to 'letting go', may undermine the project of self-knowledge. Second, most psychoanalysts understand defence mechanisms as not within the remit of the will, and so an act of will is not enough to undo them. Defence mechanisms are *purposeful* in aiming to reduce psychic pain, but do not involve *choices*. They are part of the nature of the mind, and they interact with the will, but they are not within or directly under the control of the will. Rather, they may be described as the psychic equivalent to the reflex mechanism of withdrawing one's body from a painful stimulus. The psychic pain, or threat of pain, is sufficient to redirect the attention away from the passion without the intervention of the will.[71]

What, then, supports the development of acceptance and vulnerability? The ability to tolerate and work through the pain the process of recovery involves, I want to argue, is essentially born of and sustained by compassion for oneself. The ability to tolerate, to bear, suffering – anxiety, guilt, shame, anguish – without denying the reality of that which causes it is usually identified as part of compassion. Of course, we normally think of compassion as directed towards others; here I argue we need compassion for ourselves. If our response to our fallibility, vulnerability, and dependency is disgust or contempt, we cannot move towards acceptance. Again, compassion is frequently associated with tolerating that which can strike us as disgusting or contemptible. Acceptance is the perspective of compassion.

A second point secures the role of compassion further: the passions with which we feel ourselves in conflict, as in akrasia, often seem intolerable because they threaten our sense of ourselves as acceptable, as *lovable*. Acceptance involves compassion because it precisely countermands this sense – it is possible for me to tolerate the emotion and the pain it brings, and hence to come to know and understand it, because the fact that I feel this emotion does not mean I am unlovable. Compassion for oneself and one's passions is an attitude towards one's passions that allows them to exist, to be felt, because it pulls the sting that leads us to distort our experience of ourselves, to deny or misunderstand the passions we have.[72]

Within the last 50 years, many psychoanalysts have come to understand a form of compassion, some would say love, as essential to the therapeutic process. The analyst Hans Loewald, whose work was influential in this respect, argues that 'in our best moments of dispassionate and objective analyzing we love our object, the patient, more than at any other time and are compassionate with his whole being. In our field scientific spirit and care for the object ...flow from the same source'.[73]

The point of referring to analysis is this: that the analyst demonstrates the nature of acceptance. As the patient interacts with the analyst, and repeatedly experiences their acceptance, they slowly develop the ability to adopt this compassionate understanding themselves. This is, of course, not the only way we can become compassionate towards ourselves, particularly those parts we wish to disown. But it supports the claim that it is needed for acceptance.

***

What I take myself to have argued for, and here I may disagree with Cottingham, is not, in fact, a journey of self-discovery. What I have described in this section is a set of capacities, dispositions, and attitudes of a person who is able, insofar as anyone of us is, to have the 'sense of attunement with that totality' of the self Cottingham rightly places as an essential condition on the good life. The journey is only necessary for those who lack such attunement, but there could be some happy souls who have not lost touch with parts of themselves, who managed to stay attuned, more or less, throughout the process of growing up. What I hope to have shown is that this structure of mental states, of acceptance, vulnerability, courage, and compassion, is beyond the powers of reason alone to bring about; it is what reason can't do.[74]

Notes

1. Cottingham, 1998, p. 130.
2. Cottingham, 1998, p. 162.
3. Cottingham, 1998, p. 209.
4. Cottingham, 1998, p. 24.
5. Cottingham, 1998, p. 27.
6. Cottingham, 1998, Ch. 2, Par. 3.
7. Cottingham, 1998, p. 44.
8. Cottingham, 2005, p. 75.
9. Plato, *Protagoras*, 358c.
10. Cottingham, 1998, p. 59.
11. See, for example, Rorty, 1980; Roberts, 2003, Ch. 4; Nussbaum, 2001, Ch. 4; Taylor, 1985; and Gardner, 1992. Goldie, 2000, p. 76 also defends the opacity ('cognitive impenetrability') of emotions, though does not discuss whether this is a consequence of unconscious influence.
12. Cottingham does talk specifically of the 'non-rational elements of our makeup' (Cottingham, 1998, p. 143), and goes on to discuss a case of sexual akrasia. But it would be a mistake to think that psychoanalysis – or even Freud – emphasises sexual motivation above all. There is nothing in psychoanalysis that would suggest some passions and not others have an unconscious source that makes them prone to motivate akrasia. We can be akratic with respect to love, lust, anger, fear, greed, and so on, and all may receive a psychoanalytic account.
13. Cottingham, 1998, p. 28.
14. Cottingham, 1998, p. 96.
15. Descartes, 1650, article 212.
16. Descartes, 1650, article 153.

17. Descartes, 1650, article 153.
18. Descartes, 1650, article 148.
19. Cottingham, 1998, p. 103.
20. Cottingham, 1998, pp. 48, 51.
21. Cottingham, 1998, p. 140.
22. Cottingham, 1998, p. 135.
23. Cottingham, 1998, p. 47.
24. Cottingham, 1998, p. 59.
25. Cottingham, 1998, p. 111.
26. Cottingham, 1998, p. 131.
27. I am not persuaded of this. The unconscious influences on our passions can extend throughout our lives, and can upset the public life of reason, even if this influence is stronger and more apparent in our private lives.
28. Cottingham, 1998, p. 143.
29. Cottingham, 1998, p. 143.
30. Cottingham, 2005, p. 63.
31. Cottingham, 2005, p. 142.
32. See Freud, 1894; Freud, 1968; and Bateman & Holmes, 1995.
33. Gardner, 1993, p. 145.
34. The mechanisms operate by *phantasy*; see Isaacs, 1948; Gardner, 1993, Ch. 6; Wollheim, 1984, Chs. IV, V.
35. Lear, 2003, p. 205.
36. See Lacewing, 2005, for further discussion.
37. Lear, 2003, pp. 48–9.
38. Cottingham, 1998, p. 152.
39. Cottingham, 1998, p. 162; the quote is from Freud, 1933, p. 80.
40. Freud, 1926, p. 205.
41. Freud, 1940, p. 177.
42. Freud, 1940, p. 179.
43. Nussbaum, 2001, p. 232.
44. Sorabji, 2000, p. 155.
45. Clark, 1986, p. 461.
46. Cottingham, 1998, p. 12.
47. Lear, 2003, pp. 11, 13.
48. Freud, 1913, p. 142.
49. Freud, 1910, p. 225.
50. Variations on this view of emotions as orientations to the world can be found in Sartre, 1962, and Wollheim, 1999.
51. Lear, 2003, p. 204.
52. Lear, 2003, p. 49.
53. For example, Roberts, 2003, and Nussbaum, 2001.
54. For a more detailed presentation of this argument, see Lacewing, 2004.
55. I am talking here of what Freud called *Nachträglichkeit*.
56. Lear, 2003, pp. 47 and 201.
57. Cottingham, 1998, pp. 163 and 165.
58. Cottingham, 1998, p. 144.
59. Lear, 2003, pp. 117–8.
60. Thanks to Dawn Phillips for this.
61. Jung, 1933, p. 147.
62. Freud, 1914, p. 155.

63. Freud, 1914, p. 152.
64. Lear, 2003, pp. 117–9.
65. Lear, 2003, p. 118.
66. To distinguish possible forms, and the structural relations of the self involved in the different forms of 'ownership', would make more precise the line of argument I present here. However, this is not something I am able to do at present, in part for reasons of space. But see, for example, Frankfurt, 1988.
67. See Wollheim, 1984, Ch. VII.
68. Wollheim, 2003, p. 35.
69. Freud, 1926, p. 224.
70. Freud, 1926, p. 205.
71. See Wollheim, 1984, Ch. II; Gardner, 1993, Ch. 6; Gardner, 1991; Hopkins, 1991. For critical discussions, see Pataki, 2000, and Marshall, 2000.
72. I am not claiming that compassion is in any way sufficient for knowledge of one's emotions. There are many other factors that may interfere.
73. Loewald, 2000, p. 297. See also Loewald, 1960, p. 229. It was no part of Freud's understanding of psychoanalysis that the analyst displayed a form of love for his or her patients. While he thought love played a crucial role, so as to write to Jung, 'Psychoanalysis is in essence a cure by love' (6 Dec 1906), he was speaking of the love the patient developed for the analyst. Without 'the aim of pleasing the analyst and of winning his applause and love', the patient would be unable to overcome his resistance to the painful discoveries that emerge. In Freud and Jung, 1974.
74. Thanks to the editors, Louise Braddock, Richard Gipps, and members of the St John's Research Seminar group in psychoanalysis for helpful comments.

Bibliography

All references to Freud are taken from *SE: The Standard Edition of the Complete Psychological Works of Sigmund Freud* (London: The Hogarth Press and The Institute of Psychoanalysis, 1953–74)

Bateman A. & Holmes J., *Introduction to Psychoanalysis* (London: Routledge, 1995)

Clark D.M., 'A cognitive approach to panic', *Behaviour Research and Therapy*, 24 (1986) 461–70

Cottingham J., *The Spiritual Dimension* (Cambridge: Cambridge University Press, 2005)

Cottingham J., *Philosophy and the Good Life* (Cambridge: Cambridge University Press, 1998)

Descartes R., *The Passions of the Soul* [1650], trans. Voss S.H. (Indianapolis: Hackett Publishing Company, 1989)

Frankfurt H., *The Importance of What We Care About* (Cambridge: Cambridge University Press, 1988)

Freud S. and Jung C., *The Freud-Jung Letters*, McGuire W. (ed.) (London: Routledge, 1974)

Freud S., *An Outline of Psychoanalysis* [1940], *SE* XXIII

Freud S., *New Introductory Lectures on Psychoanalysis* [1933], *SE* XXII

Freud S., *The Question of Lay Analysis* [1926], *SE* XX, 177–250

Freud S., 'Remembering, repeating, and working through' [1914], *SE* XII, 145–56

Freud S., 'On beginning the treatment' [1913], *SE* XII, 121–44

Freud S., 'Wild psycho-analysis' [1910], *SE* XI, 219–30

Freud S., 'The neuro-psychoses of defence' [1894], *SE* III, 45–61

Freud A., *The Ego and the Mechanisms of Defence* (London: The Hogarth Press, 1968)

Gardner S., *Irrationality and the Philosophy of Psychoanalysis* (Cambridge: Cambridge University Press, 1993)

Gardner S., 'The nature and source of emotion', in Hopkins & Savile (eds) *Psychoanalysis, Mind and Art* (Oxford: Blackwell, 1992)

Gardner S., 'The unconscious', in Neu J. (ed.) *Cambridge Companion to Freud* (Cambridge: Cambridge University Press, 1991)

Goldie P., *The Emotions* (Oxford: Oxford University Press, 2000)

Hopkins J., 'The interpretation of dreams', in Neu J. (ed.) *Cambridge Companion to Freud* (Cambridge: Cambridge University Press, 1991)

Isaacs S., 'The nature and function of phantasy', *International Journal of Psychoanalysis* 29 (1948) 73–97

Jung C., 'Problems of modern psychotherapy', in Jung C., *Modern Man in Search of a Soul*, trans. Baynes C.F. (London: Routledge, 1933)

Kekes J., *Moral Wisdom and Good Lives* (Ithaca: Cornell University Press, 1995)

Lacewing M., 'Emotional self-awareness and ethical deliberation', *Ratio* XVIII (2005) 65–81

Lacewing M., 'Emotion and cognition: Recent developments and therapeutic practice', *Philosophy, Psychiatry and Psychology* 11 (2004) 175–186

Lear J., *Therapeutic Action* (London: Karnac, 2003)

Loewald H., 'Analytic theory and the analytic process', in his *The Essential Loewald Reader* (Hagerstown, MD: University Publishing Company, 2000)

Loewald H., 'On the therapeutic action of psychoanalysis', *International Journal of Psychoanalysis* 41 (1960) 16–33; reprinted in *The Essential Loewald* (Hagerstown, MD: University Publishing Company, 2000)

Marshall G., 'How far down does the will go?', in Levine M. (ed.), *The Analytic Freud* (London: Routledge, 2000)

Nussbaum M., *Upheavals of Thought* (Cambridge: Cambridge University Press, 2001)

Pataki T., 'Freudian wish-fulfilment and sub-intentional explanation', in Levine M. (ed.), *The Analytic Freud* (London: Routledge, 2000)

Roberts R., *Emotions* (Cambridge: Cambridge University Press, 2003)

Rorty A., 'Explaining emotions', in Rorty A. (ed.), *Explaining Emotions* (Berkeley, CA: University of California Press, 1980)

Sartre J.P., *Sketch for a Theory of the Emotions*, trans. Mairet P. (London: Methuen, 1962)

Sorabji R., *Emotions and Peace of Mind* (Oxford: Oxford University Press, 2000)

Taylor C., 'Self-interpreting animals', in his *Human Agency and Language*, (Cambridge: Cambridge University Press, 1985)

Wollheim R., 'On the Freudian unconscious', *Proceedings and Addresses of the American Philosophical Association* 77 (2003) 23–35

Wollheim R., *On the Emotions* (Yale: Yale University Press, 1999)

Wollheim R., *The Thread of Life* (Cambridge: Cambridge University Press, 1984)

Part III The Meaning of Life

7
Meaning, Morality, and Religion

Roger Crisp

1. Meaning

One might expect philosophers to have a lot to say about the meaning of life, so it comes as something of a surprise to find how relatively quiet they have been on the topic in recent years.[1] In that context, John Cottingham's book *On the Meaning of Life* has particular philosophical significance, enhanced by the boldness, depth, and originality of its arguments.[2] In this paper, I want to examine some of Cottingham's central claims in that book about the role of morality and religion in the meaningful life.[3] I shall disagree with much of what he says, but Cottingham will be well aware that philosophical criticism can constitute a form of the most sincere admiration and respect. That is certainly the spirit in which I write. Cottingham's work strikes me as exceptional in contemporary analytic philosophy in its combining acuity and breadth with a grounding in deep historical understanding and an unusual profundity and seriousness of purpose.

First, then, we must define our terms. The question of the meaning of life can be understood in several quite different ways. Consider someone – Amy – who finds herself working 14 hours every day for a management consultancy, with no time even for spending her considerable salary. When she asks herself what the meaning of life is, she may well mean *her* life, and be wondering whether there is anything in it that makes it worth living or good *for her*. Let me call this the *well-being question*.

Amy may answer the well-being question affirmatively. In fact, she quite enjoys her job, and the buzz of weary satisfaction as she reflects upon what she has achieved at the end of a hard day. But she may still reflect upon whether there is anything in her life that *matters*, or should matter, *to her*. In other words, she can drive a wedge between the question of whether her life is good, overall, for her, and the question of whether, were she to find out that she had some terminal condition which would kill her within a year, she should be concerned. This may sound incoherent, so consider this analogy. A satisficer may agree that the chilled Coke in the fridge would be pleasant, and add overall to her well-being. But she may decide that she is already sufficiently well off that it would not be irrational for her to stay at her desk and leave the Coke where it is.[4] An avowed good, that is to say, need not be thought to ground a reason. In the same way, Amy may allow that her life is over-all good for her, but not good enough to give her any reason to care about when it ends. In many cases, she would presumably link well-being directly to reasons – if, for example, only by acting in some way could she avoid some severe suffering. But we need only one case in which well-being can come apart from reasons to care or to act for there to be space for an independent question about whether one's life matters, or should matter, to one. Let me call this the *intrapersonal significance question*.

Now imagine that Amy decides that not only is her life good for her, but that there is enough well-being in her life for it to matter to her whether it continues or not. She might then consider her life from the point of view of others: 'Is there anything in my life, or about my life, which matters, or should matter, to other people?' Amy may reflect upon the fact that, however good she is at her job, she is probably replaceable. She may wonder about global capitalism and her role in it. She may have no friends or family who would miss her if she were knocked over by a bus. And she may then conclude that, though her life is one that is overall good for her and that matters to her, there is really no reason for anyone else to be concerned about whether she lives or dies. This is the concern of the *interpersonal significance question*.

But let us assume that Amy does conclude that her life has interpersonal significance. She may still ask whether that life is a good human life. Imagine that Amy has great musical talent, and gave up a promising career as an opera singer to take her present job. She may ask herself – perhaps in the light of some conception of human nature – whether the life she is now living counts as a good one, or is as good as that she might have lived as a singer. Let me call this the *perfectionist question*.

Finally – and here we are getting close to what I suspect most people have in mind when they ask about the meaning of life – Amy may ask quite simply whether her existence matters, without qualification: the *significance question*. She may have a life of well-being, a life of justified significance to her and to others, and a life exercising her intellectual and practical capacities to the point that it may plausibly be called a good example of how a human life is best lived. But, still, does it matter? This question may occur to Amy as she steps back from her existence and considers it in the light of the cosmos, which might be infinite in space and time and even if finite provides a backdrop for her life of such a scale that anything she might have thought of brute significance in her life begins to fade away to nothing. This is what we may call the sub-question of *scale*. Cottingham puts the worry behind it eloquently:

> We humans may pride ourselves on our intellectual and cultural achievements, but against the backdrop of unimaginable aeons of time through which clouds of incandescent hydrogen expand without limit, we are a strange temporary accident, no more significant than a slime or mould that forms for a few years or decades on a barren rock face and is then seen no more.[5]

But, as the quotation from Cottingham itself suggests, there is more to the question of significance than the question of scale. The universe consists in inert matter, devoid of value: 'nature is predominantly blind, irrational, dead'.[6] The issue here concerns how such a universe can make room for anything of value – the sub-question of the *metaphysics of value*.[7]

Cottingham's concern is primarily the significance question, and its two constituent or sub-questions, that of scale and of the metaphysics of value. But much of what he says is relevant to the other versions of the question of the meaning of life I have listed.[8]

Cottingham's response to the question of the metaphysics of value is essentially a critique of evaluative subjectivism:

> [M]eaning and worth cannot reside in raw will alone: they have to involve a fit between our decisions and beliefs and what *grounds* those decisions and beliefs. That grounding may, as some religious thinkers maintain, be divinely generated; or it may be based on something else – for example certain fundamental facts about our social or biological nature. But it cannot be created by human fiat alone. ... [V]alue is typically *grounded* not in arbitrary preference but in objectively assessable features of the world. And characteristically, our value terms reflect this 'grounding' by what philosophers term 'thick concepts': they don't just say, thinly, 'wow, that's good!', but rather they carry, packaged-in with them so to speak, those factual features in virtue of which we judge the object to be good.[9]

This appeal to our ordinary evaluative practice leaves unanswered the question of how these allegedly objective evaluative properties can exist in an inert universe, so Cottingham remains open to the charge that they are 'queer' to the point that we should expunge them from our metaphysics.[10] I suspect that this may be because Cottingham does not feel the force of the objection in the first place, grounded as it is in a scientistic conception of the world.[11] The examples he mentions are fairly homely: the curative properties of a medicine, the uplifting quality of a piece of a music, the skill of a colleague. On the face of it, there is nothing 'queer' about these properties; and on further reflection a metaphysics which could make no room for them or anything like them would itself seem pretty odd. So I myself think Cottingham is justified in not spending time on elucidating and defending a positive metaphysics of value.[12]

Cottingham's arguments, then, are primarily directed towards answering the question of scale, and here he does provide a full formal and substantive account of meaning. Having spelled out the cosmic context of the question, he goes on to three further aspects of meaningfulness in an activity or a life as a whole. The first is non-triviality: 'to appraise something as meaningful excludes its being trivial or silly'.[13] This condition seems almost analytic in the light of the question of significance: to say that something is trivial just is to say that it does not matter.

The second feature Cottingham mentions is 'achievement-orientation'. A meaningful activity must be 'directed towards some goal, or requiring some focus of energy or concentration or rhythm in its execution'.[14] This condition is less obvious, though it can perhaps be interpreted in a sufficiently broad way to deal with potential counter-examples. One such might be the experience of being 'lost' in listening to some piece of music. There seems no great difficulty in allowing that such listening can count as an activity. But it is harder to see how it could be goal-directed in the ordinary sense of that phrase. One might claim that it is, in the Aristotelian sense, an end in itself; but then it would be hard to see it as 'achievement-oriented'. Nor need there be any energy in or rhythm to its execution; indeed 'execution' seems an odd word to use of it. The work must be done here by the notion of concentration, which should be understood broadly so as not to require any conscious direction by the actor (the listener is, after all, 'lost'). Listening to music can be, strictly, 'aim-less', but it cannot be entirely 'thought-less' for it plausibly to count as meaningful. But what about the *composition* of music? Imagine that Mozart had written his greatest works when in a

kind of trance or coma, inscribing the notes on the page almost automatically. Here the question will arise whether this is even an 'activity'
in the correct sense, and hence the further question whether meaningfulness can include more than such activities. Perhaps being, as it were,
the locus of great significance is in some cases sufficient for meaning.

The final aspect of meaningfuless is hermeneutic: 'for something to be
meaningful to an agent, that agent must *interpret* it or *construe* it in a certain
way ... meaningfulness in action implies a certain degree of *self-awareness*
or *transparency to the agent*'.[15] As far as the question of intrapersonal significance goes, Cottingham's first claim here is undeniable. But it is not
clear why some experience – such as being lost in music, or some religious
or quasi-religious self-transcendence – might not be said to be of sufficient
value for a positive answer to the significance question. Many potentially
meaningful activities do indeed seem to involve self-awareness, but it is
unclear why this should be a necessary condition of meaningfulness.
Cottingham goes on to relate this hermeneutic aspect of meaningfulness
to autonomy: 'someone who is in the grip of psychological distortions or
projections, and whose goals are therefore not self-transparent, risks an
erosion of their status as an autonomous agent engaged in meaningful
activities'.[16] We see again the assumption that meaningfulness can emerge
only in agency or activity. And I suggest that we also see here a fourth
condition on meaningfulness: autonomy. But it may be that certain
activities are of such great value that they bring great significance to a life
even if they are heteronomous as well as non-transparent. Imagine that
Mozart composed largely because he was put under great pressure by his
father to do so, and that – quite unknown to him – his main motivation
in composing was to please his father or to do what he knew his father
would approve of. Does that make his life insignificant?

2. Morality

I have raised some initial doubts about the boundaries Cottingham
draws around the concept of meaning. But now for the sake of argument
let me accept them. Consider someone engaged in some non-trivial
activity, setting and achieving important goals in an autonomous and
entirely self-transparent way. Cottingham worries that a dedicated torturer in some corrupt political régime may meet the conditions for having
a meaningful life,[17] but it seems that this conclusion could be avoided
by noting that meaningfulness must rest on objective value of some
kind. It cannot come merely from subjective commitment.[18] But the
case of someone engaged in properly profound projects, such as those

involving the production of great art, is more difficult, and in this connection Cottingham mentions the standard philosophical example of Paul Gauguin, 'who selfishly dumped his family to pursue a self-indulgent but highly creative life in Tahiti'.[19] Can his life not be said to be meaningful? Cottingham denies that it can.

Note first that the view that Gauguin's life lacked meaning because of his immorality implies that leaving one's family to produce great art is indeed immoral. It seems unclear whether even the morality of common sense is committed to this position. I suspect that many people would say that Gauguin's behaviour was excused by the quality of his paintings. And on certain views, such as a version of hedonistic utilitarianism, it would have been immoral for him to remain at home.

Cottingham could strip out from his view any commitment to a particular moral theory, claiming merely that meaning is inconsistent with immorality (whatever that turns out to be). His first worry about the opposing view is indeed at the level of moral theory:

> If there is no overarching structure or theory that confers meaning on life, no normative pattern or model to which the meaningful life must conform, then a meaningful life reduces to little more than an engaged life in which the agent is systematically committed to certain projects he makes his own, irrespective of their moral status.[20]

The kind of overarching theory or normative pattern Cottingham has in mind here must itself be a moral one, since someone who holds the view criticized in this passage may of course claim that she has an overarching theory and that a life of engagement in valuable projects does conform to a normative model. But given that this is so, then the argument seems to amount to little more than the claim that meaning requires morality, for which it is itself intended to provide evidence.

Cottingham's main line of argument does not depend on the claim that Gauguin was immoral. Rather the central idea is that doing the kinds of thing Gauguin did – whether or not they were immoral – are not consistent with having a meaningful life.[21] The argument rests on a certain picture of human psychology. According to Cottingham, human beings are subject to various imperatives, including a social imperative to cooperate, an emotional imperative to seek recognition and affection, and a rational imperative to engage in criticism and justification with others. In the light of these imperatives, we can see that there is an instability in a conception of meaning that allows projects to be assessed independently of their effect on others. Someone who pursues their projects without concern for others is closing off their emotions and their rational capacity so that they are no longer open to dialogue, and in this sense they are less human (that is, presumably, less characteristically, rather than less biologically, human). The upshot of this is that the pursuit of meaning in an immoral way (or in the way Gauguin pursued it) is self-defeating. It will result in a kind of 'psychic dissonance', in which the person's lack of concern for others in pursuit of her project will clash with her emotional need for relationships with others that require concern for them.[22] A truly meaningful life can be achieved only by *openness* to emotional and rational interaction with others which allows one's projects to be *integrated* into the pattern of one's overall life commitments.[23]

The idea that viciousness results in lack of psychological integration is of course an ancient one.[24] Cottingham's version of the argument relies not on any idiosyncratic conception of the soul or the person, but on the plausible idea that a good life for a human being requires a degree of emotional and rational engagement with others. Note first, however, that this is a point about what I called in the first section above the perfectionist question, not the significance question. It might be that a life could be extremely significant while at the same time being a poor example of a human life, or indeed a poor human life. Second, because Cottingham's argument is an empirical one, it is hostage to the facts. We have already seen that the real Gauguin is not an appropriate example, but there are many others who have a strong claim to meaningfulness in their lives alongside a lack of concern for (certain) others. Among philosophers two recent and salient examples are Russell and Wittgenstein, both of whom retained their characters and their interest in philosophy until the end. But we can anyway make the case using the imaginary Gauguin who deserts his family to produce great art. There is little reason to think that such a person would be unable to establish close personal relationships with at least certain others.[25] Human beings – all human beings – compartmentalize their attitudes towards others in the form of what is sometimes called 'partiality'. Indeed Cottingham himself has written some of the most acute work in defence of partiality.[26] Structurally, the mind of Gauguin is no more or less unstable than that of Cottingham's ideally virtuous person, who is able significantly to privilege the interests of his friends and family over those of strangers.

The argument so far has focused in particular on the emotions. But Cottingham claims that in the mind of the immoral achiever we shall also find a dissonance in rationality, and at one point he uses an argument from Kant:

> Legislating a privilege for oneself which one will not extend to others shows a defective rationality; for to make use of others as a mere means to one's selfish ends is to cut oneself off from the operation of that rational dialogue which defines our humanity.[27]

This passage demonstrates the same kind of optimism about a rational justification of morality that one finds in Kant himself. But, as with Kant, the argument fails on two counts. First, our imaginary Gauguin need not legislate any privilege for himself alone. He may act purely on the basis of his desires, for example, or he may be some kind of Nietzschean who believes that the strong should prevail and is willing to extend the privileges of strength to all of the strong. Second, it is highly unlikely that the view that lack of concern for (all) others is not required by rationality removes from its proponent the opportunity of rational dialogue with others. Egoism may be false; but its proponents are not irrational, in any ordinary sense of that term.

In the case of aesthetic and certain other achievements, Cottingham has another compartmentalization argument:

> [G]reat art is great precisely because of its humanity – its heightened vision of the pathos and tragedy and comedy and precariousness of the human condition; and it verges on the absurd to suggest that such a vision is best cultivated through a coarsened and blunted sensitivity to the needs of those fellow humans with whom one is most closely involved.[28]

This argument does not apply to all achievements – those in science, athletics, logic, and many others. And even in the case of art I suspect it is something of an exaggeration. What matters in the kind of art we are talking about is the capacity to understand human needs and to represent them. Both of these capacities can co-exist with a lack of concern for those needs, and perhaps – as in the case of cruelty – with an ability to relish those needs' not being met.

Cottingham sees this argument as related to Aristotle's thesis of the reciprocity of the virtues or excellences, the idea that the virtues 'cannot be fully present in isolation'.[29] Aristotle's thesis, however, rests on a monolithic conception of practical rationality, according to which the capacity one has to see and do what is required of one must carry across to any other sphere of human life. Most people find this implausible in the case of the clearly moral virtues: Can someone not be the soul of generosity but somewhat cowardly when things come to the crunch? When we extend the claim to cover non-moral excellences such as painting – which itself involves perceptual and motor capacities largely irrelevant to moral virtue – it seems even less likely.

3. Religion

Cottingham's vision of meaningfulness is a religious one. He allows that religion may not be necessary for meaning,[30] but believes that a religious life is significantly more likely to be meaningful than a secular one.[31] The reason for this is that religion is a way of resolving certain concerns which otherwise might undermine the achievement of meaning. In this section, I shall express some doubt both about these concerns, and about whether religion, as Cottingham conceives of it, can meet them. But first we should address the question of what Cottingham means by religion.

Cottingham's approach to religion is essentially a practical rather than a cognitive one, amounting to what he calls the 'Adam Bede position': 'religion is about something else besides doctrines and notions'.[32] What matter primarily are 'practices of spirituality' rather than beliefs, and these practices 'are able to give meaning to the lives of those who adopt them, not in virtue of allegiance to complex theological dogmas but in virtue of a passionate commitment to a certain way of life'.[33] That way of life has at least the four following elements:

1. A view of life as a gift, stemming from a source of truth, beauty, and goodness, and the world as transfigured by those values.
2. Seeing one's life as hinging on responsibility, freedom, and the choice between good and evil.
3. Living a life structured by traditions of worship, acts of 'submission' that provide moral and spiritual awareness and an opportunity for change within oneself.
4. Being mindful of the truth that life is made meaningful by love, and that 'only in the truly outgoing impulse can a created being transcend itself, and begin to reflect the self-giving radiance of its creator'.[34]

Note that only (3) here is clearly a matter of practice. The other three elements are all cognitive, and (1) and (4) imply acceptance of one of the main elements of classical theism: God as creator. So I take it that Cottingham's position is that by engaging in religious practice we shall find ourselves developing cognitive dispositions of acceptance – which we might call 'beliefs' – which are characteristic of theism traditionally understood.[35] But is this not an irresponsible way to acquire such beliefs, in the light of Clifford's principle that 'it is wrong always, everywhere, and for anyone, to believe anything on insufficient evidence'?[36] Cottingham's response is Pascalian.[37] One central aspect of the Pascalian view is said to be that it is 'pre-rational', involving a 'passionate commitment' or attitude to life rather than assent to doctrines.[38] Exactly how the cognitive components of elements (1) and (4) relate to this passionate commitment is left somewhat unclear by Cottingham. But I take it that the result of the strategy is indeed meant to be a belief in God as creator, which is not grounded on argument or evidence, but is the result of habituation. The passionate commitment, as he puts it, 'bypasses the need for prior rational conviction'.[39]

At this point an issue of psychological stability arises for Cottingham's own position. How plausible is it to claim that someone can believe P in the full knowledge that she has no rational grounds for it?[40] I suggest that it is not plausible. This is not to say that those who engage in religious ritual with the motivation Cottingham is suggesting might not end up in a position where it *appears* to them that P is the case, even though in fact – from the rational point of view – they suspend judgement on it. Consider the following analogy. You are in a desert and thirsty, and it appears to you that there is an oasis at the bottom of the sand dune you are on. You know that the desert contains oases, and that illusions of oases in this desert are as common as veridical experiences of them. The question, then, is whether experiencing these appearances in the religious case – having what we might call a quasi-belief – can itself be beneficial.

The benefits Cottingham mentions are:

> the care of the soul, tranquillity of mind, release from the false pursuits of egoism and material gain, a closer awareness of the mystery of life, an affirmation of its profundity and its blessings.[41]

Whether these benefits are more or less likely to result from religious quasi-belief is an empirical question. I am not aware of any research on this question, so Cottingham's claim can be taken only as a hypothesis to be investigated. It is true that those who engage in religious practices do report higher levels of 'subjective well-being'.[42] But it could be that these are people who have not suspended rational judgement and have embraced theism. Nor is it clear to me that even theists are less materialistic or egoistic, or more aware of the mystery of life and its profundity, than atheists. Perhaps, again, more research is required here; or it may be that such research would be so bound up with conceptions of God, morality and happiness that any results would themselves be philosophically highly contestable.

But I have not yet discussed the very problems that religious quasi-belief is meant to solve. These problems arise from two potential threats to meaningfulness from our 'sense of possible failure and futility'.[43] The first is universal, in that from a universal perspective we now know that nothing lasts for ever and that therefore any success can be at best temporary. This relates to the sub-questions of scale and the metaphysics of value which in the first section I saw as aspects of the significance question: 'If all human activity is part of a vast inexorable process ending in destruction, then why should anyone make the effort to struggle to achieve what is good and worthwhile?'[44] The second threat is more particular and is constituted by the potential for failure in any human project: 'in view of the obstacles which the pursuit of goodness often encounters, it seems that the path to a meaningful life offers an existence fraught with struggle, with chances of achieving a successful outcome that are often decidedly slim'.[45]

In the face of these concerns, one might adopt an attitude of resignation to fortune and hope for the best in one's own case. But this attitude, Cottingham argues, is both ethically repugnant and psychologically unrealistic. It is repugnant in going against the compassionate and egalitarian principle that

> every human creature is eligible for salvation: that the unique dignity and worth of each human being confers infinite value on every one of us, providing us, just in virtue of our membership of the human family, with all we need, provided we turn ourselves sincerely towards the good.[46]

And the attitude is unrealistic in its expecting of each of us that we shall 'have the confidence to embark on an arduous and demanding voyage with no special reason to hope for a fair wind'.[47]

The first threat, that of finitude, need not be as paralysing as Cottingham suggests. It is true that many human projects are oriented towards goals external to themselves, and would be a waste of time were those goals to be destroyed immediately on their being achieved.

Cottingham himself provides the example of someone whose life's work is creating a hospital which is destroyed on the day it is due to open. But, to return again to the aesthetic, many works of art have survived for many years, and have been experienced by many people, and from our human perspective that is surely enough for our motivation not to be sapped.

The second threat is a subtle one. On the one hand, Cottingham himself allows that we have no rational justification for theism and so no reason not to think that whether one has a meaningful life is a matter of luck.[48] So the egalitarian principle itself amounts only to a hope.[49] We return again to the issue of psychology. If we engage in religious practices to the point that we have acquired a quasi belief in that principle, will that enable us to begin a journey to meaningfulness we would otherwise lack sufficient confidence to undertake? It may be so in certain cases. But there is a great deal of evidence that many people have had the confidence to begin such journeys without that quasi-belief or actual belief in God or the egalitarian principle. And this is only what we should expect given the nature of the projects we have in mind: they are seen by those who initiate them as objectively valuable.[50] Sometimes they may be difficult, and one might need a belief in objective value to retain momentum. But one need not attempt to engender in oneself the quasi-belief that one is guaranteed success merely through sincere trying. Further, and this is a point well worth noting in the context of a discussion of motivation, human beings have, as Cottingham says, 'the extraordinary ability to feel joy in the tackling of difficult and challenging tasks'.[51] One of the things that motivated (the real) Gauguin was a need to make money. But he also recognized the value of what he was doing, and the value of his doing it, and enjoyed painting to the point that he could easily do it even when others had not yet appreciated his genius.

To conclude. It appears that the meaning of life, as Cottingham understands it, requires neither moral virtue nor religion. But how much does *that* matter? Very often, when people ask about the meaning of life, they are wondering what reason they have to continue with their life (and if their wondering is independent of reasons, then it seems, from the practical point of view, inconsequential). It seems to me that the answer to the very first question I listed in my first section – the well-being question – may be sufficient to meet that concern, if the answer is that one's life is overall worth living. Further, it seems to me not implausible to claim that it is well-being, rather than significance or meaning construed in a perfectionist or other non-welfarist way, which provides the only reason any of us have to act. Why should I do anything, except in so far as it benefits myself or others, even if it will add to the cosmic significance of my life? From this perspective, the question of the meaning of life, understood independently from well-being, itself appears to have little practical significance.[52]

Notes

1. Thaddeus Metz describes the area as a 'backwater' (2002, p. 781), and notes that the number of philosophical publications from 2002–7 is 'not enormous' (2007, p. 214).
2. John Cottingham, 2003.
3. I shall also make reference to other works by Cottingham, in particular 1998 and 2005. But the main focus of my discussion is the sustained argument on the meaning of life in 2003.
4. See Slote, 1984, pp. 143–4.
5. Cottingham, 2003, pp. 3–4; see also pp. 33–5.
6. Cottingham, 2003, p. 3.
7. There are of course further sub-questions, depending on the context in which the question of significance is asked. Thad Metz offered me the example of someone who thinks that meaning can come only from our fulfilling God's plan, so the significance question might be couched as: 'Does anything in our lives matter, given that there is doubt over whether there is any divine source for meaning?' In other words, a sub-question here consists in the significance question 'Does my life (or human life in general) matter?' asked against the background of some doubt or other about the possibility of meaning.
8. I do not wish to claim priority or special importance for any of these questions. What matters is that one is clear on which is, or are, being asked. Nor do I intend to rule out the possibility of some more fundamental question which unites those I have listed, though I cannot myself come up with one.
9. Cottingham, 2003, pp. 17, 20.
10. See Mackie, 1977, pp. 38–42.
11. See for example, Cottingham, 2003, p. 60; Cottingham, 2005, p. 110; John McDowell, 1983, pp. 1–16.
12. In *The Spiritual Dimension*, Cottingham appears to have become more pessimistic about what objectivity alone can achieve without theism. In a godless world, Cottingham suggests, there would be no way, independently of agents' contingent desires, of ascribing to certain features of actions (their being cruel or kind, say) the objective property of providing a reason (Cottingham, 2005, p. 53). Further, if our moral aversion to cruelty is merely a contingent result of our genetic and cultural history, it is hard to see how we could have an objective reason not to be cruel (Cottingham, 2005, p. 56). I prefer to take the other horn in the *Euthyphro* dilemma (which Cottingham himself appears to take in 2003, pp. 65–6 and 72). If God says there is a reason not to be cruel, that is because there is, independent of his say-so and indeed his existence, a reason not to be cruel. (See Metz, 2005, p. 224.) Nor

is it clear to me why we should not draw a wedge between our aversion to cruelty, which may be contingent, and the property of cruelty itself, which may, as a matter of necessity, ground objective reasons in all possible worlds, including those in which human beings have not developed an aversion to cruelty. 7 + 5 would equal 12 even had we not developed the capacity to add.

13. Cottingham, 2003, p. 21.
14. Cottingham, 2003, p. 21.
15. On self-awareness and transparency, see also for example, Cottingham, 1998, ch. 4, sect. 6; 2005, ch. 4.
16. Cottingham, 2003, p. 22.
17. Cottingham, 2003, p. 21.
18. It could be that Cottingham is himself making this point at the top of p. 25 of 2003. But there he seems to stress the importance of autonomous projects, as if the torturer's choice must be somehow heteronomous.
19. Cottingham, 2003, p. 25. I shall treat 'Gauguin' as an invention, since the truth about the real Gauguin is not straightforward. In 1882 Gauguin lost his job because of a stock market crash. He tried hard but with little success to support his family by working with art dealers, and in 1884 moved to Rouen in the hope of making money from odd jobs. When that failed, the family took refuge with his parents-in-law in Denmark. His hosts strongly disapproved of him, and he returned to Paris in June 1885, accompanied by his second son. It is true that he had been absent from his family for significant periods even before the trip to Denmark, and that he failed to support them after the separation, but true also that until his death he barely managed to support himself. His first visit to Tahiti was not until 1891. In a preface written in 1921 for *The Intimate Journals of Paul Gauguin*, after setting out the 'fantastic Gauguin legend' Emile Gauguin writes: '[M]y mother ... agreed to let him go ... because she respected his passion for art. It was brave of her. It meant that she was to assume the burden of maintaining and educating the children' (Gauguin, 1952, p. viii). And in the preface to his edition of Gauguin's *Letters to his Wife and Friends*, Maurice Malingue puts the blame for the break-up of the family firmly on Gauguin's wife (Malingue, 1948, pp. ix–xi). Bernard Williams, who is perhaps primarily responsible for the view among modern philosophers of Gauguin as selfish, describes the case of someone he calls 'Gauguin' without 'feeling limited by any historical facts' (Williams, 1981, p. 22). The paperback cover of *Moral Luck* is illustrated with Gauguin's masterpiece *D'où Venons Nous ... Que Sommes Nous ... Où Allons Nous?* Williams would have appreciated the irony of that second question in this context. (I am grateful here to Linda Whiteley for assistance and discussion.)
20. Cottingham, 2003, p. 26.
21. Cottingham, 2003, pp. 26–31.
22. At this point in his argument, Cottingham returns to the case of the torturer, saying 'it is (unhappily) conceivable that a job that involves cruelty and bullying may produce excitements that may make it horribly attractive to certain individuals; that is not in dispute. The point is that it cannot, for the reasons just given, constitute a coherent model for a meaningful human life' (Cottingham, 2003, p. 28). It is important to remember that the

defender of the claim that the value of his painting gives meaning to Gauguin's life is not committed to the claim that there is meaning in torturing.

23. On integrity, see for example, Cottingham, 1998, ch. 4, sects 7–8; 2005, ch. 4, sects 4–5; 2003, p. 172. I read Cottingham as claiming that integrity is partly constitutive of the meaningful life, and not merely some instrumental means to it. (I am grateful to Thad Metz for suggesting that I clarify this point.)

24. See for example, Plato, 1902, 444a10–b8.

25. On p. 29 of 2003, Cottingham makes a Humean point that a fulfilled human life must include 'minimal concern for our fellow creatures'. But our imaginary Gauguin might surely have some degree of concern for every other human being (he would go to some small trouble to protect them from some terrible danger, for example). It's just that he is quite willing to use some people to advance his valuable projects.

26. See for example, Cottingham, 1986; Cottingham, 1991; Cottingham, 1996.

27. Cottingham, 2003, pp. 28–9.

28. Cottingham, 2003, p. 30. For similar lines of argument, see Murdoch, 1985, pp. 66–8 and 87–8. This is one of several deeply Murdochian strands in Cottingham's thought.

29. Cottingham, 2003, p. 30. See Aristotle, 1894, 1144b32–1145a2.

30. Cottingham, 2003, p. 95.

31. In Cottingham, 2005, p. 147 n. 7, however, he claims that his advocacy of the spiritual life is undogmatic, accepting that there may be non-spiritual ways of dealing with the human predicament.

32. Cottingham, 2003, pp. 87–91. See also Cottingham, 2005, ch. 1.

33. Cottingham, 2003, p. 90.

34. Cottingham, 2004, p. 91.

35. See also for example, Cottingham, 2005, p. 112: belief in God comes as a *result* of trust in a living community of faith.

36. Cottingham, 2003, pp. 92–3.

37. Cottingham, 2003, pp. 93–9. Compare also another response to Clifford: James, 1956.

38. Cottingham, 2003, p. 96.

39. Cottingham, 2003, p. 96. It is clear from the surrounding argument that 'prior' could be omitted from this sentence. *The Spiritual Dimension* is also largely cognitively non-committal, though Cottingham allows that a religious adherent may claim that we acquire *knowledge* of God through praxis (Cottingham, 2005, p. 12) and there are elements of Jamesianism in his religious epistemology (see for example, Cottingham, 2005, p. 133 n. 15). He states that, for the purposes of his discussion of self-discovery through religious praxis, it is to be left an open question whether there is an 'objective correlate' towards which our creativity leads us (Cottingham, 2005, p. 73). His chapter on religious language concerns the role of metaphor, not the question of justification (Cottingham, 2005, p. 100). And the book ends with the claim that, '*if the message of faith is true*', we might 'begin to learn how to be grafted onto the true vine that is the image of the best that humanity can become' (my italics).

40. I am here excluding cases of 'basic beliefs' and suchlike. See Cottingham, 2005, p. 129.

41. Cottingham, 2003, p. 95. It is somewhat surprising to find Cottingham, in 2005, pp. 155-6, accepting the objections to 'indifferentism' that it involves an instrumentalist attitude to religion and the view that reasons for adopting a religious worldview can be independent of the truth of such a view.
42. See for example, Helliwell, 2003.
43. Cottingham, 2003, p. 67; see also pp. 67-79.
44. Cottingham, 2003, p. 68.
45. Cottingham, 2003, p. 69.
46. Cottingham, 2003, pp. 69-70.
47. Cottingham, 2003, p. 70.
48. 'To be religiously motivated to pursue goodness is to strive to act rightly ... knowing that there is no guarantee of success' (Cottingham, 2003, p. 74).
49. It is interesting to contrast Cottingham's position with that of Kant on the *summum bonum*: pt. 1, bk. 2, ch. 2, sect. 5.2.
50. Compare Metz, 2005, p. 227.
51. Cottingham, 2003, p. 70.
52. For helpful comments on previous drafts, I am most grateful to Thad Metz and to the editors.

Bibliography

Aristotle, *Ethica Nicomachea*, Bywater I. (ed.) (Oxford: Clarendon Press, 1894)

Cottingham J., *The Spiritual Dimension* (Cambridge: Cambridge University Press, 2005)

Cottingham J., *On the Meaning of Life* (London: Routledge, 2003)

Cottingham J., *Philosophy and the Good Life* (Cambridge: Cambridge University Press, 1998)

Cottingham J., 'Partiality and the virtues', in Crisp R. (ed.), *How Should One Live? Essays on the Virtues* (Oxford: Clarendon Press, 1996), 57-76

Cottingham J., 'The ethics of self concern', *Ethics*, 101 (1991) 798-817

Cottingham J., 'Partialism, favouritism and morality', *Philosophical Quarterly*, 36 (1986) 357-73

Gauguin E., 'Preface', in *The Intimate Journals of Paul Gauguin*, trans. Van Wyck Roberts (Melbourne: Heinemann, 1952)

Helliwell J., 'How's life? Combining individual and national variables to explain subjective well-being', *Economic Modelling*, 20 (2003) 331-60

James W., 'The will to believe', in his *The Will to Believe and Other Essays in Popular Philosophy* (New York: Dover, 1956), 1-31

Kant I., *Critique of Practical Reason*, Gregor M. (ed.) (Cambridge: Cambridge University Press, 1997)

Mackie J. L., *Ethics: Inventing Right and Wrong* (Penguin: Harmondsworth, 1977)

Malingue M., 'Preface', in Paul Gauguin's *Letters to his Wife and Friends*, Malingue M. (ed.) (London: The Saturn Press, 1948)

McDowell J., 'Aesthetic value, objectivity and the fabric of the world', in Schaper E., (ed.), *Pleasure, Preference and Value* (Cambridge: Cambridge University Press, 1983), 1-16

Metz T., 'New developments in the meaning of life', *Philosophy Compass*, 2 (2007) 196–217

Metz T., 'Baier and Cottingham on the meaning of life', *Disputatio*, 1.19 (2005) 215–28.

Metz T., 'Recent work on the meaning of life', *Ethics*, 112 (2002) 781–814.

Murdoch I., *The Sovereignty of the Good* (London: Ark, 1985)

Plato, *Res Publica* in *Platonis Opera*, Burnet J. (ed.), vol.4 (Oxford: Clarendon Press, 1902)

Slote M., 'Satisficing consequentialism', *Proceedings of the Aristotelian Society*, suppl. vol. 58 (1984) 139–76

Williams B., 'Moral luck', in his *Moral Luck* (Cambridge: Cambridge University Press, 1981), 20–39

8
The Meaning of Life: Subjectivism, Objectivism, and Divine Support

Brad Hooker

1. Introduction

Few can write as expertly and eloquently on such a wide range of philo-sophical areas as John Cottingham. Very few are as disposed as he to try to look at matters from others' points of view. And he is spectacularly good at foreseeing how others will react to various ideas and arguments. This combination of talents and virtues makes him one of the very best people with whom to discuss philosophy ... and life. It is thus a privilege for me to carry on the discussion with him by contributing a paper to a volume in his honour.

A maximally meaningful life involves subjective commitment to and pleasure from objectively good ends. But let us not consider only the ideal case. What is needed for a life to have at least some meaning? I will argue that a life can have at least some meaning purely because of its subjective, introspectively discernible, qualities. Then I will defend the somewhat objectivist view that a life can be meaningful without the person whose life it is realizing that it is meaningful. Cottingham closely connects religion and the meaning of life. My essay will close by commenting on this connection.

2. A subjectivist sufficient condition

Consider an example suggested by P. F. Strawson. Imagine a sybarite, by which I mean someone whose life is dedicated to the development of 'an exquisite sense of the luxurious'.[1] Someone whose overriding goal is to develop an exquisite sense of the luxurious would presumably need considerable resources in order to obtain luxuries of a high enough quality and in enough variety to train and maintain his powers of discrimination. Partaking in luxuries is typically expensive. And an exquisite sense of the luxurious cannot be obtained without actually partaking in luxuries. Reading about luxuries, hearing others talk about them, even watching others enjoy them might bring vicarious pleasures. But reading and hearing about luxuries and watching others enjoy them are not on their own sufficient for developing an exquisite sense of the luxurious. One must actually taste the caviar, sleep in the fine beds, live in multiple palaces, travel by private limousine and private jet, soak up the Mediterranean sun while lying on the deck of a well-appointed yacht, and so on.

Admittedly, some people are born into immense wealth or come upon such wealth in the course of their lives in some other way. But is anyone so rich that he or she could not use extra wealth to help develop his or her exquisite sense of the luxurious? Let us not let this question sidetrack us. As a matter of empirical fact, the vast majority of people who happen to be focused on obtaining luxuries for themselves *do* have to worry about 'whether they can afford' buying what they desire. The *typical* sybarite is obsessed not only with luxury for himself but also with the money or power needed to obtain or sustain this luxury.

Clearly, the money and power here is *merely* instrumentally valuable. The exquisite sense of the luxurious, however, is not thought of as *merely* instrumentally valuable by our sybarite. Admittedly, someone could think of a developed sense of the luxurious as merely a means to (say) increased pleasure. But what we are interested in for the moment is someone who thinks of an exquisite sense of the luxurious as non-instrumentally valuable.

Joseph Raz distinguished between two kinds of non-instrumental value, namely *constituent* value and *ultimate* value. For something to have constituent value is for it to have value as an intrinsic part of a larger whole that has value. For something to have ultimate value in Raz's sense is for its value not to derive from its relation (for example contribution) to something else.[2] Here is an example illustrating Raz's distinction: things that constitute benefits to someone[3] – constituents of that person's good – have constituent value, but the person's good has ultimate value.

We are focusing here on the sybarite who thinks of the exquisite sense of the luxurious as not merely instrumentally valuable. But which kind of non-instrumental value does this sybarite think that the exquisite sense of the luxurious has? The possible answers are of course: (1) that the exquisite sense of the luxurious has constituent value, (2) that the exquisite sense of the luxurious has ultimate value, and (3) that the exquisite sense of the luxurious has both constituent and ultimate value.

Obviously, if we show either that the exquisite sense of the luxurious does not have constituent value or that the exquisite sense of the luxurious does not have ultimate value, we have refuted the view that the exquisite sense of the luxurious has both constituent and ultimate value. So let us move on to the question of whether the exquisite sense of the luxurious has ultimate value.

An *exquisite* sense of the luxurious requires the development and exercise of capacities beyond that of sub-human intelligence. My dog prefers soft fabrics to rough ones, rich food to bland, two outings per day to one, and so on. But no one could without irony accuse him of developing an *exquisite* sense of the luxurious. There are many differences in degrees of luxury that we can judge and he simply can't. My dog can, at best, develop a *crude* sense of the luxurious.

If we can develop an exquisite sense of the luxurious and animals cannot, does an exquisite sense of the luxurious have ultimate value? On the one hand, from the fact that we have some capacity that animals don't have, it hardly follows that our exercise of this capacity has ultimate value. On the other hand, some impressive capacities are involved in having an exquisite sense of the luxurious.

For example, an exquisite sense of the luxurious can involve concentration, understanding of complex phenomena, the ability to make subtle distinctions and fine discriminations, and perhaps even the ability to formulate nuanced analyses. It can require considerable background knowledge, and partly consists in certain kinds of knowledge. An exquisite sense of the luxurious also involves feelings, in particular feelings of attraction towards the more luxurious and pleasant feelings in the experience of greater luxury. So, acquiring considerable knowledge and powers of discernment and training and fine-tuning one's feelings are all part of developing an exquisite sense of the luxurious. An exquisite sense of the luxurious can thus be quite an achievement. However, to the extent that we explain the value of an exquisite sense of the luxurious in terms of knowledge and achievement, I cannot see that we are demonstrating that an exquisite sense of the luxurious has ultimate value (in its own right). In fact, I can think of no plausible argument for the ultimate value of an exquisite sense of the luxurious.

So turn now to matter of constituent value. Having important kinds of knowledge and achieving complex goals are some of the constituents of a good life.[4] But that leaves open whether an exquisite sense of the luxurious is a constituent of the good life in its own right. Indeed, it is tempting to think that an exquisite sense of the luxurious has value only as a means to pleasure, or as a kind of achievement, or as a kind of knowledge.

Let me consider those three possibilities at greater length. Suppose we accept that having an exquisite sense of the luxurious not only requires lots of background knowledge but is also partly constituted by certain kinds of knowledge. Well, not all knowledge is equal. In fact, there is a spectrum from the most profound to the most trivial. As an example of the most trivial, consider my knowledge that there are exactly five flies in this room. Of course there could be situations where such knowledge is very important. But, absent special circumstances, such knowledge is quite banal. An example of profound knowledge is knowledge of the most explanatorily powerful facts. Now we can ask whether the knowledge involved in an exquisite sense of the luxurious is too trivial to infuse a life with meaning.

As a kind of knowledge, an exquisite sense of the luxurious doesn't seem especially important. It can be concerned with fine differences between things, when being concerned with those fine differences seems self-indulgent and a waste of attention and time. But here perhaps we can distinguish between a focus on the subtle differences between aesthetic entities and a focus on the subtle pleasures derivable from experiencing subtle and refined aesthetic features. An appreciation of the subtle differences between aesthetic entities can be admirable even if a focus on the attendant pleasures is not.

Turn now to the idea that an exquisite sense of the luxurious can be important as a kind of achievement. Relevant here is a passage from Cottingham:

> [T]o appraise something as meaningful excludes its being trivial or silly. Pastimes like golf appear somewhat borderline here: it seems they just about qualify as meaningful, but only provided they have a substantial and important recreational function ... or else play some further role, for example by promoting health or furthering a professional sporting career. ... [T]o be meaningful an activity must be *achievement-oriented*, that is, directed towards some goal, or requiring some focus of energy or concentration or rhythm in its execution.[5]

Clearly, developing an exquisite sense of the luxurious can be taken as seriously as golf, can be achievement-oriented, and can require some focus of energy and concentration.

Cottingham assigns high value to the self-aware development of distinctively human capacities, especially ones that involve habituation, and refinement. Another account of value in a similar vein is Thomas Hurka's.[6] Hurka thinks human achievement especially important, and he holds that achievement is greater where it involves greater complexity, hierarchy in goals and sub-goals, and difficulty.

Now, using a club to stroke little balls into little holes from long and short distances and on different types of terrain might initially sound like a silly activity. But being good at this does involve power, perceptiveness, planning, and precision, all of which take considerable practice. In short, it requires complex skills, the development of which takes complicated training of human capacities. There is something impressive about and meaningful in the development and refinement of capacities, even if these capacities are then used to achieve a goal that seems valueless taken on its own (for example, stroking balls into holes). Hurka's examples about sporting achievements seem to me to make this point compellingly.

However, John Tasioulas offers a further explanation of why playing games (including those sports that involve games) can be intrinsically valuable. Tasioulas postulates *play* as a basic good.[7] This theory, however, seems in danger of finding value in games that seem not necessarily to contain any value (for example, games of chance and daredevil games). Of course, participating in games has value as a means when doing so gives people pleasure (either in anticipation, or at the time, or later), or fosters good social relations, or develops or sustains abilities important for other good purposes, or just gives people relief from thinking about other things. The live question is whether participating in games is *always* valuable. Tasioulas seems committed to saying that, wherever participating in a game is a matter of *play*, it has some value.

He stops short of committing himself to the thesis that an activity cannot be an instance of play unless the activity generates (or is expected to generate) some enjoyment. But, for the sake of argument, suppose that an activity cannot count as play unless it is expected to generate some enjoyment and deepening of personal relationships. Given this supposition, we can accept that play always involves at least some intrinsic value. But the question then is: does the value come from the play, as such, or really only from the contribution to pleasure and relationships?

Tasioulas takes play to be a basic human good, presumably standing shoulder to shoulder with other basic human goods – pleasure, important knowledge, achievement, and deep personal relations. None of these four basic human goods, as I understand them here, has any of the others as a necessary component of it. In other words:

1. Pleasure can obtain in the absence of important knowledge, achievement, and deep personal relations.
2. Important knowledge can obtain in the absence of pleasure, achievement, and deep personal relations.
3. Achievement can obtain in the absence of pleasure, important knowledge and deep personal relations.
4. Deep personal relationships can obtain in the absence of pleasure, important knowledge, and other kinds of achievement.

I need to add clarifications about, and qualifications to, these four claims. One is that there *typically* are interconnections among knowledge, achievement, deep personal relations, and pleasure. For example, deep personal relations typically involve taking pleasure in the other's success and company. But a deep personal relation might bring you more pain than pleasure, for example in cases where the person you love has a life of unrelenting intense suffering, and this fact combined with your love for her makes you very miserable.

I also acknowledge that acquiring important knowledge, developing a deep personal relationship, and training yourself to take pleasure in certain things can be achievements. But acquiring important knowledge, developing a deep personal relationship, and getting or being disposed to get pleasure can be the product of luck rather than aim and effort. So acquiring important knowledge, developing a deep personal relationship, and getting or being disposed to get pleasure can fail to be achievements. Thus, one could have important knowledge, deep personal relationships, and pleasure without achievement.

I further admit that deep personal relations are impossible without some degree of knowledge of one another. Jack and Jill don't really have a deep personal relation if most of Jack's beliefs about Jill's guiding ideas and motives are false. So when I say that deep personal relations can obtain in the absence of important knowledge, I mean in the absence of important knowledge apart from the important knowledge internal to the relationship.

With those clarifications and qualifications in hand, we can say that none among pleasure, important knowledge, achievement, and deep personal relations takes any of the others as being a necessary component of it. Now, for play to stand shoulder-to-shoulder with these basic human goods, play should be able to obtain in the absence of pleasure, important knowledge, achievement, and deep personal relations.

Thus, let us consider a case where play occurs without pleasure, important knowledge, achievement, and a social dimension. Imagine a game of chance played alone. Tasioulas's theory seems committed to finding value in this game of chance, since it is an instance of play. But I think there is no value or meaning in games of chance played alone without pleasure.

Some might be suspicious that nothing could count as a game unless it is embedded in some sort of social practice. If that were right, then even a game of chance played alone must involve participating in a social practice to at least some minimal extent. But it is absurd to insist that nothing can be a game unless embedded in a social practice. Suppose that I decide that, if the number of birds I see within the next 16 seconds is even, then and only then will I give myself some treat. In no interesting way is this very simple game of chance a social practice; it is an individually designed game played alone.

Unlike an individually designed game of chance played alone, the development of an exquisite sense of the luxurious must involve the development of human capacities to a level that qualifies as an achievement. Hence, since the development of human capacities to the point of some degree of achievement can constitute a benefit to the agent in the case of sports achievements, I cannot see how to deny that the development of an exquisite sense of the luxurious can also constitute a benefit to the agent.

But perhaps Cottingham does have an objection to counting all such things as meaningful:

> [T]o count toward the meaningfulness of a life these varied activities [artistic, athletic, intellectual, and so on] have to be more than just performed by the agent with an eye to personal satisfaction; they have to be capable of being *informed* by a vision of their value in the whole, by a sense of the worthwhile part they play in the growth and flowering of each unique human individual, and of the other human lives with which that story is necessarily interwoven.[8]

Is it true that artistic, athletic, intellectual and other activities cannot add to the meaningfulness of someone's life in cases where all this person cares about is personal satisfaction? Indeed, can we even make sense of the idea that all someone cares about is personal satisfaction? If Bishop Butler was right, personal satisfaction is impossible without desires for other things. The source of personal satisfaction resides in believing your desires for other things are being or have been fulfilled.

Now, is some concern for the 'growth and flowering' of *each* individual a prerequisite of artistic, athletic, intellectual and other activities' counting towards the meaningfulness of a life? On the face of it, that certainly doesn't seem to be a prerequisite. For there have been many lives that were undeniably meaningful because of their activities, and yet did not contain concern for the growth and flowering of *every* individual. Tribalism has been the norm until fairly recently in human history. And very many people who cared not at all about 'outsiders' have had meaningful lives because of their activities. Of course some of these meaningful activities were for the benefit of others *inside* the tribe. But this circle of concern is far too narrow to satisfy Cottingham's condition.

We must be careful to distinguish between what needs to be true of a life in order for it to have *some* meaning and what needs to be true of a life in order for it to be *fully* or even *maximally* meaningful. Someone who is successful in various complex activities but not concerned about how these activities play a part in the flowering of others may not have a fully or maximally meaningful life. Someone who is successful at promoting the welfare of those within his narrow circle may have a less meaningful life than someone successful at promoting the good of a much wider circle. But these less meaningful lives are hardly meaningless.

Return one more time to our sybarite. Let us assume this person has developed an exquisite sense of the luxurious (which is a kind of achievement) and has taken pleasure in experiencing various luxuries. We can call this person the successful sybarite. Is the achievement and pleasure in this life enough to make the life at least *a little* meaningful?

Well, such achievement and pleasure constitute benefits for the sybarite, or, in other words, constitute additions to his personal good or welfare. I do not mean merely that such achievement and pleasure *seem* to him to constitute benefits to him. I mean they *really do* constitute benefits to him. Achievement and pleasure are constituent values.

If having a life containing benefits for oneself does by itself imbue this life with at least some meaning, then the successful sybarite has a life with at least some meaning. But is having a life containing benefits for oneself enough to imbue that life with at least some meaning? We might think that the answer is no. Our thought might be that for one's life to be meaningful it has to have some kind of significant impact on the world outside oneself. The life of refining and indulging one's tastes for luxury could well have no significant impact on the lives of anyone else. This is what I think makes it so difficult to accept that a successful sybarite's life must have at least a little meaning.

However, there is a powerful argument against the view that for one's life to be meaningful it has to have at least a little significant impact on the world outside oneself. Your good effects on someone else's life can imbue your life with at least some meaning. But if your good effects on someone else's life can imbue your life with at least some meaning, why can't the benefits you obtain for yourself imbue your life with at least some meaning? I think the answer is that they can.

Is this form of argument a good one? Consider a parallel argument: That you benefit others is to your moral credit. If benefiting others is to your moral credit, so is benefiting yourself. So benefiting yourself is to your moral credit.

I reject that parallel argument. Morality seems to me essentially inter-personal in the sense that it is exclusively concerned with how people treat or react to others. True, there are limits to the amount of self-sacrifice morality can plausibly demand. But this is not because there is a duty to do what is best for oneself, which could then oppose or outweigh moral duties to do things for other people.

For two reasons, I won't pursue further here whether benefiting one-self is to one's moral credit. The first reason is that I discuss it elsewhere.[9] The second reason is that, were I to be wrong about whether benefiting oneself is to one's moral credit, this would definitely not threaten the view I have expressed about meaning. I expressed the view that, since benefiting others can imbue your life with some meaning, benefiting yourself can also imbue your life with at least some meaning. The case for the view that benefiting yourself can imbue your life with meaning is strengthened if benefiting yourself would be to your moral credit.

Earlier, I distinguished between the claim that a life is a little mean-ingful and the claim that a life is fully or maximally meaningful. I do *not* think that benefiting yourself can imbue your life with *maximal* meaning. On the contrary, I think it can imbue your life with only some meaning. In this section, I have argued that the fact that someone's life contained some achievement or pleasure can give that life some degree of meaning. If my arguments in this section have been correct, then there is a subjectivist sufficient condition for the agent's life having at least some meaning.

3. An objectivist sufficient condition

Just as it is important to distinguish between the claim that a life is a little meaningful and the claim that a life is fully or maximally mean-ingful, it is important to distinguish between the claim that a life is *in fact* meaningful and the claim that a life *seems* meaningful to the person who lives it. Certainly, how meaningful a life really is can be different from how meaningful it seems to the person who lives it. This possible difference is a presupposition of such common judgements as 'I thought my life had meaning, but now I see it didn't' and 'He thinks his life is meaningless, but it isn't'.

Cottingham claims, 'meaningfulness in action implies a certain degree of *self-awareness* or *transparency to the agent*'.[10] It cannot plausibly be denied that a *maximally* meaningful life will contain self-awareness. And in a maximally meaningful life, the agent will get some felt satisfaction from this meaning. But a life can have at least some meaning without the person who lives it realizing that her life has this quality.

Imagine a professor who cared overridingly about his research. He also of course taught courses, assessed his students' work, and supervised graduate students. To keep matters simple, let us imagine that he was in a department containing enough people with aptitude and appetite for administrative work that he didn't have to do any. So his professional life consisted entirely of research and teaching.

Suppose he didn't care about being a good teacher. Indeed, he thought of teaching as being valuable only as a means of improving his presentational skills and as necessary for keeping his job. For all four decades of his professional life, he thought that his life would be meaningful if but only if his research turned out to have been important.

But suppose that in fact this person was just naturally a superb teacher. With virtually no effort or planning, he was able to zero in on the most important knowledge and skills for his students to acquire. He had a natural gift for clarity, succinctness, tempo, and tone. Students thus found his teaching riveting and inspirational. In fact, he was so good that he was the best teacher any of them ever had. And, since he had four decades worth of students, there are very many people out in the world and in this professor's own profession whose lives and careers were transformed by his teaching talents.

When we arrive at this professor's deathbed to say goodbye to him, he expresses bitterness that his research didn't end up being successful. We reply that his teaching did prove hugely successful. We point to the fact that he inspired students to take their work much more seriously than they had before. We talk about how many of his former students came away from his courses or supervision with the knowledge, skills, and self-confidence that put them on the path to success in their careers and in their personal lives. Bemused, he reminds us that he never cared about being a good teacher. We remark that everyone is well aware of this but that his nonchalance about teaching added to his charisma and lent his teaching an air of urgency, since students inferred that he might stop teaching at the end of any semester. We implore him to accept that he was an enormously successful teacher despite, maybe even partly because of, his lack of interest in it.

The next development in our story might be that the professor says, 'Ah, I see now that my life wasn't completely meaningless after all. My main focus, that is, my research, didn't work out, but what gave my life some meaning was something else, which I never even noticed until you pointed it out now'. Such deathbed re-evaluations are the most poignant scenes in innumerable plays and novels. They are hardly unbelievable.

Deathbed re-evaluations of a life can be correct. It is not true that, because the professor didn't particularly care about teaching during the four decades he did it, his sublime success as a teacher could not have made his life at least a little meaningful. No human is an infallible judge of a life's meaning, not even the person whose life is being judged.

How much does it matter that the professor had this deathbed conversion? Well, everyone would be glad he did. But it is important not to overestimate the importance of his actually reaching this final judgement on his life. His conclusion was that, although he had not earlier thought so, his life had been meaningful. At his conversion, time $t2$, he believes his earlier life, his life during time $t1$, was meaningful. The content of the judgement he reaches about the meaningfulness of his life during $t1$ does not refer to his views at $t2$. In other words, his judgement at $t2$ was not that what made his life during $t1$ meaningful (or enabled it to be so) was that he reached the conclusion at $t2$ that his life during $t1$ was meaningful.

Now suppose he dies before we are able to get to his deathbed – that is, he dies with his old view that his life was completely meaningless because the one thing he cared about, his research, was unsuccessful. Admittedly, his life would have contained more meaning if he had reached the correct judgement that it had been meaningful. Indeed, arguably, his life would have contained more meaning the earlier he reached this correct judgement. Nevertheless, his never reaching that correct judgement does not preclude its correctness. His life was meaningful even if he didn't see that it was until right before death – indeed, even if he didn't ever see that it was.

One possible reply to this line of thought is that I have misdescribed the situation. I described the professor as having been a hugely successful teacher. Cottingham writes, 'our assessment of the value of a project ... is at least partly success-oriented: we require it not just to be undertaken in the right spirit, but to *achieve* something'.[11] Now certainly the professor had teaching as an on-going project. But, first of all, this is a project to which he attributed only instrumental value. Second, arguably his project was teaching well enough to keep his job, rather than teaching as well as he could. The relevance of this is that, arguably, hitting a target at which he wasn't shooting can hardly be called success or achievement (except ironically).

At this point, I think we better consider two possibilities. One is that actually, *deep down*, he always did care about teaching as well as he could, but this wasn't transparent to him. People can be motivated by concerns they don't realize they have. The other possibility is that during his four decades of teaching he really didn't at any level care about teaching as well as he could. I will consider these two possibilities in turn.

If he cared all along about teaching as well as possible though he wasn't aware of this fact, then his success in this project obviously does add meaning to his life. His life would have had even more meaning if he had been aware of his concern to teach as well as he could. But success in a project one had can be at least somewhat meaningful even if one didn't realize this was a project one had.

The second possibility is more threatening to my line of argument. This is the possibility that his being an especially good teacher really wasn't ever one of his aims, either conscious or subconscious. Can an outcome really add meaning to an agent's life if at no level did he aim at that outcome?

Well, if the outcome consists in or results from the development of his talents, and especially if the outcome benefits one or more individuals, then this outcome can add meaning to an agent's life even if he didn't care about it. One or another by-product of our projects can turn out to make our lives meaningful even if the by-product wasn't the aim. I have two arguments for that claim.

One of these arguments is what I'm going to call fit with phenomenology. We often discover, I think, that a by-product of our aim turns out to be more meaningful than achieving the aim itself. For example, we sometimes end up thinking the journey was more meaningful than reaching the destination. Or we cultivate friends for some instrumental purpose and end up thinking the friendships more important than the purpose they were supposed to serve.

Here is my other argument for the claim that one or another by-product of our projects can turn out to make our lives meaningful. Very often we have a primary purpose in pursuing some end and secondary purposes in pursuing that end. An example is that Dostoyevsky's primary aim in writing his novels was to pay off his gambling debts; his secondary aim was to write great literature. People's primary aims are often ones like making money, impressing their mothers, gaining power, and so on. But these primary aims often work together with secondary aims to produce great literature, prevent wars, make important contributions to science, help those in need, and so on. And in many cases where both the primary and secondary aims were achieved, it is achievement of the agent's secondary aims, not the achievement of primary ones, that adds most meaning to the agent's life.

The fact that the achievement of a secondary aim can add more meaning to someone's life than the achievement of a primary aim shows that the amount of meaning added to someone's life by the achievement of her aim need not correspond to how much she cares about it. Admittedly, it doesn't follow that some outcome can add meaning to her life even it is no part of any of her aims. But once we have rejected the idea that the strength of an agent's concerns dictates the amount of meaning in the objectives she achieves, I cannot see why we would stop short of admitting that meaning does not depend on concern.

In this section, I have argued that the fact that someone's life had some objectively good qualities or produced some objectively good outcomes can give that life some degree of meaning. I have argued this is true even if the agent derived no pleasure from having these qualities or producing these outcomes. Likewise, I have argued this is true even if having these qualities and producing these outcomes were not the agent's aims. If my arguments are right, then there is an objectivist sufficient condition for the agent's life having at least some meaning.

4. Is divine support necessary?

In this final section, I will consider some of Cottingham's views about the connection between the meaning of life and religious belief and practice.

First, Cottingham and I disagree about what alternatives are left on the table, so to speak. He writes, 'it cannot ... be claimed that the universe as disclosed by modern science, and as reflected in our ordinary experience, is *inherently resistant* to a religious interpretation of its significance'.[12] I disagree. What we observe in nature and what we know of the concepts of omniscience and goodness combine to provide what seems to me to be overpowering evidence that there is no all-powerful, perfectly good God.

Admittedly, there might have to be some degree of possible evil if free will is to be meaningful (something for humans to need to avoid) and if the guilty are to get punished. And even an all-powerful being might not be able to dictate or change logically or metaphysically necessary truths. But I cannot see how these concessions provide grounds for accepting that the continued existence of an all-powerful, perfectly good God is compatible with the degree of natural evil in the world. There is much more in the way of tsunamis, plagues, decay, disease, and more generally innocent suffering than can be reconciled with an all-powerful, perfectly good God. So, as Hume observed, if there was an intelligent designer, it was a very imperfect intelligent designer.

Cottingham believes recognition of the extent of human and natural evil in the world does not rationally require abandonment of belief in an all-powerful, perfectly good God.[13] As I indicated, on that point we disagree. But his argument for religious belief is not that the balance of evidence and metaphysical argument come down on its side. Rather, his argument is instead a pragmatic one – that we can personally and morally benefit from religious belief. He writes,

> [I]f the ultimate nature of reality contains no bias towards the good as opposed to the vicious, if there is nothing to support the hope that the good will ultimately triumph, if essentially we are on our own, ... then at the very least it is hard to see how we can achieve the necessary confidence and resolution to follow the path of goodness ...[14]

> [B]ecause it would be humanly impossible to devote my life to the good if I thought I was striving after 'a conception which at bottom was empty and had no object', it is appropriate for 'the righteous man to say "I will that there be a God ... I firmly abide by this and will not let this faith be taken from me".'[15]

> [B]ecause of the fragility of our human condition, we need more than a rational determination to orient ourselves towards the good. We need to be sustained by a faith in the ultimate resilience of the good ...[16]

> The theist believes, sustained by faith, that the careful use of reason, and the sensitive and reflective response to our deepest inclinations, points us towards a life which is the life that a being of the greatest benevolence, goodness, mercy, and love has desired for us, and has destined us to achieve.[17]

The relevance of all this to the meaning of life is that Cottingham holds we find life much more meaningful if we conceive of ourselves as operating in an order created by God. Thus, 'the pursuit of meaning for beings whose existence is inherently fragile requires more than the rational engagement in worthwhile projects; it requires a certain sort of religious or quasi-religious mindset'.[18]

The problems with pragmatic arguments for holding this or that belief are familiar. First of all, sincere belief is not something we choose. Second, the benefits to be had from holding a belief are not evidence of its truth. Third, the goodness of knowing the truth might be worth the lost benefits of believing some falsehood. Let us assess these three problems.

The idea that sincere belief is not something we choose is partly right and partly wrong. We might not be able to choose right now what we will believe right now. But we can choose to immerse ourselves in practices and communities with the foreseen consequence that we will come to share the beliefs that animate those practices and bind together those communities. And those who are impressed by the pragmatic argument for religious belief, for example, Pascal and Cottingham, stress the importance of communal religious practice.

The point that benefits to be had from holding a belief are not evidence of its truth is also one that those running the pragmatist argument for religious belief can accommodate. Their argument is not that the benefit of religious belief is evidence of its truth. Their argument is the benefits that would eventually result from the actions involved in immersion in religious practice give us good reasons for immersion in those practices.

But whether that ends up working in favour of religious belief depends on whether pragmatists have a good answer to the point that the goodness of knowing the truth might be worth the lost benefits of believing some falsehood. At least in the present context, the pragmatist answer to this will certainly be that they do not accept that religious belief must involve believing some falsehood.

In the dialectic we are considering here, that is a fair reply. Before he comes anywhere close to pragmatic considerations, Cottingham concludes that the various arguments against the existence of God are inconclusive.[19] If he is correct about that, then of course we cannot assume, against a pragmatist argument for belief in God, that such a belief would involve commitment to a falsehood. In short, the pragmatist argument for belief in God enters the dialectic only after the conclusion that the various arguments against the existence of God are inconclusive.

I above endorsed the familiar argument that the problem of evil does provide a conclusive argument against the existence of an all-powerful, perfectly good God. So I disagree with Cottingham before we get as far as the pragmatic argument. Having noted that, let us now take the pragmatic argument on its own terms. In other words, let us suppose Cottingham is correct that the various arguments against the existence of God are inconclusive.

I am not up to the task of cataloguing all the possible benefits and costs of religious belief. What I am able to do is comment on Cottingham's suggestion that, as I quoted above, 'if essentially we are on our own, ... then at the very least it is hard to see how we can achieve the necessary confidence and resolution to follow the path of goodness.'[20]

True, some people cannot sustain moral commitments without the buttress of religious belief. And many people have felt that life would be meaningless if there were no God. However, it is also true that many people *have* sustained moral commitment without the buttress of belief in God, and that many people *have* felt that life is meaningful even if there is no God. Indeed, my observation of secular societies (and secular sub-cultures within religious societies) is that moral commitment and a sense of meaningfulness normally survive abandonment of religion. (I admit this is merely a personal observation.)

In any case, clearly there is no conceptual necessity that the demise of religious belief will be followed by the demise of moral commitment. Nor is there any conceptual necessity that life will be or seem meaningless without God. On the other hand, I admit that life can be more meaningful if God exists than if God doesn't exist, and can be felt to be more meaningful in conjunction with belief in God than without that belief. If there is a God, there is an especially important being who can love (or at least understand, appreciate, remember, and reward) us, even if none of our peers do. Without God, we have only our fellow creatures to look to for confirmation that our lives have had some meaning.[21]

Notes

1. Strawson, 1974, p. 26.
2. Raz, 1986, p. 177, n. 1; see also p. 200.
3. When I refer to benefits, I mean things that add to an individual's good. I do not mean what is best for someone. My knowledge might constitute a benefit to me, but friendship might constitute an even bigger benefit to me. In a case where I must choose between knowledge and friendship, my choosing knowledge might be the choice of what constitutes a benefit to me, but the loss of friendship would be an even greater loss. Here I have chosen what constitutes a benefit to me without having chosen what is best for me.
4. My hypothesis is that *having* important knowledge is a constituent value, *not* that *pursuit* of important knowledge is one.
5. Cottingham, 2003, p. 21.

6. Hurka, 2006.
7. Tasioulas, 2006, p. 242.
8. Cottingham, 2003, p. 31.
9. Hooker, 2008.
10. Cottingham, 2003, p. 22.
11. Cottingham, 2003, p. 67.
12. Cottingham, 2003, p. 62.
13. See especially Cottingham's 2005, pp. 25–36.
14. Cottingham, 2003, p. 72.
15. Cottingham, 2003, p. 99.
16. Cottingham, 2003, p. 104.
17. Cottingham, 2005, p. 52.
18. Cottingham, 2003, p. 85.
19. Cottingham, 2005, ch. 2; ch. 7, sects 1–4.
20. Cottingham, 2003, p. 72.
21. I thank Nafsika Athanassoulis and Samantha Vice for helpful written comments on an earlier draft. I also thank Roger Crisp and Andrew Moore for many years of discussion about some of the topics addressed here.

Bibliography

Cottingham J., *The Spiritual Dimension: Religion, Philosophy and Human Value* (Cambridge: Cambridge University Press, 2005)

Cottingham J., *On the Meaning of Life* (London: Routledge, 2003)

Hooker B., 'When Is Impartiality Morally Appropriate?', in Cottingham J., Feltham B., and Stratton-Lake P. (eds), *Partiality and Impartiality* (Oxford: Oxford University Press, 2008)

Hurka T., 'Games and the Good', *Aristotelian Society Supplementary Proceedings* 80 (2006) 217–35

Raz J., *The Morality of Freedom* (Oxford: Clarendon Press, 1986)

Strawson P.F., 'Social Morality and Individual Ideal', in his *Freedom and Resentment and Other Essays* (London: University Paperbacks, 1974)

Tasioulas J., 'Games and the Good', *Aristotelian Society Supplementary Proceedings* 80 (2006) 237–57

9
God, Morality and the Meaning of Life

Thaddeus Metz

1. Introduction

In recent years, John Cottingham has been the most powerful English-speaking voice defending a supernaturalist perspective on meaning in life. I take the question of what makes life meaningful to be roughly equivalent to these questions: What is worthy of our love or devotion? Which final ends do we have most reason to pursue besides achieving happiness? How can we positively connect with something higher? What is worthy of great pride or admiration?[1] Supernaturalists claim that a satisfactory answer to such questions must appeal to facts about a spiritual realm. More specifically, in the Western tradition, supernaturalists maintain that having a certain relationship with God or putting one's soul into a certain state is constitutive of, or at least necessary for, meaning in life. If neither God nor a soul exists, or if they exist but one fails to interact with them in the right way, then one's life is utterly meaningless. Cottingham is one of the few analytic philosophers lately who has defended this perspective with care and rigour.[2]

I count two major arguments in Cottingham's work that support supernaturalism. One argument is that if God did not exist, then there would be no invariant moral rules and that if there were no invariant moral rules, then our lives would be meaningless. Another argument is that if God did not exist, then we would fail to achieve the most important ends and that if we failed to achieve them, then our lives would be meaningless. A third, related argument is that if we did not believe in God, then we would lack the motivation to pursue the most important ends, and that if we lacked the motivation to do so, then our lives would end up meaningless.

In what follows, I focus on the first argument about the source of an invariant or absolute ethic. The third argument is about *belief* in God's existence being required in order to bring about meaning; it is not a defence of the supernaturalist claim that God's *existence* is itself necessary for meaning, which is my sole interest here. The second argument, that God alone could enable us to achieve supremely desirable ends, is for a supernaturalist conclusion about meaning in life, but I find it to be obscure and not very *prima facie* convincing. It is neither the traditionally Christian or Muslim view that one must have a soul (an immortal, spiritual substance) in order to receive divine grace or retributive justice from God in an afterlife,[3] nor the biblically Jewish idea that only God could effectively smite evildoers in this life.[4] Instead, the idea is apparently that God is the sole being who could structure the world so as to make it likely that the good, the true and the beautiful can be realized, at least to a satisfactory degree. However, I fail to see any reason why a personal being would be necessary to bring about this condition; an impersonal force of the Karmic sort seems to be sufficient.[5]

In any event, I concentrate on Cottingham's contention that meaning in life requires a certain type of invariant moral system that only God could ground. And supposing that criticism can be a form of flattery among philosophers, I honour Cottingham and his views by seeking to question them. Cottingham's argument raises some old Euthyphro problems regarding the ability of a God-based meta-ethic to entail an invariant morality. However, Cottingham offers important current replies to these problems, replies that the literature has not fully assessed. I suggest that the replies likely succeed, but I argue that, even if they do, they are not enough to make a God-based meta-ethic attractive in the final analysis. I contend that while such a meta-ethical position probably can *entail* an invariant morality, it cannot *explain* one as well as a naturalist view. In addition, Cottingham's argument brings up novel issues regarding the relationship between meaning and morality that warrant more exploration than the field has so far provided. Although several have maintained *that* an invariant morality is necessary for meaning in life, so far as I know, no one has argued about *which* kind of invariance is necessary. I maintain that an invariant morality of the kind that Cottingham discusses is not essential for a significant existence. However, I provide some reason for thinking that a more limited sort of invariance might well be, one that God need not ground, but that nature instead could.

I begin by explicating Cottingham's key argument in more detail (Section 2), after which I present objections to the idea that God could ground an invariant morality (Section 3). Then I explain how a purely physical world would be capable of grounding an absolute ethic, articulating a kind of ethical naturalism that Cottingham does not thoroughly address in his writings (Section 4). Next, I rebut criticisms that would likely come from Cottingham regarding the ability of this naturalist morality to ground meaning (Section 5). I conclude by suggesting an alternative strategy for the supernaturalist that I suspect is more promising than the appeal to logical dependencies between God, morality and the meaning of life (Section 6).

2. Cottingham's central argument for supernaturalism

What I take to be Cottingham's most compelling argument for thinking that God's existence is required for meaning in life is that God alone could ground the sort of moral rules that intuitively seem necessary for life to make sense.[6] A world in which apartheid, Nazism and Stalinism are not wrong, or are wrong only for some people at certain times, seems to be topsy-turvy. Of course, subjectivists *à la* Jean-Paul Sartre will not find it so.[7] However, I share Cottingham's rejection of the view that obtaining the object of an individual's contingent pro-attitude is sufficient for significance in her life.[8] Getting whatever one happens to most strongly want, making decisions in light of the ends one ranks highly, or merely believing one's life to be meaningful are not enough for meaning. Instead, there are certain conditions that one ought to orient one's pro-attitudes toward, supposing meaning is to be had. So, my debate with Cottingham is an in-house one among those who believe that meaning is to some degree logically independent of people's variable wants, choices and beliefs. The argument of Cottingham's I critically explore is that meaning cannot exist unless an invariant morality exists of the sort that could come only from God, which argument I now spell out in more detail.

I count four logically distinct features of the invariant or absolute morality that, for Cottingham, is key. First, moral norms of the right sort are *universal* in scope. A meaningful morality must be 'more than a temporary fragile disposition possessed by a percentage (perhaps a minority) of a certain class of anthropoids',[9] and 'independent of the contingencies of fluctuating human desire and uncertain historical development'.[10] For example, it must be true of any person in any place and at any time that it would be wrong for her to torture a baby for fun.

Second, in order to confer meaning on our lives when we fulfil them, moral norms must be *objective* as well. Objectivity is mind-independence, that is, for moral norms to obtain not merely because they are the object of the variable mental states of human beings or other finite persons. Here, one often finds Cottingham rejecting the importance of a morality that has 'no reality beyond the localized and temporary desires and conventions of humans'[11] and favouring an ideal of 'attuning ourselves to a creative order that is inherently good'.[12] In short, the fact that it is wrong to torture babies for fun must not be constituted by us, but instead must be part of 'the ultimate nature of the cosmos'.[13]

Third, in addition to universality and objectivity, Cottingham believes that meaningful moral norms are *necessary* truths. Here, Cottingham argues that if moral norms were a product of the particular evolutionary history of our species, then they would merely be 'contingent facts'[14] and a 'cosmic accident',[15] unable to confer meaning on our lives when we act in accordance with them. Important norms are instead 'eternal and necessary moral verities'[16] such that 'cruelty is wrong in all possible worlds'.[17]

Fourth, and finally, Cottingham believes that the relevant kind of moral norms are *normative* in the sense of providing a categorical reason for action that is (at least often) conclusive. A categorical reason for action is a reason that is binding on an agent regardless of her desires and interests, where a conclusive reason is one that outweighs all other reasons for action. So, the wrongness of torturing babies for fun must be such that it provides an all-things-considered reason not to do it, apart from any consideration of whether the agent wants to do so or whether it would benefit her.

Summing up, Cottingham maintains that the kind of morality that confers meaning is invariant or absolute in the following senses: it applies to all persons irrespective of their group membership (universality); it applies to all persons not merely because of their mental states (objectivity); it applies to all persons regardless of the world in which they live (necessity); and it provides a conclusive reason for action for all persons regardless of their desires and interests (normativity). Consider, now, why it is reasonable for Cottingham to believe that God could most plausibly ground a morality with these four features.

A God that stood apart and above finite moral agents could straightforwardly provide a set of norms that applies to all of them. If God were to command all persons to perform certain acts and to refrain from others, then those commands could ground universally applicable moral norms. Furthermore, these commands would obtain independent of the mental states of any of these agents and hence would be objective. In addition, supposing that God would exist necessarily and could not change his mind (perhaps because he would be perfect), then the command not to torture babies for fun would be necessary, 'a timeless moral truth or principle held in the mind of God, an inseparable part of the structure of the divine mind'.[18] Finally, the commands of a perfect being could straightforwardly ground a reason for us to perform an act regardless of its effect on our desires or interests.[19]

Although it is difficult to conceive of a supernatural realm and how it might operate, Cottingham provides some reason to think that an invariant morality not only can be grounded in it, but also can *only* be grounded in it. The non-naturalists who posit the existence of abstract properties that exist apart from the natural or supernatural 'reach a terminus of explanation just a little too soon for comfort'.[20] Although many contemporary philosophers find the spiritual unclear and poorly understood, the supernaturalist's suggestion of a kind of concrete substance that exists is more ontologically satisfying than the non-naturalist's suggestion of a kind of abstract property that exists independently of any substance. And, *contra* the naturalist, who is on the most firm ontological ground for positing a relationship of identity (or constitution) between natural and moral properties, Cottingham appeals to the familiar Humean rationale that, upon apprehending values, 'we humans are plainly recognizing something that goes beyond the observed facts of the natural world'.[21]

The argument for supernaturalism about meaning is interesting and compelling, particularly for those who reject subjectivism, which a very large majority of contemporary writers on meaning in life do. If you think that what makes a life meaningful are conditions that obtain independently of people's variable mental states, that apply to all persons, and that provide anyone a good reason to pursue them, then you are likely to think that parts of morality have a similar invariance and are constitutive of meaning to some degree. So, Cottingham's argument is likely to have dialectical pull for most readers, beyond having plausibility in assertoric respects.

3. Could God ground an invariant morality?

Cottingham is well aware of the Euthyphro problems facing an attempt to ground morality in God's will, and he adopts promising strategies to resolve them. Here are three of the standard worries about whether and how God's commands could entail the key features of an invariant moral system. First off, they seem unable to support an intuitively attractive morality, for if the bare fact of a command were right-making, then torturing babies for fun would be right if commanded. Second, although God's commands would be objective (in the sense of independent of our minds), they would be neither universal nor necessary if God's commands changed, something major monotheistic traditions often agree is possible and even actual. Third, for some it is hard to see how the bare fact of being commanded to do something could be normative, that is, provide an overriding, categorical reason for action.

Following Aquinas and other contemporary perfect being theists,[22] Cottingham convincingly resolves all three problems in one fell swoop, by grounding God's commands in God's perfect nature. Suppose that God's essence just is perfection, where perfection is creative, knowledgeable and benevolent personhood. Suppose, further, that perfection is unchanging, because any alteration would be a matter of 'going downhill' from an apex, because atemporality is a higher state than the 'feebleness of division' (Plotinus) that is inherent to temporal extension, and because an utterly simple being incapable of changing for lack of parts would be more independent and hence higher than a complex being dependent on parts for its existence. If God's immutable nature just were creative, knowledgeable and benevolent personhood, where all these properties were ultimately identical, then God's commands would be fixed by it. Hence, God could not command us to torture babies, for an essentially benevolent agent could not issue such a command. In addition, God's commands could not change since his nature is unchanging. And, lastly, God's commands would ground conclusive, non-instrumental reasons for action in that they would be grounded on perfection itself; normativity would, roughly, be a matter of becoming like God as much as we can or striving to 'participate, however dimly, in the divine nature'.[23]

The last remark hints at Cottingham's normative ethics, something worth articulating. While this abstract schema promises to demonstrate the way a God-based ethic could avoid many Euthyphro meta-ethical problems, it would be more compelling if it were also clear which sort normative ethic it grounds. After all, Cottingham must account for not only norms that are *invariant*, but also *moral* norms. At the normative level, Cottingham follows most perfect being theologians in thinking that God's commands would be for us to realize those aspects of our nature that approximate God's, that is, to become as much like God, 'a source that is generative of truth, beauty and goodness',[24] as we can. More specifically, Cottingham's normative ethic, which standardly accompanies the above meta-ethical manoeuvre, is the Aristotelian view that right action is a function of developing goodness, which, in turn, is a matter of actualizing our most divine capacities. Everything is good to some degree merely by virtue of existing, that is, being an offshoot of God, but some beings have more perfections or greater potentialities than others, giving them a (high) moral status. The beings on earth with the most great-making qualities are persons, and right action is a matter of them actualizing their own personhood, that is, their potential for rational behaviour, at least in those ways that God actualizes His in the spheres of intellectuality, creativity and morality. Our reason 'gives us a point of contact with the divine',[25] and its development, for example, in the domain of science, is a way to 'reflect the ultimate rationality of the creator'.[26]

It would be worth enquiring into whether an Aristotelian normative ethic necessarily falls out of a meta-ethic grounded on God's nature *qua* perfect. I think there are serious problems facing an Aristotelian normative ethic, which would cast doubt on its God-based meta-ethical foundation, if the former were entailed by the latter. For instance, it is unclear that such an ethic can recommend killing oneself in all the cases where one intuitively may or even should, since one's self-realization would thereby end.[27] In addition, the view seems to give the wrong philosophical explanation of why one ought to help others, namely, that one will be a better person or be living a more human life. A better explanation would at bottom appeal to other-regarding considerations, say, that the other person's quality of life will be improved or that her capacity for agency demands honouring. However, I do not press these criticisms here, partly because I have made them elsewhere,[28] and partly because I see no reason to think that one must believe that right action is a function of the realization of oneself *qua* rational, supposing one believes that moral properties are constituted by God's nature *qua* perfect. For example, it seems open to someone with such a meta-ethic to believe that right action is a matter of promoting the divine property of rational nature wherever one can, not fundamentally in oneself.[29] Such a view neatly avoids the two criticisms I have just mentioned.

In sum, Cottingham's appeal to God's perfect nature enables him to avoid many of the standard Euthyphro concerns about the ability of a God-based ethic to entail an invariant morality. And while some criticisms I have made *prima facie* apply to Cottingham's account of the normative content of morality, it is open to him to adjust the self-regarding basis of his view and thereby sidestep them. In the following, I raise two problems with Cottingham's God-based meta-ethic that remain. Specifically, I begin with one problem that probably can be resolved – but consideration of which should enrich our understanding of an attractive God-based ethic – and end with another that probably cannot be resolved and that gives us strong reason ultimately to reject such an ethic.

i. Entailing Normativity

The first objection questions whether Cottingham's God-based ethic can ground the claim that *only* moral norms have the kind of normativity he thinks is unique to them. Recall that Cottingham believes that moral norms provide not only categorical reason to conform to them, but also overriding reason to do so, at least in the typical case. To say that morality provides 'conclusive reason' for action is to say that it usually defeats all other considerations in cases of conflict between moral and non moral norms. The trouble is that grounding normativity in God's essence means that *all* of God's essence is normative, not merely those facets of it that are moral. If God had moral, logical and aesthetic great-making properties, and if God's nature were essentially to provide conclusive reason to be like Him as much as we can, then we would have just as much reason to follow the laws of logic and of beauty as to follow those of morality. Recall, for instance, Cottingham's remark that modern, scientific enquiry is 'one way in which our human activities reflect the ultimate rationality of the creator'.[30] One important aspect of the normativity of morality is unaccounted for, namely, the respect in which it alone provides conclusive reason for action.

The appeal to simplicity is not a source of rescue for Cottingham, for if God were simple, then there would be no real distinction between God's logic, benevolence and creativity. These three logically distinct properties would be three different ways for us to talk about what is ultimately one and the same act in God. Since we are not simple, and since these properties are really distinct in our physical universe, the claim that God's essence just is 'ultimate rationality' provides no ground for us to prize moral norms over non-moral ones. We are, for instance, given no reason not to forcibly extract someone's blood for use in a painting with superior aesthetic qualities such as, say, the shade of colour (blood might make for an utterly unique and captivating hue) and insightful and suggestive interpretation of the importance of human life (using violence to obtain blood would urge us to reflect on certain values). And we are, for another example, provided no reason not to use coercion in order to teach logic, supposing coercion were an efficient cause, for example, by forcibly putting electrodes onto a person's body and shocking her each time that she reasons fallaciously.

As a first reply, one might suspect that simplicity is actually the culprit and withdraw the suggestion that when we speak of God in different ways we are referring to what is ultimately a single condition. Here, one might suggest on Cottingham's behalf that God is a being whose moral, logical and aesthetic properties are really distinct, that God does not as a matter of fact sacrifice moral norms for any of the non-moral norms, and that our fundamental moral duty is to do what God does so far as we can.

While the invocation of simplicity does no help to avoid the current objection, the rejection of simplicity turns out also to do no help to avoid it. Even if God's essence were complex and normative, even if God never sacrificed the moral for the non-moral, and even if our duty were to be like God to the extent that our capacities allow, it would not follow that morality has normativity of the sort that Cottingham is seeking to ground in God. The problem is that God faces no (or little) conflict between moral and non-moral norms, whereas we face plenty. God never (or rarely) has to consider whether to sacrifice morality for the sake of another value, since he is all-knowing and all-powerful and can therefore find ways of reconciling them. We finite beings, in contrast, routinely encounter situations in which it would be most useful to promote non-moral values by immoral means. In such situations we cannot do as God does, and the injunctions to 'participate, however dimly, in the divine nature'[31] or to realize 'properties [that] were divinely created'[32] seem to be of no use. We simply cannot invariably perform acts that reconcile moral and non-moral goods, and so we are left without any guidance of what to do on those many occasions when we must make a forced choice, if we are enjoined to be like a being who (almost) never has to make forced choices.

As a second reply, Cottingham might suggest that the very concept of morality, unlike the concept of logic, includes the idea of providing an overriding, non-instrumental reason for action. If 'morality' alone by definition included normativity, then the present objection would fall away.

However, this suggestion is implausible for the familiar reason that it would make the amoralist logically contradictory. It is an 'open question' whether one has the most reason to be moral. Neither Friedrich Nietzsche nor Bernard Williams or Susan Wolf or a given class of undergraduates learning ethical theory is conceptually confused to question morality's authority. However, suggesting that the concept of morality (or definition of 'morality' or some related term) includes the idea of normativity counterintuitively implies that they all are.

So, consider a third reply on Cottingham's behalf. Perhaps he should appeal not (solely) to the claim that we have most reason to be like God, but (also) to the claim that we have most reason to do what God commands. Suppose that God had a ranking of commands, with the command to be moral (for example, be benevolent, love one's neighbour, and so on) being the strongest command, and other commands about following the laws of logic and so forth being ancillary commands (or even mere recommendations). Then it would appear to be the case that if two commands conflicted, one would have most reason to follow the strongest command, that is, to be moral.

The present account of normativity raises another old problem for divine command theory, namely, that God has no reason to be moral. The present view is that there is conclusive reason for an agent to perform an action just insofar as God has issued a higher-order command to the agent to perform the action. However, commands are not reflexive; that is, they do not apply to the person doing the commanding. It follows that God is not an agent who can have conclusive reason to perform an action, let alone moral ones.

To avoid this problem, Cottingham could reject divine *command* theory, in favour of a divine *purpose* theory. Although Cottingham does often speak of moral and rational actions being a function of 'submission' to God's will or to his 'commands',[33] he might instead try to appeal to another feature of God's agency, namely, his intentionality.[34] On this view, conclusively rational actions would be ones that comport with God's higher-order ends. And since, unlike commands, intentions can be reflexive in the sense that we can intend ourselves to perform certain actions, God can have conclusive reason to be moral insofar as morality is his highest-order end.

So far, so good. But, upon reflection, this purpose-based schema faces the following dilemma. Either the highest end is lexically superior to the other ends or it is not. If it is lexically superior, then it will be the case that moral norms indeed provide conclusive and categorical reason to follow them, but they will be *too* conclusive. It is implausible to think that some amount of morality, no matter how small, always trumps non-moral values, no matter how large – but that is precisely what a lexical ordering implies. For instance, imagine it were necessary for me to be ten minutes late to an appointment with a student and thereby break a promise, in order to finish watching a thrilling baseball game. Although it would be immoral, I would have most reason to do it. To avoid such a counterexample, we are forced to weaken – slightly – the sense of what it is for morality to be 'conclusive', this way: morality in general almost always wins in cases of conflict, and its most weighty injunctions not to kill and abuse probably always win.

To make room for the plausibility of the claim that morality in general does not always win, we must forsake the lexical ordering and instead, it seems, opt for a cardinal one. Here, one would provide a numerical value for each of God's ends, where the numbers would indicate not only which ends are more important than others, but also to what degree. So, a moral end might be given a score of, say, 100, a logical end one of 25, and an aesthetic one of ten. These numbers indicate not only that morality is most important, but also that the degree to which the moral purpose is more important than the logical one is much greater than the degree to which the logical purpose is more important than the aesthetic. However, once we conceive of God's ends in this way, it is unfortunately impossible to retain a robust enough sense of 'conclusivity' of morality. To illustrate, suppose that one could conform either to the highest end or to a large number of the other, very trivial ends. Rationality would counsel fulfilling the latter ends, if and because doing so would promote a greater sum of value, that is, would add up to more than 100.

If lexicality is too strong and cardinality is too weak, is there any thing else to consider? Yes. One option at this point is to draw a distinction between first-order and second-order intentions. Imagine that God's first-order intentions were moral, logical and aesthetic, for example, 'Agents do not intentionally harm innocents', 'Thinkers do not affirm the consequent', and 'Creators do not neglect form when making objects to be contemplated'. And suppose God's second-order intentions provided guidance about what to do when the first-order intentions conflicted. If second-order intentions were lexically superior to any first-order ones, and if the second-order intentions specified that first-order moral intentions in general almost always took precedence over first-order non-moral ones, then we would have resolved the dilemma.

To sum up the discussion, I started by pointing out that grounding normativity in God on the face of it makes it hard to entail that moral norms alone provide conclusive reason for action. However, a God-based ethic does appear to be able to show that only morality is (largely) overriding, once a purpose-based ethic is favoured over a command-based or imitation-based one, and once a further distinction is drawn between first-order and second-order purposes, where second-order purposes are lexically superior to first-order ones. For this reason, in the remainder of this paper, I presume that such a purpose-based account is the most promising one for a God-based morality. Although my goal is to defend a naturalist ethic and to reject Cottingham's supernaturalist one, it has been worth considering this failed objection, since responding to it has required developing the sort of supernaturalist morality that is most defensible. I now argue, however, that it is not defensible enough.

ii. Explaining invariant morality

The objection that I believe is most worrisome for a God-based ethic questions its ability to explain an invariant morality, even if it can entail one. I grant Cottingham that rules with an intuitively moral content and that are universal, objective, necessary and (uniquely) normative could be grounded in God. What I question is whether appealing to God provides the best theoretical account of these kinds of rules. Specifically, I first point out that Cottingham's appeal to a God-based meta-ethical view evinces a logical incoherence, and then note that most readers would manifest a similar incoherence if they were to adopt such a view.

If there were conclusive evidence for a God-based ethic, then the evidence for God's existence would be comparable in strength to the evidence for the existence of wrongness – but Cottingham's works indicate that it is not. Cottingham's writings make it clear that he is confident that certain acts are wrong but is not confident of whether God exists, which discrepancy entails that he is not justified in being confident that wrongness is fundamentally a function of God. Again, Cottingham cannot reasonably believe strongly that an act is wrong just because one of God's intentions is for us not to do it *and both* believe weakly (if at all) that God exists and believe strongly that wrongness exists, which he does.

To clarify the nature of the incoherence, consider that for any entailment 'If X, then Y', it would be inconsistent to claim the following three things: I know 'If X, then Y' is true; I know X obtains; I do not know whether Y obtains. Now, Cottingham claims to know that 'If wrongness exists, then God exists' is true and also to know that wrongness exists, but he denies knowing that God exists. That set of claims is incoherent. If Cottingham wants to retain the idea that he knows that a God-based ethic is true, then, to avoid incoherence, he must either claim to know that God exists or deny knowing that wrongness exists. However, as I show below, Cottingham explicitly rejects both of these claims. Furthermore, I demonstrate that Cottingham and the rest of us would be correct to reject these two claims – meaning that, to avoid incoherence, we must reject a God-based ethic.

First, Cottingham could try to argue that there is substantial evidence of God's existence, as much evidence as there is that certain acts are wrong. If that were true, then it would be coherent to claim that there is conclusive evidence that wrongness is a function of God. However, Cottingham expressly denies that we have any conclusive evidence that God exists. He maintains that, at best, the evidence does not indicate that God does not exist, such that theism is at most consistent with, but not positively defended by, the evidence. Invoking the tradition of Pascal and Kant,[35] Cottingham's conclusion is that 'there is at least the possibility of a religious interpretation of reality',[36] one that the evidence neither indicates is actual nor indicates is non-actual, thereby permitting one to have faith in God's existence without contradicting one's rational nature. Summarizing his analysis of arguments for atheism, Cottingham concludes, 'the evidence from the observable world was at best compatible with a claim about its ultimate divine source: although not ruling it out, it was not such as to support it either'.[37]

Now, the qualification that evidence 'from the observable world' favours neither theism nor atheism might suggest that Cottingham believes that there is some other kind of conclusive evidence of God's existence available. And Cottingham does at times claim to articulate a way to find 'knowledge of God',[38] to access religious 'truths that are made manifest',[39] and to have 'some form of support for the theistic interpretation of reality'.[40] The epistemic reason Cottingham discusses in this context is a certain kind of religious experience. Adamant that he is not making an abductive argument that would posit God as the best explanation of religious experience, Cottingham instead maintains that sometimes the world is 'seen as carrying traces of the transcendent divine world that is its ultimate source',[41] an experience that provides non-inferential warrant for theism. These experiences include 'glimpses. ... of a world transfigured by overwhelming goodness and beauty' and 'transformations wrought in our lives by prayer and meditation'.[42] These are supposed to be apprehensions of the world as participating in the divine, such that, for example, one does not merely perceive beauty, but rather a beauty *that has God as its source*. Not everyone has these experiences, which cannot be replicated willy-nilly in a scientific experiment. But for those who have engaged in spiritual practices over some time, that is, those who are most likely to have these experiences, they provide an immediate epistemic justification for theism. Call this the 'religious experience' defense of God's existence.

Cottingham's texts indicate two strong reasons for denying that religious experience ultimately entails that any of us has conclusive evidence of God. First off, recall that Cottingham says that the evidence 'from the observable world' is equivocal with regard to God's existence, and notice that Cottingham explicitly characterizes religious experiences as *'observational modes of inquiry'*.[43] Second, immediately after noting that religious experiences have traditionally been regarded as 'signs of the divine presence',[44] Cottingham points out that there are other, equally weighty indications of God's non-existence (for example, the quality and quantity of evil) and concludes that there is a 'stand-off when it comes to evaluating the nature of the cosmos we inhabit. ... that leaves the door open for the theist (as it does for the atheist, or the agnostic)'.[45] These two passages render consistent the tension that initially seemed to exist between Cottingham claiming that God is no more than consistent with the evidence and claiming that religious experience provides epistemic reason to believe in God. The tension is reconciled by noting that this epistemic reason to believe in God is merely *pro tanto* and is not all things considered. And if the epistemic reason is not conclusive, then Cottingham still faces the objection that the evidence for God is much less than the evidence for wrongness, where the evidence for both must be comparable if we have conclusive evidence that wrongness is a function of God.

Now, I must note that Cottingham's work suggests another way to reconcile the tension. Cottingham distinguishes between two sorts of evidence, namely, 'discursive',[46] 'demonstrative',[47] 'propositional',[48] 'empirically testable',[49] 'impartial'[50] and 'argumentative',[51] on the one hand, and (roughly) non-inferential, non-propositional and private, on the other. In light of this distinction, Cottingham's *oeuvre* could be read as saying that the former kind of evidence is inconclusive as to the existence of God, but that the latter sort is conclusive, tipping the scales in favour of theism for those who have had religious experiences. On this way of reading Cottingham, he would say that some of us do in fact have conclusive evidence of God comparable to the evidence of wrongness (just not the sort of evidence that scientists and most analytic philosophers would readily accept).[52]

If this were the right way to read Cottingham, then there would be no incoherence in his views. However, a loss of plausibility would accompany the presence of coherence; I do not think the appeal to religious experience is enough to show that the evidence of God is comparable in strength to the evidence of wrongness. First off, note that I am willing to grant that non-inferential, non-propositional and private knowledge is possible; after all, knowing that one has a headache seems to be an instance of such. However, knowing that one has a headache is about an internal state, whereas knowing that God exists is about an external condition. When seeking evidence of something external to oneself – even evidence that involves immediate justification, non-discursive apprehension and information that is not accessible to neutral observers – one ought to encounter some kind of consensus. Strong evidence of the existence of something external to individual judgment is consensus among individual judgers. If many different minds converge on the same opinion about what is beyond them, often the best explanation of the convergence is that there really is something beyond them that they are all tracking.

But Cottingham does not provide any reason to believe that religious experiences have a substantially similar content, and I doubt that such evidence is available. Eastern mystics claim to apprehend the world or its substrate as an indivisible unity entirely lacking personhood, while sub-Saharan Africans claim an awareness of spiritual persons who invariably lack some of the 'omni-properties' ascribed to God in the Western tradition. Few in these cultures claim to apprehend the world as participating in the essence of a perfect, spiritual person. And supposing there are indeed widespread differences in the content of religious experiences, the best explanation of the differences would seem to be the lack of anything external, or at least the lack of the reliable apprehension of anything external.

Furthermore, consider what follows if I am incorrect and religious experience does in fact provide some evidence, either because there is consensus when it comes to its content or because consensus is not necessary for experiential evidence. Even so, Cottingham would not have resolved the basic incoherence of the evidence of God being *not as robust* as the evidence of wrongness and of claiming that there is conclusive evidence that wrongness depends on God. The evidence from religious experience for God's existence – if evidence it is – would still be weak relative to the evidence we have for thinking that certain actions are wrong. There is plenty of strong evidence for the claim that it is wrong to torture babies for fun. I am sympathetic to the idea that it is justified *a priori*, and it is in any event justified *a posteriori* by virtue of explaining a wide array of actions and beliefs, being produced by a reliable mechanism of evenhanded reflection, and cohering with many other moral beliefs. The evidence for God's existence would be nowhere near this great, even granting Cottingham that religious experience is some evidence of God.

Hence, both in terms of exegesis and independent plausibility, Cottingham is committed to the view that there is no conclusive evidence that God exists. And he therefore cannot coherently think that wrongness is a function of God, if he also thinks, as he does, that there is conclusive evidence that wrongness exists. If there is justification for thinking that wrongness logically depends on God, then the justification for the existence of both should be comparable, but it is not, either for Cottingham or for us.

This brings us to the second major way that Cottingham could object to my claim of incoherence, namely, by maintaining that our evidence of the existence of wrongness is equivocal in the way that evidence of God is. However, Cottingham explicitly (and rightly) denies that there is merely inconclusive evidence that wrongness exists. Commenting on the fact that some people enjoy being greedy, harmful and arrogant, Cottingham says that 'despite the grizzly satisfactions so described, such actions are wrong, indeed necessarily wrong: cruelty is wrong in all possible worlds. (Those who doubt this are invited to try to construct a coherent scenario of a possible world in which such behaviour is good or right.)'[53]

The quote expresses not the weak view that if wrongness existed, cruelty would be wrong. It rather indicates the strong view that cruelty is wrong. And plausibly so. It would be poorly motivated for Cottingham to backtrack by saying that we lack conclusive evidence that anything is wrong. *For all we know*, torturing babies for fun, enslaving others so that one can become rich, raping others to feel a sense of power and intentionally shooting innocents for target practice are indeed wrong. Most (though quite clearly not all) of the debate in contemporary moral philosophy is not about whether wrongness exists, but rather about what its nature is and how it is known.

I conclude that there is an incoherence in Cottingham's views, one that is unavoidable so long as he adopts a God-based meta-ethic. On the one hand, Cottingham maintains that wrongness is constituted by God, but, on the other hand, he is more confident that wrongness exists than he is that God exists. And it is important to see that this argument is not merely an *ad hominem* against Cottingham. I submit that a large majority of readers will find themselves reasonably sure that certain actions are wrong, but not reasonably sure that God is real. If one encounters this discrepancy, then one cannot coherently hold that whether actions are wrong or not logically depends on God. To be coherent, one should hold that wrongness is a function of something other than God, since, I suggest, one is not likely to find either more evidence that God exists or less evidence that wrongness does.

In light of the substantial evidence that wrongness exists and the insubstantial evidence that God does, a more coherent meta-ethical position would be that wrongness is a function of natural properties. There is substantial evidence that there are natural – that is, physical – properties, and this evidence is comparable in strength to the evidence that wrongness exists. Hence, if a naturalist meta-ethic can be shown to entail an invariant morality, then it should be favoured over a super-naturalist for reasons of explanatory strength. Given that there is no conclusive evidence of God's existence, and that there is plenty of evidence that matter exists, a naturalist absolute morality would fit much better with what else we (think we) know about the world. What I need to do now is to articulate the way a naturalist metaphysics could plausibly underwrite an absolute ethical system.

4. How nature could ground an invariant morality

In the previous section, I argued that a God-based ethic does not best explain invariant morality since it is in severe tension with the greatly disparate degree of justification most of us intuitively have for belief in God's existence and in the existence of wrongness. A God-based ethic should be rejected if another theory not only entailed the same data, but also was not incoherent and fit better with our background knowledge. I think that moral naturalism fits the bill, and spell out such a view in this section. Cottingham does briefly address naturalist meta-ethical views,[54] but not the one that I find most easily able to entail an invariant morality, namely, a kind of moral realism that is analogous to scientific realism, the hallmark of Cornell meta-ethics for some time.[55] Consider how realism captures invariance in the scientific realm, before applying it to the moral.

Let us suppose that the claim 'Water is H_2O' is universally true, objectively true and necessarily true. That is, it is true for everyone, for someone who did not believe it would be mistaken; it is true in virtue of something independent of our beliefs about it, for it took a lot of empirical discovery to ascertain that it is true; and it is true in all possible worlds, for if something were encountered that seemed a lot like water but were composed of XYZ rather than H_2O, it would not be water. Of course, there are those who reject these assertions about the claim that water is H_2O, but my aim here is not to defend them. It is rather to point out the way that realists capture these facets of invariance in science, a way that Cottingham himself explicitly accepts.[56]

The invariance is accounted for in terms of synthetic *a posteriori* necessities and a causal theory of reference. When we claim that water is H_2O, we are expressing a real property identity such that the term 'water', which is associated with features such as being a clear, odourless liquid found in the ocean and in the rain, picks out the same thing in the world as 'H_2O', a term associated with a certain chemical composition. The co-reference of the two terms is thought to be necessary because the terms rigidly designate one and the same existent, once a certain dubbing process has taken place. This co-reference is not ascertained *a priori* in the way that the claim 'A bachelor is an unmarried male' is, but rather through *a posteriori* methods of perception, induction and abduction. Relatedly, the co-reference is not analytically true in the way 'A bachelor is an unmarried male' is, for the sense of the term 'water' does not include the chemical composition associated with 'H_2O'. In sum, we have learned empirically over time that our terms 'water' and 'H_2O' essentially refer to one and the same property.

Moral realists account for the invariance of morality in the same way. They view moral principles as synthetic *a posteriori* necessities, so that, depending on one's moral views, 'Wrongness is degradation of persons' would be analogous to 'Water is H_2O'. The term 'wrongness', which is, say, associated with actions that *pro tanto* warrant guilt or blame, picks out the same thing in the world as 'degradation of persons', behaviour that fails to treat rational creatures as having a superlative intrinsic value. The co-reference of the two terms would be necessary since the terms rigidly designate one and the same property, again, once a certain dubbing process has taken place. The co-reference has not been ascertained *a priori*, or at least *a posteriori* methods have played by far the dominant role in supporting it (particularly in the last 40 years' expansion of normative ethical theorization). And it is of course not analytically true, since it would not be logically contradictory to reject it in favour of, say, the claim that wrongness is failure to maximize utility. If one believes the evidence favours Kantianism, then the moral realist would say that we have learned empirically over time that our terms 'wrongness' and 'degradation of persons' essentially refer to one and the same class of actions. Hence, the claim 'Wrongness is degradation of persons' would be universally, objectively and necessarily true in the same way that 'Water is H_2O' is.

So far, I have explained how one might account for the invariance of moral norms on a naturalist metaphysics, basically in the same way that realists account for laws in science. However, one feature of an absolute morality has so far been unaccounted for, namely, normativity. Here is where the analogy between science and morality might seem to break down. The claim 'Water is H_2O' is not normative; that is, it does not provide a conclusive, categorical reason to do anything, not even to believe something. In contrast, claiming that it is wrong to torture babies for fun does provide overriding reason not to do something, which reason obtains regardless of one's desires and interests.

In fact, I submit that the analogy between scientific realism and moral realism can be extended to account for the normativity of morality.[57] The way that a realist ought to account for normativity is by asserting another sort of property identity, this time between wrongness and rationality. Consider the claim, 'One (typically) has overriding, categorical reason not to perform wrong acts.' There is nothing stopping the moral realist from maintaining that we have empirically learnt that the terms 'overriding, categorical reason not to perform actions' and 'wrongness' essentially (or largely) co-refer. Here, it would not be that the term 'wrongness' inherently *connotes* the idea of a conclusive, non-instrumental reason not to perform a certain act, something I denied earlier as being unable to account for the logical coherence (even if substantive falsity) of amoralism. Instead, 'wrongness' would *denote* the property of having an all-things-considered consideration not to act, a consideration independent of one's desires or interests. There would be a synthetic *a posteriori* connection between wrongness and normativity, such that it is universally, objectively and necessarily true that one has overriding, categorical reason not to perform wrong actions such as torturing babies for fun. Hence, it is incorrect to think that the naturalist is committed to the view that any reasons that exist for people to act must be 'relative to their desires or inclinations'.[58]

Consider, finally, the way to refute the Humean reason Cottingham proposes for rejecting naturalism. That objection to naturalism, recall, is that when one apprehends nature, one does not sense any moral properties; ethical norms are not 'observed'. Normativity, especially, is not part of our sense-data. This rationale supposes that naturalism must be reductive in the sense of holding that moral language is reducible to the language of physics or some other sense-based enquiry. However, at the core, naturalism is a metaphysical thesis about what exists (only the physical) and, in the meta-ethical realm, about the nature of ethical properties (they are physical). It is not essentially a view that the language of physics or of what is apprehended through one of the five senses must or even can be used to express what exists, a view that most self-described 'naturalists' reject these days. Hence, in the same way that contemporary naturalists in the philosophy of science are happy to grant that we do not literally or immediately 'see' causation or democracy but may infer that they are physical relations, so naturalists in meta-ethics maintain that we do not apprehend normativity directly through any one of the five senses, but can reasonably conclude that it is a physical relation.

In sum, as there is another, naturalist way to capture the invariance or absoluteness of morality besides an appeal to the supernatural, and since the former is more coherent than the latter, fits with our background ontology better than the latter, and is not vulnerable to Cottingham's objections, I find weak Cottingham's key claim that an invariant morality (and hence meaning) is possible only if God exists.

5. Objections and replies

Cottingham's work suggests several ways in which he would question the ability of naturalistic moral realism to ground invariance of the sort he thinks is relevant. Although I have shown that realism accounts for certain kinds of universality, objectivity, necessity and normativity, I have failed to capture the precise kinds that Cottingham seems to believe are not only necessary for meaning in life, but could also be grounded by God alone.

First off, as discussion of 'Moral Twin-Earth' has suggested,[59] moral realism seems at best able to account for truths that are universal across the human race, not across all species or from a God's-eye point of view. Suppose that another species used the term 'wrongness' to refer to some property other than degradation of persons (or whatever feature one most plausibly thinks constitutes impermissible action). Then what counts as 'wrong' for them will differ from what counts as 'wrong' for us. Cottingham, in contrast, believes that the important sort of universality is one that avoids the 'unacceptably relativistic conclusion that rightness or wrongness depend on the contingencies of species development'.[60]

This problem also applies to the scope of normativity. If another species used the phrase 'conclusive, categorical reason' to refer to some property other than wrongness, then it would not be true for them that they have an overriding reason independent of their desires and interests to avoid wrong actions, even if it would be true for all of us.

When it comes to objectivity, the realist is committed to thinking that the content of wrongness is fixed by a dubbing process dependent on human choice. Of course, the essential nature of what it is that gets referred to is a mind-independent matter, and so there is a much stronger objectivity than forms of conventionalism or social relativism. However, what it is that gets denoted by a certain term is a subjective issue, making the objectivity weaker than a God-based ethic, which removes the content of morality altogether from being a function of human disposition.

Finally, the strength of necessity is also weaker when it comes to a realist approach than a God-based one. Realism grounds a weaker kind of necessity in that it entails that truths in all possible worlds obtain by virtue of facts in only one world. Specifically, necessary truths about which actions are wrong are fixed if and only if our species has rigidly designated certain properties 'wrong'. In contrast, on Cottingham's model, there can be necessary truths about wrongness that do not obtain by virtue of facts in only one world but rather facts in all possible worlds, namely, the contents of God's mind.[61]

There are three ways that the moral realist can plausibly reply to the charge of being able to account for only a weak invariance. First, when it comes to the scope of universality and normativity, she can point out that even if another species used 'wrongness' and 'conclusive, categorical reason' to denote properties different from the ones we pick out with these terms, we could still say *of that species* that its members are acting wrongly when they degrade persons, an act that they have all-things-considered and non-instrumental reason not to do. Just as the claim 'Water is H$_2$0' is true for any species *from within our language, so would* the claim 'Wrongness is degradation of persons' be true, too. And there is no reason to think that we must give up our language when referring to other planets or the behaviour of another species.

Second, and also regarding the scope of universality and normativity, the naturalistic moral realist can try to tell a story about why all species would have a common history leading them to dub the same properties with the same terms. After all, the realist needs such a story at the level of the human race. There needs to be some reason for thinking that evolution would lead (nearly) all societies to refer to the same essential property with the term 'wrong' in the way they presumably do with 'water'. Perhaps a similar evolutionary force would apply to those beyond the human race. Familiar socio-biological rationales about the evolutionary advantages of cooperation among finite agents might do the trick of grounding moral kinds that we can expect to find among any people that resemble us.

While the second response begs for elaboration, I do not have the space to provide it here. Plus, there is a large body of literature to draw upon to bolster it, unlike the third response that the realist can make. What the realist can also say in reply to all four respects in which her invariance is more limited and weak than a God based invariance is that the former is nonetheless sufficient for meaning in life. Although a number of theorists have suggested that life would be meaningless if there were no invariant morality,[62] no one, so far as I know, has provided an account of precisely which sort of invariance is key.[63] It would be useful for me to provide some reason for thinking that if an invariant morality were necessary for meaning, it would need to be merely an invariance with the scope and strength that a physicalist meta-ethic could ground.

My strategy is to draw an analogy between the true and the beautiful, on the one hand, and the good, on the other – suggesting that the meaning-conferring invariance of the former is merely naturalist. Cottingham himself often invokes the classic triad of the good, the true and the beautiful as largely constitutive of meaning,[64] and so if I can ascertain that a naturalist invariance grounds meaning in two of these conditions, I can fairly draw a similar conclusion about the remaining one.

Intuitively, meaning can come from making scientific discoveries and creating works of art, and I think it is clear that the kind of invariance sufficient for meaning in these cases is one for which a naturalist could account. That is, when it comes to discovering scientific laws or the laws of beauty, the laws need not be ones that apply to all species, that are utterly independent of human reference, or that obtain necessarily by virtue of facts in all possible worlds. It is sufficient that these laws are ones that are true merely for all human beings, that are fixed by what we denote with certain terms and that are necessarily true by virtue of human reference in this world. For example, even if another species theoretically carved up the world in such a way that $E = MC^2$ were not true for it, Einstein's law was a fantastically important discovery. And even if another species found Picasso's works to be ugly or otherwise aesthetically revolting, they conferred a terrific amount of meaning on his life. Similar remarks, I suggest, apply to morality. Even if another species did not deem Mother Teresa (or the stereotypical understanding of her) to be morally superior, her actions made her existence significant by virtue of living up to high standards that have a species-wide invariance.

In sum, although I believe Cottingham is correct to think that meaning cannot come from the 'mere local satisfactions of our contingent wants'[65] or 'happening to produce certain desired societal goals',[66] I submit that the cases of art and science indicate that it can come from conforming to norms that are absolute for our species, something realism can ground. In reply, Cottingham would be unlikely to claim that the good is qualitatively different from the true and the beautiful. Instead, he would question my characterization of the latter's invariance. Cottingham believes that the good, the true and the beautiful must all be grounded in God, insofar as they can confer meaning in life. Cottingham believes that the truths of logic must be part of God's mind,[67] and so he will think that basic scientific laws and any aesthetic standards must be as well.

However, it is implausible to think that aesthetic standards, if they are to make a life matter, must be true for all species and in all possible worlds by virtue of God's mind obtaining in all possible worlds. There is a possible world in which there are intelligent, finite creatures with much different sensibilities and experiences than we have. Surely, what is beautiful or otherwise aesthetically pleasing and revealing for this species may differ from what is for us. And it will not do to suggest that God would have in mind a 'conditional universal', for example, 'If one is a human being, then the following is required for beauty ...'. For that is just to forsake the idea that only something 'riding free of the contingencies of our human development'[68] can ground meaningful conditions. Meaning-conferring aesthetic norms can be – and probably must be – grounded on facts relative to species (if not biological orders, then at least ontological kinds). And when it comes to science, consider that even if God did not exist, discovering laws of nature would make one's life meaningful. Even if $E = MC^2$ were not eternally and necessarily in God's mind, discovering it made Einstein's life matter. I therefore conclude that the sort of invariant morality that a naturalistic moral realism could underwrite would be sufficient to avoid the meaninglessness of a world in which, for example, Nazi polices are not *really* wrong.

6. Conclusion: a different strategy for supernaturalism

In this paper, I have critically explored Cottingham's most powerful argument for the supernaturalist thesis that the existence of God is necessary for meaning in life. This is the argument that life would be meaningless without an invariant morality, which could come only from God. I first pointed out that Cottingham's God-based ethic probably can avoid not only many traditional Euthyphro meta-ethical objections, but also objections at the normative level. Next, I considered whether it could entail the unique respect in which morality is normative, and, upon addressing various ways to develop the view, I concluded that it could. However, I then raised another objection that I maintain cannot be replied to satisfactorily. The objection is that, if we had conclusive evidence for a God-based meta-ethic, then our evidence for the existence of God and of wrongness would be comparable, but they are not, either for Cottingham or for readers more generally. That is, I argued that it is incoherent to believe that if wrongness exists then God exists, given that there is strong evidence that wrongness exists, but little, if any, evidence that God does. I also presented an alternative, naturalist meta-ethic that avoids this incoherence, fits better with our extant metaphysical knowledge, and grounds a moral system that has invariance. I raised the natural replies to be made on Cottingham's behalf, most centrally, that there is conclusive evidence of God and that the sort of invariance naturalism could ground would be insufficient for meaning in life. However, I argued that these replies are unsuccessful. Respectively, an appeal to religious experience for God's existence does not provide near the strength of evidence there is for the existence of wrongness, and analogies with science and art suggest that naturalism could underwrite a meaning-conferring kind of invariant morality. I conclude that even if Cottingham is correct that invariant moral norms must exist for our lives to make sense (a claim I have granted for the sake of argument in this paper), supernaturalism about meaning gains no support from this point.

In my view, the most promising argument for a supernaturalist conception of meaning would not appeal to logical relationships between God, morality and meaning. There is too much controversy about God-based meta-ethical views to think that this kind of argument is the most auspicious one to ground a God-based account of meaning in life. A more likely account of why God would be necessary for meaning would appeal to some facet of God that *more clearly* cannot be manifest in a purely natural world. I have argued elsewhere that if meaning must come from God, that is probably because he has certain properties such as atemporality, immutability and simplicity, properties that cannot be found in a physical universe, that classic theists such as Plotinus, Anselm and Aquinas plausibly deem to have a superlative intrinsic worth, and that would confer meaning if we oriented our lives toward them.[69] Although I am a naturalist when it comes to meaning and morality, I think that this kind of argument is the one that supernaturalists ought to explore – at least in the absence of replies from Cottingham, replies that I am certain the field should consider.[70]

Notes

1. For more on the sense of 'life's meaning', see Metz, 2001.
2. In the following I refer to Cottingham, 2003, 2005 and 2006.
3. A view that Cottingham repudiates in 2006, p. 403.
4. While not explicitly rejecting it, Cottingham's texts never suggest such a view.
5. A point I first made in Metz, 2005, p. 225. A few of the claims in this paper I initially voiced in that article, although I develop and defend them in a more thorough way here.

6. For another recent exponent of this argument, see Craig, 2000.
7. Sartre, 1948.
8. Cottingham, 2003, pt. 1.
9. Cottingham, 2003, p. 72.
10. Cottingham, 2005, 54n37.
11. Cottingham, 2003, p. 33.
12. Cottingham, 2003, p. 62.
13. Cottingham, 2003, p. 66. See also Cottingham, 2005, p. 57.
14. Cottingham, 2003, p. 71.
15. Cottingham, 2003, p. 62. See also pp. 72–3, and Cottingham, 2005, 54n37, pp. 55–7.
16. Cottingham, 2005, p. 55.
17. Cottingham, 2005, p. 55.
18. Cottingham, 2005, p. 47.
19. Cottingham, 2005, pp. 46–57.
20. Cottingham, 2005, 54n37.
21. Cottingham, 2005, p. 48.
22. Compare MacDonald, 1991; Adams, 1999.
23. Cottingham, 2005, p. 49.
24. Cottingham, 2003, p. 90.
25. Cottingham, 2005, p. 116.
26. Cottingham, 2005, p. 117.
27. A standard reply, that one's self-realization could continue in a disembodied state in Heaven, is not open to Cottingham, who rejects not only the idea that we have souls that will forever outlive the death of our bodies, but also the claim that we need such in order to find meaning or be moral (see note three above). For critical discussion of the way that Aristotle (implausibly, in my view) replies to this objection, see Wielenberg, 2004.
28. Metz, 2007, 'Toward an African moral theory'.
29. For an instance of this normative ethic, albeit without a supernaturalist meta-ethical foundation, see Hurka, 1993.
30. Cottingham, 2005, p. 117.
31. Cottingham, 2005, p. 49.
32. Cottingham, 2005, p. 51.
33. Cottingham, 2005, pp. 43, 46–7.
34. In some places, Cottingham speaks of 'conformity with his [God's] moral purposes' (2005, p. 56) or fulfilling God's 'desires' for us (2005, p. 52).
35. Cottingham, 2005, pp. 6–8, 18.
36. Cottingham, 2003, p. 62.
37. Cottingham, 2003, p. 92. See also Cottingham, 2005, pp. 6–8, 13, 24–5, 47–8, 57–8, 61–2, 118–9, 122–4, 133.
38. Cottingham, 2005, p. 12.
39. Cottingham, 2005, p. 139. See also p. 16.
40. Cottingham, 2005, p. 136.
41. Cottingham, 2005, p. 123. See also chs 2 and 7.
42. Cottingham, 2005, p. 133. See also Cottingham, 2003, p. 61.
43. Cottingham, 2005, pp. 131–2.
44. Cottingham, 2003, p. 61.
45. Cottingham, 2003, p. 62.
46. Cottingham, 2005, pp. 122, 133.

47. Cottingham, 2005, p. 118.
48. Cottingham, 2005, p. 124.
49. Cottingham, 2005, p. 136.
50. Cottingham, 2005, p. 138.
51. Cottingham, 2005, p. 133.
52. Roger Crisp has ingeniously suggested another way out, here. He points out that one could claim to apprehend conclusive evidence of God's existence if one were initially sure both that wrongness exists and that if wrongness exists then God exists. However, most of us are unsure of the latter claim; indeed, Cottingham's work is important simply because so few in the field believe it and because he marshals resources to defend it that are worth taking seriously. Furthermore, Crisp's evidence for God's existence would have to be weighed up against the counter-evidence of the sort Cottingham discusses.
53. Cottingham, 2005, p. 55.
54. Cottingham, 2005, 54n37.
55. For example, Boyd, 1988; Sturgeon, 1988; Brink, 1989; and Miller, 1992, esp. ch. 2.
56. Cottingham, 2005, pp. 29–30.
57. In way that the Cornell realists have been reluctant to do, for, invariably, they are instrumentalists about practical reason.
58. Cottingham, 2005, p. 53.
59. For example, Horgan and Timmons, 1990–1.
60. Cottingham, 2005, 54n37. See also Cottingham, 2003, p. 71.
61. For more on this distinction between types of necessity, see Nozick, 2001.
62. Besides Cottingham (2005) and Craig (2000), see Murphy, 1982, ch. 1; Tännsjö, 1988; Wiggins, 1988; and Jacquette, 2001, ch. 1. For those who deny, implicitly or explicitly, that an invariant morality is necessary for meaning in life, see Taylor, 1987; Margolis, 1990; and Ellin, 1995, ch. 10.
63. Nor has anyone provided an explanation of *why* invariance of some sort or other is required for meaning, something I plan to take up in other work.
64. For example, Cottingham, 2003, pp. 33, 90, 103; Cottingham, 2005, p. 43.
65. Cottingham, 2003, p. 62.
66. Cottingham, 2005, p. 53.
67. Cottingham, 2005, pp. 47–8.
68. Cottingham, 2005, p. 57.
69. Metz, 2000, and Metz, 2007, 'God's purpose as irrelevant to life's meaning: reply to Affolter'.
70. I am grateful for written comments from Nafsika Athanassoulis, Roger Crisp, David Martens, Frans Svensson and Samantha Vice, as well as for conversations with John Cottingham, who, more than anyone else, has prompted me to take God-based approaches seriously.

Bibliography

Adams R., *Finite and Infinite Goods: A Framework for Ethics* (New York: Oxford University Press, 1999)

Boyd R., 'How to be a moral realist', in Sayre-McCord G. (ed.), *Essays on Moral Realism* (Ithaca: Cornell University Press, 1988)

Brink D., *Moral Realism and the Foundations of Ethics* (New York: Cambridge University Press, 1989)

Craig W., 'The absurdity of life without God', reprinted in Klemke E.D. (ed.), *The Meaning of Life* 2nd edition (New York: Oxford University Press, 2000)

Cottingham J., 'What difference does it make? The nature and significance of theistic belief', *Ratio*, 19 (2006) 401–20

Cottingham J., *The Spiritual Dimension* (New York: Cambridge University Press, 2005)

Cottingham J., *On the Meaning of Life* (London: Routledge, 2003)

Ellin J., *Morality and the Meaning of Life* (Ft. Worth, TX: Harcourt Brace, 1995)

Horgan T. and Timmons M., 'New wave moral realism meets moral twin earth', *Journal of Philosophical Research*, 16 (1990–91) 447–65

Hurka T., *Perfectionism* (New York: Oxford University Press, 1993)

Jacquette D., *Six Philosophical Appetizers* (Boston: McGraw-Hill, 2001)

MacDonald S. (ed.), *Being and Goodness* (Ithaca: Cornell University Press, 1991)

Margolis J., 'Moral realism and the meaning of life', *Philosophical Forum*, 22 (1990) 19–48

Metz T., 'God's purpose as irrelevant to life's meaning: reply to Affolter', *Religious Studies*, 43 (2007) 457–64

Metz T., 'Toward an African moral theory', *The Journal of Political Philosophy*, 15 (2007) 321–41

Metz T., 'Critical notice: Baier and Cottingham on the meaning of life', *Disputatio*, 19 (2005) 215–28

Metz T., 'The concept of a meaningful life', *American Philosophical Quarterly*, 38 (2001) 137–53

Metz T., 'Could God's purpose be the source of life's meaning?' *Religious Studies*, 36 (2000) 293–313

Miller R., *Moral Differences* (Princeton: Princeton University Press, 1992)

Murphy J., *Evolution, Morality and the Meaning of Life* (Totowa: Rowman and Littlefield, 1982)

Nozick R., *Invariances: The Structure of the Objective World* (Cambridge, MA: Harvard University Press, 2001)

Sartre J.P., *Existentialism is a Humanism*, trans. Mairet P. (London: Methuen & co., 1948)

Sturgeon N., 'Moral explanations', reprinted in Sayre-McCord G. (ed.), *Essays on Moral Realism* (Ithaca: Cornell University Press, 1988)

Tännsjö T., 'The moral significance of moral realism', *The Southern Journal of Philosophy*, 26 (1988) 247–61

Taylor R., 'Time and life's meaning', *Review of Metaphysics*, 40 (1987) 675–86

Wielenberg E., 'Egoism and *eudaimonia*-maximization in the *Nicomachean Ethics*', *Oxford Studies in Ancient Philosophy*, 26 (2004) 277–95

Wiggins D., 'Truth, invention and the meaning of life', revised and reprinted for Sayre-McCord G. (ed.), *Essays on Moral Realism* (Ithaca: Cornell University Press, 1988)

Part IV   Replies and Reflections

10
The Self, the Good Life and the Transcendent

John Cottingham

1. Preamble

I should like to begin by recording my heartfelt gratitude to Nafsika Athanassoulis and Samantha Vice, for their labours in putting this volume together. As one who has edited a number of collections of papers, I know only too well how much work is involved in such a task. It is rather like running a conference: those who have never done it may join in perfunctory thanks to the organizers, but have no real idea, when they arrive to give their presentations, of the time and effort that has been expended to make the event possible. It is a particular source of pleasure that the two editors of this volume are former doctoral pupils of mine. Teaching is sometimes often looked down on in comparison with 'research' – mistakenly, in my view, since the two are integrally related, and without the discipline of having to communicate ideas face to face, philosophy can sometimes become tortuously introverted. But in any case, there can be no greater privilege than supervising really gifted students; and when they go on to take their place in the profession and become friends with whom one can continue fruitful philosophical dialogue, then 'the cup runneth over'.

As I write this, I am also moved by a powerful sense of gratitude for the careful attention that has been devoted to my work by all the friends and colleagues who have been kind enough to contribute the various essays in this volume. Much philosophical activity consists of a continuing dialogue in which ideas are presented, objections developed and responses articulated; and it is pleasing enough to have one's own work subjected to that dynamic process. But a Festschrift is more than just a further instalment of the dialectical activity we all engage in throughout our philosophical careers. It performs something of the function of the 'retrospective exhibition', displaying a gallery of ideas worked out over a span of time, and enabling one to see connections and contrasts that were not always apparent at the time. It is far from easy to evaluate one's own ideas; the eyes of critics are generally much more acute. And when the discerning eyes of one's peers uncover in one's work insights they judge worth discussing, or thoughts they consider worthy of further reflection, this is the most valuable reward for one's labours that could be imagined. I am truly grateful.

The format of 'objections and replies' is a tried and trusted one in philosophy, going back to the birth of the subject at the hands of its self-styled midwife, Socrates,[1] and receiving its most polished treatment in the early-modern period, in the criticisms and responses Descartes arranged to have included in the first edition of his masterpiece, the *Meditations*.[2] The process is an exacting one, and when the objections are as sensitive and thoughtful as those offered in the present volume, the result is wonderfully illuminating for an author. But in the contemporary philosophical scene such exchanges, as we all know, are by no means always so fruitful, and (since a 'reply slot' in a Festschrift traditionally offers an author the chance for a few general reflections before getting down to business) I should like to offer a brief preliminary word on the possible dangers of the adversarial style – a style many see as inseparable from the 'analytic rigour' that has become the slogan of contemporary anglophone philosophy.

Most professional philosophers will at some point have attended conferences at which the megastars of the subject – that handful of truly giant intellects that dominate each generation – have been questioned about their published work. Yet it is not always a salutary experience to witness the cross-fire in which fiendishly ingenious critics devise objections of mind-boggling intricacy, only to be floored by counter-arguments of equally furious complexity; there is sometimes just a tiny sense that what is at stake on both sides is less a sincere quest for the truth than the imperative of protecting the ego. There is a connection here with the theme of self-concern, which has been one of my own philosophical interests. Without a special commitment to our own projects, I have argued, the scope for a worthwhile human life would be drastically curtailed. But the projects themselves, it has to be added, exert their own requirements; and if the project in question is philosophy – defined by its founder, Plato, as the loving pursuit of wisdom – then winning an argument is, or ought to be, less important than coming closer to the truth.

'Rigour' is also a debatable virtue. As one who is more sympathetic to the so-called 'continental' tradition in philosophy than some of my colleagues, I have often felt suspicious of those on the 'analytic' side of the divide who assume that compulsively cautious throat-clearing must signal great clarity and precision of thought, as if locutions like 'it seems to me as if I may now be being appeared to red-ly' must automatically trump declarations like 'the conceptuality of redness posits itself phenomenologically in the domain of subjectivity'. Both sorts of jargon tend to make me see red. But questions of style aside, what surely matters in philosophy is that the considerable time we devote to argument and counter-argument should be sincerely motivated by a desire for a better understanding of ourselves and the world we inhabit. Ever more intricate definitions and ever more minute analysis may, but need not necessarily, contribute to that process; and as philosophy becomes more and more academicized and professionalized, they can often work against it. In the scramble to get published, managing to formulate an argument so elaborate that it is difficult or impossible for a journal referee to refute it may end up being a far less risky strategy than trying to be maximally accessible in articulating one's deepest beliefs about what we can know or how we should live.

Philosophy, as Pierre Hadot's work so eloquently reminds us, is a way of life – a way of caring about how we live.[3] It is, to be sure, a kind of intellectual caring, that involves 'following the argument where it leads';[4] and no disparaging of the tortuous excesses of analytic philosophy should allow us to forget the importance of clarity and logic, for without them we succeed in saying nothing. But it is not a purely intellectual caring. The truth, or at least the interesting truth, involves, as Heidegger observed, the disclosure of what is hidden; and what is hidden, as Freud so brilliantly saw, cannot be forced out by logic alone.[5] All of us who frequent seminar rooms and conferences will, I am sure, have had the experience of seeing a shaft of light suddenly burst forth when, after tedious swathes of grinding analysis, a speaker suddenly lets slip an example or a metaphor or an anecdote: at once the imagination, or whatever we call that not-always-accessible creative core of ourselves, is stimulated, and we see not just *what* is being said, but why it is being said – where the speaker is 'coming from'. We begin to glimpse that part of his or her worldview that he or she cares about enough to want us to share. We see (I am speaking of times when philosophy becomes a joy, not a job, when philosophical ideas take flight because they are presented not just to further a career, or to gratify the ego, but from a wholehearted conviction of their beauty or truth or goodness) – we see at last the point of all those hours of furrowed brows and chewed nails and coffee-damaged stomachs, as the strange, irregular, awkward pieces of the jigsaw start to move into place and a coherent picture, or part of a picture, begins to form.

It may be clear from some of the above that I see philosophy as a way of trying to reach an integrated view of the world; integrity, indeed, has increasingly come to seem to me the master virtue in philosophy, as in the ethical life generally. For that reason, the 'retrospective exhibition' I am confronted with in these essays is a humbling experience. In the first place, particularly as my attention has been drawn to things I said up to thirty years ago, I have been acutely conscious of how much I got wrong:

> *Par montaingnes et par valees*
> *Et par forez longues et lees,*
> *Par maint peril, par maint destroit,*
> *Tant qu'il vint au sentier tot droit ...*

> [By rocky crags and valleys steep,
> through trackless forests dark and deep,
> with many a danger night and day
> until he found the one true way.][6]

But if it has taken me so long to stumble towards what I hope is a more connected picture, I am also struck by the integrity of my interlocutors in this volume, many of whom have over many years held consistently and clearly to their distinctive philosophical allegiances, while I have been struggling. All the contributions, moreover, have re-enforced my growing conviction that there is no such thing as fruitful compartmentalization in philosophy (again, any more than in life itself). Issues of partiality and self-preference, I have been helped to see, are not just a topic in 'ethics', separate from issues in philosophy of religion or spirituality; questions about rationality and how it is related to the unconscious parts of the mind are in turn interlinked with ethical questions concerning self-development; and theoretical problems in theology are not just abstract metaphysical and cosmological puzzles but are intimately intertwined with central philosophical problems about human nature and the good life.

All this has encouraged me to think more about the position I have gradually come to adopt in my most recent work, which is that the ethical and the psychoanalytic and the religious quests are very tightly intertwined indeed, and that philosophizing itself is an integral part of all these extraordinarily demanding and vitally important processes. I am not venturing to say – would that I could – that those of my writings that are discussed in this volume form an integrated picture; but what contributors to the volume have taught me, coming at many different aspects of my work from many different perspectives, is how much implicit or explicit overlap nevertheless obtains. In offering some reactions to the wonderfully rich reflections which my discussants have so generously provided, I shall inevitably have to pass over much of value; but if there are issues which I shall be forced for reasons of space to neglect, this should certainly not be taken to imply that they have not given me much food for thought. Indeed, I am heartened by how many stimulating topics will remain for me to tackle after responding to the relatively small subsection of important points that can be addressed in the pages that follow. If I may end this preamble by beating once more the drum of philosophy as a way of living, in our subject, as in our lives, the piecemeal approach is never ultimately satisfying; so it is one of my many debts to those who have contributed to this volume that they spurred me on afresh to the task of constant self-examination, the continuing intellectual and moral search to discover what needs integrating and what needs discarding as we struggle to grow.

2. Partiality and spirituality

The integration project, to which I have just been alluding, is one that Samantha Vice, in her impressive opening paper for the volume, has firmly in her sights. As she rightly observes, much of my work on ethics has focused on our special concern for our selves and our immediate circle – a concern that some ethicists have frowned on, but which I have championed as being the core of the good life. Along with others, I have drawn on the 'integrity argument' developed by perhaps the most insightful moral philosopher of our times, Bernard Williams,[7] in order to cast doubt on the coherence of wholly detached and impersonal conceptions of a worthwhile life: is there not something self-defeating about recipes for the pursuit of the good that alienate human beings from the very selves that are supposed to be seeking that good?[8] I have also used the notion of integrity in order to mount a slightly more edged, but I think justified, ad hominem argument against those austere impersonalists who insist in their books and articles that all resources should be globally allocated on a basis approvable from a detached and impartial perspective: are they not sometimes conscious of a momentary sense of dissonance between their stated ideals and the actual distributions of time and resources (salaries and promotions and research grants) on which their comfortable careers depend? Self-awareness (to invoke another recurring concept in my work) is often in surprisingly short supply among intellectuals – and I certainly do not exempt myself from that charge, nor mean to deny that impartialists who have written on global poverty have performed a valuable service in challenging our current attitudes. If self-scrutiny is formidably difficult for human beings, those whose lives are cushioned by security and wealth may find it well-nigh impossible. This is perhaps the point of the saying about the rich man and the eye of a needle.[9] And without self-scrutiny, the chances of achieving integrity are virtually nil.

The dimension of integrity on which Vice focuses is a particularly interesting one, which, as it were, hoists me with my own petard. She brings into juxtaposition the spheres of moral philosophy and philosophy of religion and asks, in effect, how far my own advocacy of self-concern in the domain of ethics is consistent with my support for the religious idea of life as a spiritual quest? For is not the true spiritual path one that leads away from self-concern, and culminates in the abandonment of self: 'whosoever would save his life shall lose it'?[10] This is an area, as Vice notes, that I have touched on in a recent paper, where I developed the idea of the 'auto-tamieutic' perspective (from the Greek *tamieutikos*, 'relating to a steward') – one that brings into focus the special and unique responsibility each of us has for understanding and properly developing their moral character, and the unique set of abilities that has been given to them.[11] I illustrated this by referring to the New Testament parable of the talents.[12] As a result of the genetic endowments we may have inherited, and been fortunate enough to have had fostered during our upbringing, each of us possesses a unique range of abilities and capacities for the production (in the widest sense) of human goods. It is self-evidently good that, other things being equal, beings with real opportunities for the production of goods should make use of those opportunities. Moreover, the good that is the development of this talent, or the deepening of this moral character, is something that cannot be realized except in the life of the individual that is me. As I put it in the paper just referred to, 'I am the only vehicle for this good, its only potential implementer; if I do not realize it, it will eternally be lost.'[13]

Vice's question, at this point, is whether the goals of spirituality do not cut across this demand on the individual to realize his or her own distinctive opportunities for self-development. One of our greatest religious poets, Gerard Manley Hopkins, burned much of his earlier poetry on becoming a Jesuit, apparently fearing that cultivating his poetic talents might turn him too much inward and away from the service to God and fellow man, which was his highest duty as a priest. Without more knowledge of the intimate circumstances of Hopkins's life, it would be presumptuous to base any judgment on this particular case. But the general point raised by Vice seems clear enough: the 'inward turn' that exemplifies spirituality is supposed to be, as she puts it, 'in the service of an ultimate outward turn, to a value independent of oneself – whether God or morality or the Good' (p. 16). She goes on to quote Simone Weil's vision of the highest good that is 'perfect and infinite joy ... within God' – but a joy that is so absolute and detached from any of the grasping concerns of the self that it is 'of no importance whether *I* am to share it or not'.[14]

Vice has succeeded here in raising a crucial concern, which it is not easy to lay to rest. But although I am indeed troubled by the tension she points to, I think there may be something fundamentally problematic in her 'disjunctive' conception of the spiritual quest, as it may be termed – that is to say the notion that the goal of spirituality may be 'God, or morality or the Good'.

To take morality first, of the three classic ethical frameworks she mentions, utilitarianism, consequentialism and virtue ethics, all three can and should (as she accepts) accommodate the 'care of the self', in the sense that anyone who adopts any of these frameworks will presumably be interested not just in the pursuit of the relevant ethical objectives, but also in the cultivation in him or her self of the kind of character which fits one for that task. But nevertheless, given the objective conceptions of the good espoused in these systems, does it follow, as she suggests, that the care of the self will ultimately be subordinated to a 'value independent of oneself'? Well, Aristotelian or virtue ethics is, as I have argued elsewhere,[15] inherently autocentric in its perspective – not in an egotistical sense, but in the sense that the central question for ethical inquiry is taken to be the question, 'How should I live?' The primary objective is the achievement by each of us of a fulfilled or flourishing life. So there is no question here of an ideal in which the self is supposed eventually to drop out of the picture. In the case of standard deontological theory, I would argue for a similar ineliminability. Kantian respect for persons seems to me to put an indelible emphasis on the idea of the individual as *selbstgesetzgebend*[16] – as the unique individual locus of rational authority and responsibility. The self as an empirical concatenation of contingent desires may be destined for suppression or control, but the individual self as rational autonomous chooser is the core of the whole system. Finally, in the case of consequentialism, it is true that in some versions, notably the impersonalist utilitarianism of William Godwin, there is a vision of a kind of willed eradication of the self and its concerns: 'What magic', Godwin famously asked, 'is in the pronoun *my*?' How could one justify saving one's own mother from a burning building if it contained someone more worthy of rescue, judged from a detached and impartial perspective?[17] But since the very proposal of such overriding of personal ties has seemed to so many philosophical critics the strongest possible reason either for a radical softening of the consequentialist system to accommodate the legitimate concerns of self, or else for the complete rejection of the system on grounds of the violence done to human integrity, it is doubtful whether after all it offers a coherent vision of a viable ethics in which the self drops out.

If the specific moral systems so far mentioned do not quite fit the bill, Vice can and does nevertheless still claim that there is recognizable spiritual tradition concerned with the pursuit of the good in which some kind of self-extinction is the goal. She invokes the support of Iris Murdoch in reaching the conclusion that 'responsibly orienting one's life around an impartial Good can take one beyond oneself to something that has nothing at all to do with the self' (p. 27). Perhaps it can. But it is here that I feel most acutely the disquiet about that disjunction 'God or the Good'. For the two, it seems to me, are very different.

Let me at once rephrase that more carefully. God is of course identified with the Good, by many of the patristic writers from Augustine onwards, in whose eyes he takes over, as it were, the logical space previously assigned to Plato's Form of the Good; He is the source of all truth and beauty and goodness. And that inaugurated a tradition in which God and 'the good' are quite often used almost interchangeably (indeed, I sometimes talk that way myself, including later on in this essay). But God, in the Judaic and Christian traditions, is very much *not* an impersonal Good. God is, on the contrary, 'a personal being – that is, in some sense a *person*',[18] and his relationship with his creatures is intensely personal. Jesus of Nazareth was certainly not a promoter of some impersonal ideal of goodness; all the evidence suggests that he was not some kind of detached impartialist but had very close relationships indeed with particular disciples and friends for whom he specially cared.[19] Moreover, he reportedly addressed God directly as 'Father' (the Aramaic term '*Abba*' is quoted at Mark 14:36). And when the Christ of the Fourth Gospel thanks his Father that 'not one of those you gave to me has been lost' (17:12), or when in Luke the one sheep that is found causes more joy than all the others that were never lost (15:4–7), we have a vision of intimate and personal caring that is wholly incompatible with the self 'dropping out of the picture'. The Christian vision is perhaps hard for some contemporary philosophers to take on board, because they are so used to 'morality' being an abstract subject about abstract categories of obligation or value; in the moral metaphysics of Christianity, by contrast, ultimate reality is wholly and irreducibly individual and personal. This, surely, is the meaning of incarnational theology, in so far as its mystery can be deciphered: the good is never abstract, but from the beginning destined to be realized and manifested in human form, 'dwelling among us', so that its 'glory' is seen in an individual face that is 'full of grace and truth'.[20]

Iris Murdoch's metaethics, which rejects the Christian vision in favour of a bizarre neo-Platonism, seems to me, to put it crudely, too sophisticated for its own good. We would do better to hold on to the robust Aristotelian insight that if goodness does not exist in particular substances it does not exist at all. A cosmos of abstract entities hovering around, even if one could make sense of the idea, can hardly provide any plausible focus for spiritual aspirations, for to be united with something impersonal and abstract would be an experience (if that is the word) that had no meaning or concrete reality; as a logician might put it, genuine relations can obtain only between the terms of a predicate, not between a predicate and a term.

That point aside, there are, to be sure, spiritual visions in which the self is supposed to be eradicated. Buddhism provides the best-known example. But this stems from a vision of the cosmos in which all personal relationships and attachments are illusory, and enlightenment comes from recognition of *anatta* – the absence of any personal self, in a sort of merging into the impersonal flux that is all there is. Although there is a noble and demanding ethics associated with Buddhism, its ultimate goal is the complete giving up of the self and its attachments and the resulting cessation of suffering (*dukkha*).[21] The 'loss of self' found in the theistic traditions is very different. What we are urged to give up is in reality not the self, but the ego – the ugly grin of the miser scanning his portfolio of stocks and shares, or the sneering grimace of the official who revels in his power over others, or the superior smirk of the academic delighted by his own cleverness and the 'importance' of his ideas. But when such illusory goods are abandoned, what is found, and what the long hard traditions of spirituality are supposed to fit us for, is an acceptance of vulnerability that opens our hearts to the possibility of grace, so that we can in the end achieve self-realization: for 'what does it profit for a man to gain the whole world *and lose himself*?'[22] This does not have to be put in religious terms, or at least it may be construed as a truth that connects with many aspects of ordinary human experience, such as are found when two people stop trying to control or manipulate each other and begin to learn to love through letting go: strength, as Paul so eloquently put it, is made perfect in weakness.[23] But what is aimed at through that process is not the disappearance of self, but its true flowering, where two people see each other 'face to face', not through the distorting glass of the ego, but in a way that enables us to 'know, even as we are known'.[24]

3. Integrity and human living

The theme of integrity recurs in the discussion on contempt that forms Max de Gaynesford's fascinating contribution to the volume. There are times in my career, I must admit, when I have been sceptical of the merits of 'conceptual analysis' as a method in philosophy; this is no doubt a hang-over from the disquiet I used to feel about the 'ordinary language' conception of philosophizing that reigned when I was an undergraduate, when it sometimes seemed as if the great traditional aspirations of philosophy to understand the world, and how we should live in it, were all about to evaporate in a particularly drab form of lexicography in which one's nose was to be kept so close to the columns of the dictionary as to prevent any possibility of glimpsing the wider horizon. De Gaynesford's essay, by contrast, displays precisely the kind of subtle historical and literary awareness which are needed if philosophy is to make the 'humane turn' which I have advocated in my own work, and to which he alludes in his paper. Another important virtue of his approach is that it does not confine its linguistic investigations to the English language; he thus avoids that insularity and narrowness of vision found in that not inconsiderable subset of Anglophone philosophers whose linguistic chauvinism sometimes seems almost equal to that of the legendary Frenchman, who is reported to have observed, in all seriousness, that the great advantage of the French language over others was that the order of the words corresponds exactly to the order in which the ideas present themselves to the mind.

An interesting feature of de Gaynesford's discussion is his warning against 'over-moralizing' contempt. Certainly it is important, as Bernard Williams has so powerfully argued, that what we now call 'moral' appraisal is only one dimension of the commendation or discommendation which human beings bestow on each other; what is more, we do not have to go too far back in the Western philosophical tradition before finding an ethical world in which the sense of something called a 'morality system', as having a special kind of overriding normativity, is simply absent.[25] It may be very important for readers to keep this in mind, if they are not to miss the 'extra-moral' overtones involved in, for example, Lady Macbeth's contempt for her husband's unmanliness (to take but one vivid example de Gaynesford deploys). But I would want to add that understanding an evaluative practice correctly is one thing, and approving of it is another. The culture of Shakespeare's epoch was one in which contempt and scorn were often displayed in ways that manifested a cruel insistence on 'rubbing in' deficiencies, or supposed deficiencies, that properly viewed were really not appropriate subjects for anyone's taunts. 'Why *bastard*, wherefore *base*?' asks Edmund in *King Lear*,

> When my dimensions are as well compact,
> My mind as generous, and my shape as true,
> As honest madam's issue?[26]

Edmund's complaint is of course perfectly just. But one would want to go further and question the presuppositions behind the way he defends himself. Even if (like the hunchback Richard III) his dimensions had *not* been so 'well compact', would that have been deserving of contempt? I can remember from my schooldays that expressions like 'you moron!' (not to mention even more offensive slurs alluding to genetic disabilities) were routinely used; disturbingly so, in retrospect, not because all insults ought somehow to be banished from the schoolroom (where they have been part of the growing-up process since time immemorial), but because these particular kinds of insults, applied jokingly to one's ordinary classmates, unthinkingly presupposed that actual inherited abnormality would indeed have been something to despise.

It is for this kind of reason that I am not entirely happy with de Gaynesford's rejection of Kant's move, when he (Kant) condemns contempt outright, as a failure to respect someone's humanity. De Gaynesford makes the technically correct point that the negative appraisals we bestow on each other could not even get off the ground without presupposing that their object was genuinely human (as opposed to a robot or a puppet), and hence worthy of Kantian 'respect'. Nevertheless, contempt seems to me to have its natural home in cultures where whole swathes of humanity were looked down on or in some way despised – as 'low-born', as racially inferior, as mentally or physically defective, or even simply as members of the 'fair sex' (patronizingly regarded as delightful enough, but nevertheless weaker, both in mind and body, than their male counterparts):

> I lament that women are systematically degraded by receiving the trivial attentions which men think it manly to pay to the sex, when in fact they are insultingly supporting their own superiority. It is not condescension to bow to an inferior.[27] So ludicrous, in fact, do these ceremonies appear to me that I scarcely am able to govern my muscles when I see a man start with eager and serious solicitude to lift a handkerchief, or shut a door, when the *lady* could have done it herself, had she only moved a pace or two.[28]

Underlying Kant's strictures is, I think, the perfectly valid question of whether any of us should feel entitled to look down on any fellow human being. I don't think it is too fanciful to see as a subconscious influence on Kant's thinking the striking reversal which Christian ethics demands concerning the scope of those key verbs *respicere* (to respect or look up to) and *despicere* (to despise or look down on). In the *Magnificat*, perhaps the most resonant expression in all literature of that reversal, God is said to 'respect' the lowly, and 'put down' the proud – those who in their own self-conceit look down on others.[29] In allowing ourselves to be contemptuous of others, the message seems to be, we ourselves deserve to be sent to the bottom of the pile.

Despising people for low birth or poverty is one thing, but despising them for manifest and genuine moral faults is surely another. And it is here that de Gaynesford's concluding suggestion comes into play with particular force, namely that 'it is only by marshalling contempt for much of what it is to be human ... that moral theories are able to ... make their hold on us seem appropriate at all'. This brings us back to the concept of integrity; for if de Gaynesford is right, it may be that the very pursuit of integrity 'requires us to regard or to treat others with contempt' (p. 53). De Gaynesford presents this as a 'difficult issue' rather than a settled conclusion; but in so far as he is arguing for the moral legitimacy of contempt, I think his argument needs to be resisted. Part of my reason for saying this is phenomenological: there are of course plenty of moral monsters around, but when one introspects the feelings such people inspire, contempt seems to give the wrong flavour. People like Hitler are frightening, dangerous, to be resisted, but 'contemptible' sounds like a rhetorical piece of bravado. And for lesser villains, the motley army of philanderers and tax-evaders and malicious slanderers and self-aggrandizers, and so on, right down the grubby list of human failings, the appropriate response before working up contempt seems to be to remember the moat and the beam, and cast a critical eye back on oneself.[30] One is reminded of a favourite dictum of the late broadcaster and parish priest Dr Cormac Rigby: 'there is only one person about whom I ought to worry about whether they are in danger of going to Hell, and that is the person who is speaking these words.'[31]

At this point, my position may appear to have self-destructed; for does not my argument against the moral legitimacy of contempt presuppose its moral legitimacy in at least one case, namely the proper scorn and distaste a good person ought to have towards their *own* failings? As one whose recent writings have dwelt on the role in the moral life of various strategies for achieving self-improvement through increased self-awareness, including the 'spiritual exercises' so prominent in the religious tradition, must I not be disposed to accept that moral progress requires that 'distancing' of which de Gaynesford speaks – in other words a disdainful withdrawal from one's flawed self, as something unworthy and contemptible?

It would require a whole paper to deal with this complex issue in the detail it deserves. Modern moral philosophy is, on the whole, not very good at coming to terms with what is involved in concepts like acknowledgement of sin, repentance, and *metanoia*, or change of heart. But while such ideas certainly involve a firm resolve to put one's failings behind one, I am not convinced that the kind of despising and aversion signalled by the term 'contempt' is either necessary or appropriate here. One of the great contributions of psychoanalytic theory to the moral life is the idea that splitting off one part of oneself for contempt and disapproval by another part, although it may *sound* very morally impressive ('That was disgraceful! How *could I have done it!*') may actually be a ritualistic strategy of evasion, much easier to perform than the long and painful task of coming to understand what truly motivated such lapses. The point is powerfully made by Carl Jung:

> The psychoanalytic aim is to observe the shadowy presentations – whether in the form of images or of feelings – that are spontaneously evolved in the psyche and appear, without his bidding, to the man who looks within. In this way we find once more what we have repressed or forgotten. Painful though it may be, this is itself a gain – for what is inferior or even worthless belongs to me as my shadow, and gives me substance and mass. How can I be substantial if I fail to cast a shadow? I must have a dark side if I am to be whole; and

inasmuch as I become conscious of my own shadow, I also remember that I am a human being like any other.[32]

There is all the difference in the world between dramatic expressions of self-contempt and the contrite acknowledgement of failing that comes from serious self-examination.[33] Contempt is here nowhere to be seen; but integrity, or the struggle to achieve it, is the guiding light of the whole project.[34]

4. Partiality, saints and samaritans

The path towards an integrated moral life has many pitfalls, and one of them, which may have become visible towards the end of the previous section, is the fearful gap between what we are and what we aspire to be. Grovelling and self-abasement, though they may be mistaken for proper contrition, are not the solution; what is required, in the necessary declaration *mea maxima culpa*,[35] is a clear-eyed awareness of what has gone wrong, and a resolute refusal to shift the blame. A vivid portrait of what goes awry when lack of integrity leads to evasion of responsibility is provided in one of the novels of C. S. Lewis, in the character of 'Mark Studdock', an intelligent but morally weak young sociologist whose ambition leads him into agonies of indecision about whether to resign from 'NICE' (the 'National Institute for Co-ordinated Experiments'), a sinister but powerful and well-funded research organization that he knows in his heart to be corrupt:

> Mark had said he wanted to think: in reality he wanted alcohol and tobacco. He wanted never to see the Deputy Director again, and he wanted to creep back and patch things up with him somehow. He wanted to be admired for manly honesty among the opponents of NICE, and also for realism and knowingness at NICE. Damn the whole thing! Why had he such rotten heredity? Why had his education been so ineffective? Why was the system so irrational? Why was his luck so bad?[36]

Those who talk in uncompromising terms about repentance and personal responsibility, particularly when they use traditional terminology of the kind found in some of the medieval philosophers and theologians, may put people off by seeming to adopt a 'holier than thou' attitude. But distaste for moral preachiness may lead to the very real danger that some of the most profound ethical insights of the Western ethical tradition, to be found in a long line of religious thinkers from Augustine and Aquinas onwards, may nowadays not receive the attention they deserve. Many, of course, are in any case put off by the metaphysical framework within which such religious writers operate, which they find unacceptable. But leaving that aside, a further reason why Aquinas tends to figure far less prominently than, say, Aristotle in university ethics courses, or (to come down to early-modern moral philosophy) why the secularist ideas of Bentham have tended to eclipse the more religiously oriented theories of Samuel Clarke or Joseph Butler, may be that theistic conceptions of morality are seen as incorporating an ideal of holiness altogether too exalted for ordinary human use. Of course the currently much debated 'problem of demandingness' is actually one that arises as much for secular consequentialism as it does for theistic ethics. But it is the latter approach that nonetheless tends to be regarded as the more unpalatable, with what is often seen as its implied division of humanity into the saved and the damned, the saints and the sinners. And certainly for a philosopher to say 'I follow the goal of utility maximization' is less likely to appear to be putting oneself on a pedestal than saying 'I subscribe to the Christian command to love one's neighbour as oneself'.

It may have been worries of this kind that led me, in some of my earlier writings on partiality, to distance myself from what I then took to be the unrealistic and impracticable Christian injunction to love one's neighbour, and to support John Mackie's dismissing of it as 'the ethics of fantasy'.[37] In the typically intelligent and erudite paper which he has contributed to this volume, David Oderberg aptly takes me to task for misinterpreting the thrust of the Christian tradition, and I must sincerely thank him for getting me to revisit these issues.

Oderberg's general stance is to defend and support my views about the moral legitimacy of self-preference or self-love, but to take issue with the philosophical framework within which I presented my views, and to argue that the metaphysical structures of Christianity (and natural law theory) are much more hospitable to those views than I then (at the time of writing the articles he discusses) supposed. I think he is quite correct in many of his arguments; and also that in bringing out the crucial relationship between normative moralizing and its metaphysical foundations, he has drawn attention to something that is all too easily overlooked in the way contemporary moral philosophy is practised. This connects with my recurring theme of integrity. In developing, quite some years ago now, my views on partiality and impartiality, it would be accurate to say, not so much that I operated from a suspect metaphysical base, as that I did not really see that any metaphysical grounding was needed for ethics at all. The methodology I followed, in common, I think, with many contemporary writers on ethics, was to consult various assorted moral intuitions I happened to have, to try to develop principles or positions consistent with those intuitions (or at least a significant number of them), and to attempt to expose inconsistencies or paradoxes in the rival positions of others. And if asked to list any further objectives, I would have had to reply, in the immortal words of the satirical magazine *Private Eye*, 'Err ... that's it!' There was no overarching 'worldview' (looking back, I can now see that my early philosophical education was designed to make me suspicious of such things); and if from time to time I drew on elements to be found in the systems of Plato, or Aristotle, or Descartes, or Mill, or Hume or Nietzsche, this was really more or less on a 'cafeteria' basis, with the aim of making the views already arrived at as philosophically attractive and articulate as possible.

This is something of a caricature, but I think it is one that many observers of the contemporary scene in moral philosophy may recognize as not diverging too far from the way things are often done in our subject. It is rather (I now think) as if we were to roam around the countryside, finding secure places to pitch our tents, utilizing the materials that happen to be to hand in constructing the encampments, securing them against possible attack, and mounting sorties to snipe at rival encampments – but all without any map of the territory, or any real idea of what the point of the journey is or what our final destination may be. *Et par forez longues et lees* ... Not that an overarching metaphysical schema is a panacea. It may lead to dogmatism, to forcing one's views into the straitjacket of received doctrine, or to myopia towards valuable insights from other traditions. But without at least the attempt to fit one's results into a systematic and properly-grounded theory of the good life, there will always be the risk that a view arrived at in a given area may conflict with results reached elsewhere. Integrity is not an optional extra, since ethical truth, like all truth, is in the end indivisible (no truth can conflict with any other truth).

To come to (some of) Oderberg's specific arguments, in his approach to self-love he not only agrees with my view of its ineliminability in any sound ethics, but actually outdoes me in zeal for defending it, to the extent of identifying it as central even to the life of the saint: 'the path from sinner to saint never deviates from the path of self-preference' (p. 61). The ideal of the sainthood, however, presents particular problems for moral philosophers, and Oderberg neatly identifies a tension in my attitude to it in the partiality articles. On the one hand I wanted to dismiss it (along the lines hinted at a moment ago) as unrealistic, too exalted to be incorporated in a viable ethic for most human beings; but on the other hand I admitted to its being an admirable ideal. Yet, asks Oderberg 'how can morality consist of a set of norms for the mass of mankind yet be overlaid by an ideal that is completely *at odds* with what those norms require?' For Oderberg, there must be a *continuity* between the norms governing the mass of humankind, given our nature, and those governing the saint: 'the norms are in fact *the same*, though the saint follows them par excellence'(p. 60).

Oderberg's position is one I have considerable sympathy for (and which deserves much more discussion than I can give it here), but it cannot, I think, be quite right as phrased. He asks, rhetorically, whether we ought not all to aspire to sainthood. Well, if by a saint is meant what is typically meant, one who gives up all for God, or one who (as in the monastic ideal) unflinchingly follows the path of poverty and celibacy and obedience devoting every day to long hours of prayer and meditation and *lectio divina*, and ministering devotedly and without favouritism or preference to those in need, then the answer surely has to be 'no'. The standard Christian view is that the religious (in the technical sense) life is a vocation which the majority cannot and should not aspire to. For everyone to attempt it would quickly produce disaster, both spiritual and material. Celibacy, to take but one element in such a life, is certainly not an 'extension' of ordinary sexual life, having a continuity with the passionate and inward-turning life of sexual partners; rather, it is a withdrawal from, or renunciation of, that life, in order better to devote oneself to the (wholly non-sexual) love of God. By its very nature it cannot be an ideal all should aspire to. St Paul said he could wish all to be celibate like him,[38] but he cannot (or should not) have meant this seriously unless he wanted the human race rapidly to come to an end. The life of the 'holy' man or woman (which is what a 'saint' means) is by its very nature a life possible only for a minority. In a way such forms of life depend for their existence on the existence of ordinary society – ordinary families to provide their recruits, ordinary farmers and merchants to provide the infrastructure they need for their continued existence (as an itinerant mendicant friar needs others to grow the food he eats). There need, incidentally, be nothing ethically dubious about this: even an organism that is technically 'parasitic' can be perfectly benign, and sainthood can be as spiritually valuable to society as the yeast is to the bread.

None of this means there cannot be a kind of sacramentality or sanctity in the everyday lives of ordinary people who are not 'holy'; but there is nothing, I think, to be gained by denying that the norms and ideals for such mundane lives, and the self-referential commitments and ties that govern them at the most fundamental level, will be very different from anything appropriate for the life of one who is 'set apart' from the world.

In respect of the command to love our neighbours, however, Oderberg seems to me on much stronger ground. The essence of his criticism is that I mistakenly identified the Christian ethic with the impartialist ethic of (some types of) consequentialism. That is an identification in which I was encouraged by utilitarian propagandists such as Godwin and Mill,[39] but Oderberg's arguments have convinced me that it is wholly mistaken. The account of Christian beneficence he proceeds to offer is an intensely personalist one (having some affinities, indeed, with my own critique, above, of Vice's advocacy of an impersonalist 'good'): loving others in the Christian sense is a matter of responding to them *one at a time*, in ways that are rooted in particular circumstances and contingencies of commitment or involvement. Against this background, we have the basis for interpreting the parable of the Good Samaritan in a way which does not construe the obligation of beneficence in an unreasonably globalist or impersonalist way. As Oderberg puts it (making a useful distinction between the *manner* and the *measure* in which one is supposed to love our neighbour as oneself): 'our general inclination to do good to ourselves and others in equal *manner* is also an inclination to do good in unequal *measure*, depending on which relations of proximity I am in with respect to other people [and also on] the severity of the need of those who are my proximates' (p. 66, emphasis supplied).

All this is valuable, even if the notion of 'proximates' does not quite succeed in allaying worries about the demandingness of the maxim of neighbour-love. For since Oderberg allows that being relevantly 'near' to someone may be a pure accident (as it was on the Samaritan's journey down from Jerusalem to Jericho), but may also be self-imposed (as in the aid worker who chooses to go out to the wilds of Borneo), and since in an era of global communications we can all see the plight of those in need across the planet just as vividly as the Samaritan saw the plight of the traveller he came across who had been mugged and left for dead, it remains unclear exactly how much sacrifice the command of Christ requires of us. The Thomist point made by Oderberg, that it cannot require us to sin in order to assist others, is of course right, but does not really address the precise challenge to affluent Western philosophers, who are not being asked to imperil their souls, but only to give up their ipods. These are of course fearfully tricky issues, and (to revert to a point

I made in the earlier articles, and to which I still strongly adhere) the demands of integrity require us not to run any flags up the mast, which we are not prepared to sail under, in the actual choices we make every day of our lives. Nevertheless, I am happy to agree that the general metaphysical framework which Oderberg outlines, and to much of which I now subscribe, offers much better prospects for a resolution than the assorted alternatives which I explored in my earlier writings.[40]

5. Reason and the good life

I can now perhaps accelerate the pace a little by taking together the three absorbing contributions, by Nafsika Athanassoulis, Seiriol Morgan and Michael Lacewing, which form the middle section of this volume. Although widely divergent in approach and in content, they all explore, in different but very perspicuous ways, the role of reason in determining and maintaining a worthwhile life, and they all focus on a certain scepticism about 'ratiocentric ethics' which I articulated in *Philosophy and the Good Life*. Philosophers, in a way, make their living through confidence in the power of reason, and in that book I explored what I took to be a serious challenge to that confidence. Confidence begins at home, and if, as Sigmund Freud famously argued, the rational ego can no longer be regarded as 'master in its own house',[41] then the traditional project of moral philosophy, to formulate the conditions for the good life, and implement their realization, looks seriously threatened.

The three contributors mentioned are among a sizeable number of moral philosophers who have taken this challenge seriously; and I certainly cannot complain about the general critical reaction to *Philosophy and the Good Life* since it was published, which has been extremely encouraging. But it is perhaps worth adding that there are also a considerable number of philosophers who, politely enough but nevertheless firmly, decline to see what the problem about the 'challenge to reason' is supposed to be. Part of the reason for this is no doubt that any mention of the word 'psychoanalytic' or 'Freud' still causes a certain instant 'switch-off' effect in certain quarters of the analytic academy – rather as does mention of God or religion. Indeed, I have very occasionally worried that some unconscious rebelliousness or contrariness in my psyche has caused me to devote so much of my work in moral philosophy to defending its integral links with two domains of thought that are anathema to so many of my philosophical colleagues. The essays of Athanassoulis, Morgan and Lacewing are welcomingly reassuring on this point, since, though they are far from agreeing with everything I say, their eloquence and expertise in the techniques of analytic philosophy has clearly been no bar to their complete appreciation of what the issues are, and why they are important for moral philosophy.

i. The hegemony of reason

Nafsika Athanassoulis's illuminating essay takes up my targeting of Aristotle as a 'rational hegemonist' – one who, while acknowledging that rationality is by no means the only powerful element in the psyche of a virtuous and flourishing individual, nevertheless assigns it a leading role in the control and management of the good life. She rightly takes the phenomenon of *akrasia* to be the key issue here. For *akrasia*, the knowing and genuinely regretted selection of an alternative known to be the worse option, is nothing else than the derailing of reason's control over the good life; the ability of a moral philosophy to account for it, and to take steps to remedy it, is a litmus test for evaluating its resources. Athanassoulis takes us carefully though the resources offered by Aristotle, and acutely identifies why *akrasia* presents such a puzzle: it is 'implausible' to suggest that 'morality exerts an attraction, but ... only a rather weak one'; for 'how could recognition of the noble and the good be attractive but only mildly so?' On the other hand, the picture of human nature as enabling us to perceive the good, but being utterly 'ravaged by contrary extreme desires,' leaves it unclear how we are so often able to desire the good and unproblematically act upon it. In expounding Aristotle, Athanassoulis goes on to question my interpretation of Aristotle as putting reason in charge and so leaving himself unable to account properly for *akrasia*. Moral choice, she argues, may on his account be thought of as either *orektikos nous* or as *orexis dianoêtikê*; that is to say it is a unified synergy of reason and emotion. Ethical understanding for Aristotle is not just a matter of reason's laying down the law, but a complex process of maturity, built on the right early training, whereby we come to 'perceive, appreciate, affirm and be motivated by' the good (pp. 87–110).

   This analysis of Aristotle's resources strikes me as very sound. But I am not convinced that it refutes or 'defies' the interpretation of Aristotle as a 'ratiocentric' moral philosopher. Athanassoulis offers a persuasive picture of Aristotle as holding that 'the emotions shape reason as much as reason shapes emotions', and an understanding of this subtle interactive process is certainly a valuable corrective to certain types of Platonic and Stoic models which see reason as set 'over against' the emotions, either automatically succeeding or inexplicably failing to control them. Nevertheless, it seems to me that since it lacks a developed concept of unconscious mentation, the Aristotelian account presents us with a picture of moral formation as operating in an essentially transparent domain. And hence, once the relevant sensitivities are appropriately shaped, through training and maturation, it is a complete mystery why they should suddenly break down. Aristotle (and as I noted in *Philosophy and the Good Life* this is to his credit)[42] recognizes that what must be involved when the palpably lesser good is selected must be *some* kind of loss of transparency or cognitive clouding: although the akratic man has got the knowledge (or in Athanassoulis's terms, the relevant perceptive, appreciative, affirmatory and motivational understanding), his mind somehow fails to activate it fully. His understanding, even if he rehearses it to himself, becomes mere verbalizing, like the famous drunken man 'babbling' the verses of Empedocles.[43] But *why* this occlusion of ethical understanding? Only with something like the psychoanalytic picture of *projections*, of which the subject is consciously unaware, but under whose influence the lesser good gains its mysterious allure for the akratic subject, can we begin to see how ethical understanding, with all its associated perceptual and emotional sensitivities, becomes strangely distorted. There is nothing wrong with Aristotle's account; it is just that it needs supplementing – supplementing by the kind of systematic insight psychoanalytic theory can provide into how reason, even when allied to and integrated with non-intellectual sensitivities and perceptive powers, nonetheless fails to rule the roost.

ii. The temptations of reason

The psychoanalytic account of *akrasia* just alluded to was one I endeavoured to develop in more detail in my account of the imaginary case of 'Cecil',[44] which is discussed with great subtlety in Seiriol Morgan's essay. Cecil had his life blown off course by a disastrous affaire, and the fantasy of starting a 'new life' with what turned out be a wholly unsuitable partner. Yet his inexplicable opting for the lesser good in place of the solid relationship he already enjoyed was not just a piece of 'weakness' in the face of appetite, but the effect of an allure, projected from the depths of his unconscious, whose nature was, at the time, opaque to him. As Morgan nicely puts it, what was involved was 'the turning against him of his evaluative sensitivity itself'. Using quite different materials from the ones I deployed, Morgan then provides an independent argument (one I am happy to take on board) for the conclusion that 'the Aristotelian model of the virtuous person as able to have full confidence in her own motivational response to the world is an unattainable illusion, and a dangerous one at that' (p. 134).

The bulk of Morgan's paper offers an interesting defence of Immanuel Kant against the charge made by quite a few, including myself, that his account of the ethical life is suspect, because (to use my terms) it is unacceptably 'ratiocentric'. In so far as I had Kant in my sights in *Philosophy and the Good Life*, it was in quite a schematic way, as but one example of the ratiocentric approach, and on the basis of his most famous text, the *Grundlegung*. Morgan, by contrast, offers a very illuminating exposition of some of the ideas in the later and less studied text, *Religion within the Bounds of Mere Reason*,[45] which exhibit a distinct 'scepticism about the powers of practical reason' (p. 115). The point which strikes me as central here is that Kant, if Morgan is correct, came to see that any moral theory worth its salt must be able to offer an account of 'how immoral inclination gets its motivational grip on the will'. It needs to tackle the question of what precisely is it that leads the will to take the satisfaction of some desire as a reason for action, in the face of a clear rational perception of the demands of the categorical imperative.

Once again we are face to face with a variant of the problem of *akrasia*; and I think it is fair to say that the approaches taken by both Morgan and myself converge on the central psychoanalytic insight that solving the problem is primarily a matter of developing a sufficiently rich moral psychology, along broadly Freudian lines. (One might add that the continuing debates on weakness of will in the philosophy of action seem very unlikely to make much progress on this by using the tools of logic and conceptual analysis alone.) As far as Kant's own solution (as interpreted by Morgan) goes, it rests on the idea that reason is entirely vulnerable to 'being crippled by the darker elements of the psyche' – an account, of course, to which my support for the psychoanalytic framework makes me in principle likely to find illuminating. But despite the 'remarkable congruities' which Morgan uncovers between Kant and Freud, there are (as I am sure he would accept) very significant discontinuities.

One in particular that troubles me concerns the Kantian label of 'radical evil' to describe the aetiology of akratic lapse; as Morgan puts it 'any one of us might at any time find our inner attraction to evil welling up despite ourselves, and casting some dark and self-centred course of action in a seductive light' (p. 126). There seems to me an uneasy amalgam here of the grim Calvinist idea of an innate predisposition to evil, and the more mainstream Platonic and Christian idea that evil tends to appear *sub specie boni*, under the guise of the good. My disquiet, I should add, does not stem from any antipathy to the concept of original sin (which may be the unacknowledged source of the Kantian talk of 'radical evil') – far from it: one of the great fallacies of the secularist optimism found in some of the more disastrous ideologies of the twentieth century was precisely the failure to recognize inherent flaws in the human species, and the naïve assumption that ameliorating economic conditions and removing existing structures of exploitation would be all that was necessary to usher in the golden age. But as the story of the Fall suggests, such inherent flaws are more perspicuously understood not as a matter of an 'inner attraction to evil', but rather as a turning away from a known good when some lesser good – often carrying a concealed terrible cost – is speciously presented in a way that makes it seem almost irresistible: 'and when the woman saw that the tree was good for food, and that it was pleasant to the eyes, and that it was desired to make one wise, she took of the fruit thereof, and did eat, and gave also unto her husband with her: and he did eat.'[46]

Before moving on, I should perhaps mention one point on which I think Morgan's otherwise very illuminating treatment of Freud goes astray. This is in the objection he raises to the Freudian framework, namely that it offers 'a therapeutic methodology to be used *by* analysts *on* patients, in order to effect their release from pathological symptoms' – an external, quasi-scientific or 'third-personal' approach which he takes to be in tension with the true first- and second-personal perspective of the moral philosopher (p. 128). This, I think is unfair. Freud frequently made it clear that the required kind of psychoanalytic knowledge could not simply be imparted by the therapist from the outside, but had to be internalized by the patient through their own complex efforts (such as through the 'dreamwork'):

It happens in analysis that an experienced practitioner can usually surmise very easily what those feelings are which have remained unconscious in each individual patient. It should not therefore be a matter of great difficulty to cure the patient by imparting this knowledge to him ... If only it were so! ... There are various kinds of knowing, which psychologically are not by any means of equal value. *Il y a fagot et fagots*, as Molière says ... When the physician conveys his knowledge to the patient by telling him what he knows ... it does not have the effect of dispersing the symptoms.'[47]

Therapy is never the passive receipt of a narrative supplied by the analyst, but a demanding labour which the subject must undertake in significant measure in his or her own terms. In *Philosophy and the Good Life* I described (albeit taking Jung rather than Freud as my guide) a model of 'transformational analysis' which envisages an eventual release from the consulting room altogether, to allow the subject to take full control of their continuing path of moral growth towards self-understanding.[48] Morgan concludes his paper by observing that notwithstanding my strictures against ratiocentric eudaimonism, I still believe that the business of moral philosophy is to show us how to live the good life. This is indeed quite right; it is just that I believe that moral philosophers should have the humility to acknowledge that they need all the help they can get.

iii. The limits of reason

The question of the self-sufficiency of moral philosophy is taken up in Michael Lacewing's very rich paper, where he brings a highly sensitive grasp of the psychoanalytic process to bear on developing and reinforcing the critique of ratiocentrism offered *Philosophy and the Good Life*. I have a sense that in our general approach to moral psychology we are very much on the same wavelength, so that there is much of his analysis to which I have little to add except enthusiastic agreement. The scope and power of reason, however, and the associated question of what moral philosophy can accomplish, is an area where Lacewing suggests my critique of ratiocentrism may not have gone far enough; so it is perhaps worth my saying something on this central issue.

Suppose the moral philosopher can have at his disposal, as it were, all the results of psychoanalysis – a complete understanding of the ways in which the plans of reason can be blown off course by the distorting projections generated from the unconscious parts of the mind. Could he, armed with this information, resume the traditional eudaimonist task of mapping out and implementing the conditions for the good life? This is a question which some of the things I said in *Philosophy and the Good Life* may have suggested that I was prepared to answer affirmatively; and the way I have just put the point in response to Morgan's conclusions may suggest the same. But in the light of Lacewing's arguments I think this now needs some careful qualification.

Lacewing remarks that my approach 'can sometimes emphasise the acquisition of knowledge at the expense of other elements'. This is perhaps a besetting sin of philosophers, and although I tried to guard against it in *Philosophy and the Good Life*, Lacewing's reactions have shown me that I did not do so explicitly enough; I think it is only in my most recent work (in *The Spiritual Dimension*) that I have begun to see how it needs to be addressed. The correct response, I would now argue, is not to retreat from cognitivism, but to take seriously the idea that there are types of knowledge that have what I call *accessibility conditions*.[49] The scientific models that dominate much of philosophy and psychology tend to assume that what can be known must be in principle accessible to anyone, always assuming that reason's implements, the appropriate experimental and logical techniques, are properly deployed. Yet in central areas of moral philosophy and moral psychology (and I think in religion too), there may well be truths whose significance is accessible only on condition that there is some kind of transformation in the subject. Lacewing himself puts his finger on it: 'gaining knowledge of the meanings of one's passions and choices is not knowledge one can acquire *without changing as a person*' (p. 152). The Freudian concept of *Nachträglichkeit* (one of Freud's most brilliantly worked out ideas, and one which most moral philosophers, in my view, have scarcely begun to assimilate)[50] is part of the story here. Past events, often not properly understood at the time, are constantly reinterpreted and re-evaluated, both consciously and unconsciously, in the light of changes which the subject later undergoes. It is not just a matter of dormant knowledge that needs to be recovered; rather, the grinding of the lens through which the meaning can be discerned is an exercise that requires the hard work of psychological and moral change. Whether we describe the relevant process as beyond our powers as rational beings or within the broad scope of those powers, but with caveats about how those powers cannot be exercised in splendid isolation from our other human capacities, is perhaps a matter of emphasis. What Lacewing and I would surely agree on is that the model of reason inspecting the data, and drawing its lordly conclusions about future planning of the good life is just the kind of fantasy of control that shows there is a great deal more work to be done.

Since I am always talking about the need for a 'humane turn' in moral philosophy, I will risk ending this section by quoting a celebrated sonnet about the 'Ancient Torso of Apollo', penned by the most psychoanalytically insightful of poets, Rainer Maria Rilke.[51] Apollo stands, of course, for light and rationality, and in his decapitated torso, which nevertheless seems to see right into us, there is a powerful symbol of the indestructible power of the unconscious. But I will not violate the principles I have just been articulating by trying to uncover all the layers of meaning for the reader's rational inspection. Like all work that engages with those parts of ourselves that are not fully accessible to consciousness, the sonnet may need to be revisited many times, and not just by the analytic intellect, before its meaning crystallizes. But since no ponderous philosophical formula seems apt for capturing the vitally important themes which, with the help of Lacewing's discussion, I have just been pondering, I cannot do better than leave the reader with Rilke's luminous poem, and the famous and resonant injunction with which it ends:

> *Wir kannten nicht sein unerhörtes Haupt*
> *darin die Augenäpfel reiften. Aber*
> *sein Torso glüht noch wie ein Kandelaber,*
> *in dem sein Schauen, nur zurückgeschraubt,*
>
> *sich hält und glänzt. Sonst könnte nicht der Bug*
> *der Brust dich blenden, und im leisen Drehen*
> *der Lenden könnte nicht ein Lächeln gehen*
> *zu jener Mitte, die die Zeugung trug.*
>
> *Sonst stünde dieser Stein entstellt und kurz*
> *unter der Schultern durchsichtigem Sturz*
> *und flimmerte nicht so wie Raubtierfelle;*
>
> *und bräche nicht aus allen seinen Rändern*
> *aus wie ein Stern: denn da ist keine Stelle,*
> *die dich nicht sieht. Du mußt dein Leben ändern*

> [We could not see his lost, unheard of head
> where the eyes' berries ripened. Yet, despite,
> his torso glows still, like a candle-light,
> his glance grown dimmer, but yet never dead:
>
> its gleam endures. Else could the subtle line
> of the white chest not blind you, nor the curve
> of those pale loins so smilingly down-swerve
> to that dark core which held the seed divine.
>
> Else would this marble not seem whole and tall
> beneath the shoulders' long, translucent fall
> nor glisten so, like a wild creature's fleece;
>
> nor every edge burst forth like the bright blade
> of a star's point: of him, no single piece
> but looks you through. Your life must be remade.][52]

6. Religion, meaning and morality

I come now to the final section of the volume, where the distinguished essays by Roger Crisp, Brad Hooker and Thad Metz have raised, with outstanding clarity, many key questions concerning the topics that have interested me in my most recent work, on the relation between the religious and moral domains, and the problem of the meaning of life. In the first of the three remaining sections of this essay, I will consider some of the reflections offered by Crisp.

Roger Crisp's beautifully argued discussion of the meaning of life is particularly challenging to me because it becomes clear by the time he reaches his conclusion that he himself does not think the notion of the significance of a life matters very much in the end. As a welfarist, he holds that the only ultimate reason I ever have to pursue any course of action is that it will benefit myself or others. And hence, as he says in his final sentence, 'the question of the meaning of life, understood independently from well-being ... appears to have little practical significance' (p. 179).

If I may adapt Crisp's example of 'Amy' to a rather different purpose, drawing on some of the elements of a worthwhile life (interpersonal, intrapersonal, and so on) which he distinguishes, let us imagine Amy as one of the fortunate beneficiaries of the affluence and comfort and stability which has steadily increased for typical inhabitants of the so-called 'Western' world since the second World War. Let us assume that circumstances of her life are such as to provide all the basic biological and social preconditions for human flourishing, such as being healthy, well nourished, emotionally nurtured, free from repression or exploitation, able to make her own decisions without interference, and so on. The social and ethical culture in which she finds herself allows, let us assume, for the flowering of a significant range of her talents and capacities, and also for the cultivation not just of a variety of enjoyable and satisfying activities, but also for the development of those moral sensibilities and dispositions that are indispensable for human beings, if they are to live together in a stable and mutually fulfilling way.

Thus blessed, need Amy have any disquiet about meaning in her life? One thing that might trouble her is that the fulfilling existence enjoyed by herself and her peers is made possible, in its present form, at the cost of systematic ravaging of the planet's ecological resources and the shameless exploitation or neglect of the lives of millions of fellow human beings in other parts of the world. This, one might think, is an issue about morality, not about meaning, and indeed Crisp mounts some elegant objections to a number of arguments in which I tried to exhibit morality and meaningfulness as integrally interlinked. Let me therefore say a word about these, before proceeding to evaluate the wider question of whether our positive evaluation of Amy's fulfilled life might somehow be undermined by doubts about its meaningfulness.

Some of my arguments in *On the Meaning of Life* were about whether the viciously immoral but subjectively fulfilling life could be meaningful (for example, the life of someone like Adolf Eichmann, the dedicated mass murderer who seems to have derived great satisfaction from his work); but the issue can usefully be broadened to encompass whether meaning can attach to morally imperfect but not revoltingly evil lives (such as that of the totally self-absorbed artist 'Gauguin'),[53] and even to lives many would not see anything much wrong with, such as Amy's flourishing and locally sensitive, but globally somewhat morally myopic life. My principal strategy in dealing with all such cases (as will by now be no surprise to readers of the present essay) was and remains to invoke the importance of *integrity*. The argument is not supposed to be a logically watertight one, immune to any counter-examples an ingenious philosopher might dream up, but amounts to an empirically plausible (I think) hypothesis: that for the great bulk of humankind, the compartmentalization that in varying degrees will have to be maintained by an Eichmann or a Gauguin or an Amy will in the end create a psychic dissonance that undermines the very flourishing we are supposed to be presupposing in the first place.

Crisp responds here by denying that compartmentalizing and flourishing are in tension. He cites Wittgenstein and Russell as actual examples of morally defective people who had fulfilled and meaningful lives, and also turns the tables on me by suggesting that the very partialism that I have defended will necessarily involve some compartmentalising: 'the mind of Gauguin is no more or less unstable than that of Cottingham's ideally virtuous person, who is able significantly to privilege the interests of his friends and family over those of strangers' (p. 173).

These are powerful criticisms, for which I am very grateful, since they have spurred me to reflect further on my position. To develop a proper answer would require a great deal more space than I have here, but my short response can fall into two parts. In the case of my virtuous 'partialist' (to use a convenient but somewhat awkward label), I do not accept that what is going on is compartmentalisation. Rather, the love shown to one's dear ones can (as suggested by David Oderberg in his paper in this volume)[54] embody a clear and consistent vision of general benevolence, but realized towards others taken 'one at a time', as dictated by the particular structures of involvement and commitment that necessarily shape an individual human life. In the case of 'Gauguin', Crisp offers what at first seems a reasonable enough picture of an egotistical artist who can nevertheless 'establish close personal relationships with at least certain others.' But 'close personal relationship' is a somewhat imprecise notion. Our 'Gauguin' can no doubt successfully acquire a series of wives and mistresses – indeed rampant egoists can often be rather good at amassing a string of devoted lovers (what I have elsewhere called the 'Ingmar Bergman syndrome').[55] But if one means by a 'close personal relationship' one that allows for the kind of openness and caring and vulnerability that brings out what is most truly human and truly precious in us, then I simply deny that someone who, ex hypothesi, is prepared to treat his closest intimates as discardable in the pursuit of artistic fame can do so without either a hardening that is likely to impair the very artistic sensitivity he requires, else the kind of psychic dissonance that will impact on flourishing.

To return to the broader question of whether Amy's fully flourishing life (in the welfarist sense) need be threatened by doubts about its meaningfulness, this may seem partly a matter of temperament. The twentieth-century French existentialists, to be sure, painted a vivid picture of that sense of disorientation that arises when our confidence in meaning is eroded and we are face to face with absurdity or futility. No doubt many could get through life without being explicitly troubled by the kinds of vertiginous *Angst* or nausea portrayed by Sartre and Camus. Yet the existentialists were, I believe, only giving somewhat elaborate (and possibly exaggerated) philosophical expression to something fundamental to human nature. The ineradicable 'restlessness' of which Augustine eloquently spoke[56] and that powerful desire to reach beyond the given which Pascal referred to when he declared that 'humankind transcends itself'[57] are but two expressions of a inherent aspect of human nature – its hunger for ultimate meaning and purpose. Crisp notes, in effect, that other things besides a belief in the transcendent may be able to satisfy that hunger: even without such a belief, 'many people have had the confidence to begin ... journeys [to meaningfulness]' (p. 178). That seems true; but I doubt whether such embarkations are in the end psychologically stable, since they will involve a kind of willed suppression of the transcendent aspirations that are, whether we like it or not, part of our psyche. To plan one's life within what is taken to be an entirely 'closed' cosmos, where one's projects have no purpose other than to further aims one sees oneself as having as a result of a purely accidental chain of biological, historical and cultural contingencies, seems an enterprise that a reflective person cannot sustain without risking a certain psychic disorientation. This of course launches us on momentous issues that are much too vast to be settled here; so I will simply close this section with a quotation from Thomas Nagel, not himself an advocate of religion, which nonetheless at the very least poses a challenge to those who, like

Crisp, feel no strong pull towards the transcendent route, or who even doubt that the underlying worry about the meaningfulness of life has much practical significance:

> Given that the transcendental step is natural to us humans, can we avoid absurdity by refusing to take that step and remaining entirely within our sublunar lives? Well, we cannot refuse consciously, for to do that we would have to be aware of the viewpoint we were refusing to adopt. The only way to avoid the relevant self-consciousness would be either never to attain it or to forget it – neither of which can be achieved by the will.[58]

7. Sybarites, professors and religious morality

Brad Hooker's thought-provoking paper, written with the conciseness, clarity and philosophical acuity that are his trademarks, raises several significant questions about my views on value and meaning, and about the transcendent structures that I take to be the essential support for both. He takes, first, an ingenious example, that of the 'successful sybarite', whose overriding goal is to develop (in Peter Strawson's phrase) an 'exquisite sense of the luxurious'. And he uses this example to establish what he calls a 'subjectivist sufficient condition' for an agent's life having (at least some) meaning.

The argument is that, since benefiting others can imbue one's life with meaning, it is hard to deny that benefiting oneself can imbue one's life with (at least some) meaning. With this I would agree, provided that 'benefiting' is understood properly. I would certainly consider, for example, that someone who 'benefits himself' by devoting himself to what Pierre Hadot calls the 'care of the soul' – that is to say by systematically striving to orient himself towards the good, and to grow in knowledge and love of the good – is thereby achieving a meaningful life. Indeed, he is, I would say, fulfilling the purpose of human life. Hooker, however, understands what could qualify as 'benefiting' in a fairly relaxed way; if I understand him correctly, he would maintain that I am benefiting myself by ensuring that my life contains 'some achievement or pleasure'. Developing an exquisite sense of the luxurious, he then observes, can be 'quite an achievement', given the complex knowledge and discrimination certain kinds of luxury require from their devotees. So the satisfying achievements of the successful sybarite, even if they do not have any significant effect on anyone else, are enough to give his life some meaning.

I have to say I find this view very counter-intuitive. The life of such a person strikes me as a paradigm case of a futile life – one which, if we were to look back on it after the person's death, we should have to say had been completely and utterly pointless and meaningless. To see this, let us beef up the case a bit by generously adding in some extra 'value' through the supposition that such a life ropes in a significant number of other people to the same or similar pursuits. Even with this widened scope of so-called 'benefit', I should still have to agree with Kant's stern verdict:

> [T]hat there is any intrinsic worth in the real existence of a man who merely lives for enjoyment, however busy he may be in this respect, even when in so doing he serves others – all equally with himself intent only on enjoyment – as an excellent means to that one end, and does so, moreover, because through sympathy he shares all their gratifications – this is a view to which reason will never let itself be brought round.[39]

Kant may have had a certain puritanical disapproval of 'enjoyment', which I would not share, but that does not affect my main objection to Hooker's use of the sybarite. My disquiet about Hooker's conclusion is not some disapproval of pleasure, nor any quarrel about the 'achievement' which certain kinds of luxury-oriented pursuits may technically involve, but something far more fundamental. It concerns how such a sybaritic person has chosen to make use of the precious gift of life.

At the risk of causing the 'switch-off' effect, I will venture to quote the story from Luke (12: 16–21), about the rich man who spent a lot of time organizing storage barns for his lavish surplus wealth (it was no doubt quite an achievement to supervise all this), and then said to himself 'Soul, you have many goods laid up for many years, take your ease, and [enjoy your luxurious pursuits]'. He received a chilling reply from God: 'You fool! This very night your life is required of you!' Let me at once say what I think is *not* the point of this story: (1) The point is *not* that you never know what is going to happen tomorrow (though that of course is true enough). To such a point, Hooker could quite reasonably reply that this does not negate the value and meaning already achieved today and yesterday. (2) The point is *not* that the rich man had an immortal soul which was now destined to pay the price in the next world. Nothing is mentioned about a last judgement, and even if it had been, that would simply have been to reinforce, not to replace, the existing moral point of the story. John Henry Newman was nearer the mark when he has the guardian angel tell Gerontius *'already in thy soul the judgment has begun!'*[60] The point, rather, is the sheer idiocy of the choice this man had made, the sheer foolishness of his whole mindset, as he grubbed around to secure his exquisite comforts and neglected to ask what his life was really for.

It is a mistake, I think, to conceive of value in atomistic terms, as if it consisted, as it were, of little tokens which, if they can be credited to an account, automatically enhance it. Aristotle once observed that *eudaimonia* could only be assessed in a complete life,[61] and I think the holistic lines along which he was thinking were approximately right, but his point is not quite what I am getting at. Even a few moments of life may be enough to give it ultimate meaning and value, if what happens in those few moments is that the subject undergoes a shift of outlook and becomes, in her whole being, oriented towards truth and beauty and goodness. These may seem overblown ways of speaking, but it is hard to find other language. I do not mean that such a person becomes a saint, simply that if their soul were 'required of them' – that is, on the *supposition* (forget metaphysical and ecclesiastical doctrine for a moment) that an all-good, all-compassionate and all-seeing judge were to look into their deepest inclinations and desires, and to assess the quality of their actions in every last detail – then he would find room for mercy. 'I have smoked some exquisite cigars' does not look quite enough.

Concerning Hooker's very interesting second section, about the 'objectivist sufficient condition' – that is, the idea that if someone's life produces objectively good outcomes this imbues it with meaning even if the subject does not recognize or aim at those outcomes – I have fewer qualms. I would only add that the life of his imagined professor, who dies frustrated at what he sees as the failure of his life even though his friends (rightly) recognize it as very worthwhile, has an obviously tragic quality to it, which makes it hard to see it as qualifying as what most people would call a meaningful life. Far better, far more meaningful (as Hooker indeed concedes), if there can be a fit between the professor's aspirations and the good he achieves.

In Hooker's third section, about the support religion offers for the notion that a life can be meaningful, there is a great deal of common ground between us, since Hooker is prepared to concede that the existence of God would make life maximally meaningful; though he ends by hinting that in God's absence our fellow creatures might provide some 'confirmation' of meaning (a suggestion which it would be interesting to explore). Hooker's general stance, however, refuses to allow that the notion of religious support is even 'on the table' as a possible candidate for a provider of meaningfulness; for he thinks the traditional problem of evil makes the universe as disclosed by modern science inherently resistant to a religious interpretation of its significance. The perhaps somewhat imprecise phrase 'inherently resistant' was one I myself introduced in *On the Meaning of Life*. If we are here talking about a *logical* incompatibility (Hooker may mean this when he says the problem of evil offers a 'conclusive argument'), then I think most parties to the debate now accept that it could not possibly be demonstrated that an all-powerful, all-good being could have no conceivable reason to allow the amount of evil found in the world.[62] If, however, what is meant is that the amount of evil found makes the existence of God vanishingly *improbable*, then if we lay aside evils caused by the free actions of human beings (whether there is of course a long tradition of theodicy going back to Augustine, which many have found persuasive), the issue turns on whether the constant dangers and suffering generated by the ordinary natural conditions of the planet (Hooker mentions tsunamis, plagues and disease) undermine any reasonable belief in a divine being of the supposed supreme power to prevent it and benevolent desire to avoid it. This is an issue I addressed in *The Spiritual Dimension*,[63] where I suggested, roughly, that change and decay are inseparable from material existence, and so ineliminable even by an omnipotent creator of a material world.

There is of course much more to it than that; and in any case (as I also argued in that book) the issue is not really one for which a 'solution' can be offered through intellectual debate alone.[64] The adoption or rejection of a religious worldview, together with the associated attitudes to death and suffering, are in my view things that are determined at a much deeper level (just as you do not decide whether to marry someone, or to have children, simply as a result of rational argument). This, incidentally, is where some atheist critics systematically distort things by entirely identifying religious allegiance with the adoption of a quasi-scientific explanatory scheme – the 'God-hypothesis', as Richard Dawkins has irritatingly called it.[65]

Hooker concludes his essay by noting, with complete justice, that 'many people *have* sustained moral commitment without the buttress of belief in God, and that many people *have* felt that life is meaningful even if there is no God'.[66] I hope I have made it sufficiently clear in my writings that my advocacy of religion carries no slightest shred of a suggestion that those lacking religious belief cannot be upright and morally committed human beings (indeed, at the risk of embarrassing him, I might add that Brad Hooker himself provides an absolutely paradigm case). I explicitly denied in *The Spiritual Dimension* that religious allegiance was universally necessary, let alone sufficient, for living a moral life.[67] What I did suggest was that given the weakness of human nature, most human beings were going to find the painful and exacting voyage towards self-discovery and the struggle to achieve integrity in the moral life very difficult indeed without something like the supporting disciplines of spiritual *askesis*. It could well be that the current ethical culture of the increasingly secularized Western world is living off borrowed capital in this respect: the effects of a 2000-year-old tradition of spirituality do not dissipate overnight. What the future holds remains to be seen.

8. Religious metaphysics as grounding for morality

I come finally to Thaddeus Metz's polished and intricately argued paper, in which, notwithstanding his radical differences with me over the acceptability of theism, he has done me the signal service of expounding my arguments, and unpacking their implications in meticulous detail, and has also offered a generous bonus by suggesting possible lines of reply to the some of the objections that might be raised against my position.

In the first part of his paper, Metz refers to four features applying to central moral truths which I take to favour a supernaturalist metaethics: *universality*, *objectivity*, *necessity* and *normativity*. First, cruelty (for example) is to be avoided, and compassion to be cultivated, by *all* rational creatures (not just by this or that group or society); second, these truths about cruelty and compassion, and so on, obtain independently of what people's attitudes towards the relevant actions may be; third, these truths apply absolutely, in all possible worlds; and fourth, it is incumbent on us to act on them – we have (as some would put it nowadays) conclusive 'reasons' to avoid cruelty and to show compassion. A God-based ethics appears to support these four features very well. Although I am no metaphysician, so feel tentative about occupying this territory, I am sympathetic to a fairly mainstream theological conception of moral truths as eternal verities, held in the mind of God, the supremely perfect being who exists in all possible worlds. And (though I have not gone into this much in my work) I would be attracted by a similar account of logical and mathematical truths, and indeed of central aesthetic truths. There are of course alternative accounts on offer of the four features identified by Metz, notably certain kinds of non-naturalism and of Platonism, but I would agree with Metz's comment (on my behalf) that whatever its problems, 'the supernaturalist's suggestion of a kind of concrete substance that exists is more ontologically satisfying than the non-naturalist's suggestion of a kind of abstract property that exists independently of any substance' (p. 205).[68]

In expounding my views, Metz raises the important question of why, if all these kinds of truth are grounded in the divine substance, moral norms should have a special kind of overriding normativity: should not we have 'just as much reason to follow the laws of logic and beauty as to follow the laws of morality'? I'm slightly puzzled by the thought that logic falls lower down the scale of normativity than morality: in one way, of course it is true that killing is worse than affirming the consequent; but in another sense, a rule like 'you can't have your cake and eat it' seems just about as overriding as one could imagine. Let us however take the relation between beauty and goodness, which is an interesting one for religious ethicists. Certain somewhat bleak versions of Christianity have put the beautiful and the 'fine' (what the Greeks called *to kalon*) very far down the list of values, almost as if any distraction from the stern imperatives of morality should be as far as possible eliminated. But a remarkable episode reported in the first gospel puts a different complexion on things. When a woman in the house of Simon the leper uses an 'alabaster box of precious ointment' to anoint the head of Jesus, the disciples round on her for this morally disgraceful act of waste ('could it not have been sold and given to the poor?'). But Christ tells them not to bother the woman: 'she has done a *fine* deed.' (*ergon kalon*, Matthew 26:10). There is a vital and non-negotiable place in life for the fine and the beautiful. The example, of course, concerns the overriding of what Kant called an imperfect moral duty (helping the poor), and Metz is quite correct that our intuitions would never support its overriding a perfect duty (for example, if the woman had stolen or killed to get the perfume). So there remains a crucial priority issue here; but since Metz generously offers an ingenious solution on my behalf (p. 211), which seems to me likely to work, I am happy to accept his assistance without further comment.

Traditionally, the main argument against a God-based ethic of the kind I support has been the so-called Euthyphro dilemma (that making the good dependent on God's will is either explanatorily vacuous, or else liable to generate morally counter-intuitive results);[69] but reassuringly Metz considers that the way I deal with the problem (along with several other recent writers) is satisfactory.[70] He goes on, however, to raise an even more serious charge – namely that of logical incoherence: 'On the one hand, Cottingham maintains that wrongness is constituted by God, but, on the other hand, he is more confident that wrongness exists than he is that God exists' (p. 216). This is not just an ad hominem argument against me; anyone who thinks there is a conclusive argument for a God-based ethic should, according to Metz, regard the evidence for God's existence as comparable in strength to the evidence for the existence of wrongness. And that is a very hard bullet to bite.

I agree that it is, but I confess to finding the logical presuppositions of Metz's argument very implausible. I can surely maintain that apples are constituted by quarks, and yet be far more confident of the evidence that apples exist than of the evidence that quarks exist. Or I can surely maintain that the properties of the number zero are essentially consti- tuted by complicated properties involving relations between sets of sets, yet be far more confident that the number of coins in my pocket is nil than I am about the existence of sets (I may have just read an ingenious paper refuting their existence, which I cannot see how to get round). But even leaving these analogies aside, I would not in any case want to insist on the 'conclusiveness' of the argument for a divine-based metaethic. My general position in *The Spiritual Dimension* is that the adoption of a religious worldview does not hinge on the plausibility, let alone conclusiveness, of philosophical arguments; it depends, rather, on coming to see the world in a different way, as the result of various moral and spiritual transformations that open one to certain realities previously occluded. I do however maintain that the worldview so arrived at must (on pain of sacrificing one's integrity) be at least conformable with the results of philosophical and scientific inquiry. So I would be content to align myself with the position recently taken by the theologian Brian Hebblethwaite, who resiles from any attempt to reason people towards faith by conclusive arguments, but who offers a 'buttress' for faith already arrived at, by indicating how belief in God would plausibly fit in (not as the only possible explanation, but at least in a satisfying way) with how we conceive of the kinds of moral and logical necessity under discussion:

> Theistic metaphysics offers the best explanation of all the necessary features of the contingent world, its mathematical expressibility, its conformity to the laws of logic, and the properties and abstract ideas that it instantiates – all the features discerned but not explained by pure Platonism. For theistic metaphysics, mathematics and logic reflect the consistency and rationality of God's necessary being, while abstract ideas and properties are God's creative ideas. So all the necessities in the created world, and indeed in any possible world, depend on either the nature or the will of God.[71]

Towards the end of his paper, Metz argues in support of a complex alternative to supernaturalist metaethics which he thinks accounts just as well for the properties of universality, objectivity, normativity and necessity that attach to moral truths. This is so-called 'Cornell realism' developed over the last 20 years or so – a type of naturalism which regards moral truths as synthetic a posteriori necessities (like 'water is H_2O'). Just as we learn by scientific investigation that the terms 'water' and 'H_2O' necessarily pick out the same stuff, so (we are invited to believe) ethical theorists have discovered that the class of actions picked out by the property *wrongness* cannot but coincide with the class of actions picked out by the property of, for example, producing damaging consequences, or undermining the flourishing of persons. The end of an already long paper is no place for me to launch into a discussion of the intricacies of Cornell realism, which have generated a massive literature. When I first encountered this view, I must admit that I regarded it (with its reliance on complicated Kripkean metaphysics) as too cumbersome to have much chance of general appeal; I was reminded of the verdict passed by Locke on Malebranche's occasionalism, 'tis an opinion that spreads not, and is like to die of itself, or at least do no great harm'. But I have since come to think that either this or whatever turns out to be the best articulated naturalistic account might, as far as it goes, be perfectly serviceable from a theistic perspective.[72] After all, if the universe is created by a supremely benevolent God, then it is surely to be expected that the good for his creatures will be intimately related to their nature. Nevertheless, *nature* is, as I have argued elsewhere,[73] a highly ambiguous concept: as applied to humans it can on the one hand designate simply those characteristics and inclinations we happen to find ourselves having; but can also (as in the natural law tradition) have a more strongly normative flavour, referring not just to how we are, but to the best we can become. Without a divinely based teleology, something like an ideal pattern of life or goal for human existence, I cannot see how we can distinguish among which of the 'natural' inclinations and satisfactions of our species have ultimate normative force. The systematic indulgence by a powerful tribe of their impulses towards conquest and genocide might if sufficiently successful, usher in a millennium of stability, prosperity and personal flourishing for the winners, and I can see no ultimate conclusive reason which, for the naturalist, would count against such a course of action.

Irrespective of the viability or otherwise of naturalism in its modern sophisticated forms, I take comfort from the thought that Metz and

I would surely concur in thinking that that the ethical subjectivism and relativism so prevalent when I was an undergraduate are non-starters. If our central moral insights do, as he and I agree, represent truths that hold universally, are independent of our contingent inclinations, require our allegiance, and cannot be otherwise, then we have a picture of moral reality that is already strikingly consistent with what religious ethicists have held for many centuries. At all events, there is much I have learned from his paper, and much about which I shall have to think further.

9. Envoi

In completing this essay, I see I have broken a lifelong rule that articles or chapters should never exceed eight thousand words. But perhaps transgressing that limit to respond to nine substantial papers is not so inexcusable. I should like to end where I began, with an expression of sincere gratitude for these 'gifts now prepared for me'. Like all worthwhile gifts, they are not of transient interest, but will give me a great deal to appreciate and ponder on for a long time to come.

Festschriften are things that automatically conjure up images of retirement. Like many academics, I hope to continue working and writing when my more formal commitments in other areas taper off. But rites of passage are nevertheless important, and we should not delude ourselves about the adjustments needed as one phase of life gradually merges into another. So if this volume is, in a sense, a launch, I am grateful that it has been such an enjoyable one – one that has helped me to look back with pleasure on the terrain so far traversed, and to anticipate with relish the voyage that lies ahead. If I may be forgiven for quoting a last piece of poetry, my thoughts at this point are perhaps best summed up in some favourite lines produced by the Roman poet Horace when he asked himself what he should hope for:

> *Frui paratis et valido mihi*
> *Latoe, dones, et, precor integra*
> * cum mente, nec turpem senectam*
> * degere nec cithara carentem.*

> [May I enjoy the gifts now prepared for me;
> give strength, I pray, and grant me integrity
>   of mind, aging without dishonour,
>   and the sweet chords of the lute to guide me.][74]

Notes

1. Socrates, remarking that he himself was the son of a midwife, describes himself as a 'midwife of the soul' in the *Theaetetus*, [*c.* 380 BC], 148–50. The idea that philosophy proceeds dialectically clearly goes back to Socrates himself, and is preserved in the dialogue form adopted throughout Plato's writings (though in some of the his later works it becomes not much more than a stylistic device).
2. René Descartes's *Meditationes de prima philosophia* ('Meditations on First Philosophy') was published in 1641, along with six sets of objections together with the replies of the author; the second edition of 1642 contained a seventh set. The terms 'Objections' and 'Replies' were suggested by Descartes himself, who wrote 'I shall be glad if people make me as many objections as possible, and the strongest ones they can find. For I hope that in consequence the truth will stand out all the better.' (From a letter to his editor, Marin Mersenne, of 28 January 1641.)
3. Hadot, 1995, Ch. 3.
4. Plato, *Republic* [*c.* 380 BC] 394d. The actual phrase is: 'wherever the argument takes us, like a wind, there we must go' (*hopê an ho logos hôsper pneuma pherê, tautê iteon*).
5. See Heidegger, 1927, §44, p. 262; and Freud, 1916–17, Lecture XVIII.
6. Chrétien de Troyes, *Yvain* [*c.* 1175]; my translation is somewhat free, but preserves the rhyme-scheme and metre. I should add that I identify merely with the struggle of the Chevalier du Lion, without presuming to claim arrival on the right road.
7. Williams, 1972, pp. 108–17, and Williams, 1981, pp. 1–20 and 40–53.
8. Compare Cottingham, 1986, p. 365.
9. 'It is easier for a camel to go through the eye of a needle, than for a rich man to enter into the kingdom of God' (Matthew 19:24). There is some fascinating commentary on this text at *http://www.biblicalhebrew.com/nt/camelneedle.htm.*
10. Luke 9:24. This is almost certainly one of the core authentic sayings of Jesus. Closely parallel texts occur later in Luke (17:33), in Matthew (10:39), and also (unlike many of the sayings found in the synoptic gospels) in John (12:25).
11. Cottingham, 'Impartiality and Ethical Formation', §2.
12. A man travelling into a far country called three servants, and gave to the first five talents, to the second two, and to the third one. On return he called them to account, and found the first servant had used his five to make five more, and the second had used his two to make two more; but the servant who had received but one had 'hidden his talent in the earth'. The first two are highly praised, but the third is censured and punished (Matthew 25: 14–30). Certain philosophical readers, for no doubt perfectly understandable reasons tend to 'switch off' when they hear a biblical reference, supposing that the argument must be degenerating into religious dogma. But such a reaction (like that of those who refuse to go to Shakespeare plays because his poetry has been ruined for them by their early experiences in the schoolroom) is one that I continue to try to coax people out of. Whatever one's attitude to religion, biblical scripture is at the very least a fertile source of examples for moral philosophy, and the widespread failure to make use of it, whether it arises from prejudice or caution, or simply from an upbringing

that bypassed the relevant texts, seems to me a sad waste of one the great riches of our intellectual and moral culture.

13. Cottingham, 'Impartiality and Ethical Formation', §3.
14. Weil S., *Gravity and Grace* [*La pesanteur et la grâce*, 1947], tr. E. Crawford and M. von der Ruhr (London: Routledge, 2002), p. 37; cited in Vice, 'The Insignificance of the Self', p. 17; emphasis supplied.
15. Cottingham, 1991, pp. 798–817, esp. p. 813.
16. Autonomy, for Kant, is 'the basis of the dignity of human nature and of every rational nature', according to which our will must be considered as *selbstgesetzgebend* ('giving the law to itself'), Kant, 1785, Ch. 2, 4:436 and 4:431.
17. Godwin W., *An Inquiry concerning Political Justice* [1793], from Book II, ch. 2. The pedagogue in me cannot forbear to note that 'my' is in fact not a pronoun, but a pronominal adjective.
18. Swinburne, 1996, p. 4.
19. Compare his weeping at the death of his friend Lazarus ('see how he loved him!' said the bystanders; John 11:35–6), or his special relationship with the 'beloved disciple' (for example, John 19:26-7).
20. John 1:14.
21. Harvey, 2000, Ch. 1.
22. Luke 9:26; emphasis added.
23. *He gar dynamis en astheneia teleitai* (II Corinthians 12:9).
24. I Corinthians 13:12.
25. See Williams, 1993, *passim*, and Williams, 1985, Ch. 10.
26. Shakespeare W., *King Lear* [*c*.1606], Act I, Scene 2.
27. The word 'condescension' has shifted its connotations from positive to negative since Wollstonecraft's day. To be condescending, in the eighteenth century, was the aristocratic virtue of displaying a gracious lack of hauteur towards the lower ranks of society.
28. Wollstonecraft M., *A Vindication of the Rights of Women* [1792], Ch. 4.
29. Luke 1:46–55.
30. 'How canst thou say to thy brother, Brother, let me pull out the mote that is in thine eye, when thou thyself beholdest not the beam that is in thine own eye? Thou hypocrite, cast out first the beam out of thine own eye, and then shalt thou see clearly to pull out the mote that is in thy brother's eye.' (Luke 6:42; cf. Matthew 7:5).
31. Rigby C., *The Lord be with You* (Oxford: Family Publications, 2003), p. 81.
32. Jung, 1933, p. 40. I explore this theme at length in Cottingham, 1998, Ch. 4, §6.
33. Particularly illuminating here is what Michael Lacewing says about the notion of 'acceptance' (in a psychoanalytic context) – a process which, as he rightly insists, is not at all to be identified with moral approval or moral complacency (p. 157).
34. This, I take it, is part of the meaning behind the haunting words of Psalm 51 (or 50 in the Vulgate numbering): *cor contritum Deus non despicies* ('a contrite heart O Lord wilt thou not despise'). Contempt is made redundant by the hard work of contrition. The psychoanalytic addition (by no means incompatible with many traditional Christian approaches) would be that a good therapist neither starts from a position of contempt, nor

requires the client to start from there (and so, mutatis mutandis, for confessor and penitent).

35. 'Through my own most grievous fault' (the phrase, from the *Confiteor* – the confession at the start of the Mass) is a liturgical analogue of the full acknowledgement of responsibility that many secular accounts would insist on as a necessary part of the process of dealing with wrongdoing; compare Duff, 1985.
36. Lewis C.S., *That Hideous Strength* [1945] (London: Pan Books, 1955), p. 134.
37. Cottingham, 1983, p. 87. Cf. Mackie, 1977, pp. 129–34.
38. I Corinthians 7:7.
39. For Godwin (and his latter-day disciple Peter Singer), see Oderberg, 'Self-Love', p. 66, n. 36. John Stuart Mill's propaganda is equally marked: 'In the golden rule of Jesus of Nazareth we read the complete spirit of the ethics of utility To do as you would be done by, and to love your neighbour as yourself, constitute the ideal perfection of utilitarian morality' (Mill, 1861, Ch. 2)
40. Although I must ruefully accept the justice of Oderberg's rebuke for my earlier flirtation with the Nietzschean conception of value as generated by a subjective act of will (in Cottingham, 1997–8, pp. 1–21), it should in fairness be made clear that this is a conception I have since wholly and emphatically repudiated – both in Cottingham, 2003, Ch. 1, and in Cottingham, 2005, Ch. 3. See also Cottingham, 'The Good Life and the "Radical Contingency of the Ethical"', forthcoming, 2008. As for my espousal of a 'neo-Pagan' approach (in 'The Ethics of Self-Concern'), I would only note that my very schematic 'bell curve' representation of Aristotle's doctrine of the mean was certainly not meant to suggest lateral symmetry (I am of course well aware that the mean of any given virtue will be closer to the vice of excess in some cases, and closer to the vice of deficiency in others). And as for the Christian conception of virtue being 'linear' (it would have been better to say 'rectilinear'), when Oderberg repudiates my interpretation of, for example, Christian charity as insisting that the more we give the better, he does not seem to me to give sufficient attention to just how hard a saying is the injunction Christ gave to the rich young man: 'sell *all you have* and give to the poor' (Matthew 19:21).
41. 'But man's craving for grandiosity is now suffering the ... most bitter blow from present-day psychological research which is endeavouring to prove to the "ego" of each one of us that he is not even master in his own house, but that he must remain content with the veriest scraps of information about what is going on unconsciously in his own mind' (Freud, 1916–17, Ch. 18).
42. Compare Cottingham, 1998, Ch. 4, §6.
43. 'Within "having knowledge but not using it" we can see a difference in the having, so that there is such a thing as having knowledge in a way and yet not having it, as with someone who is asleep or mad or drunk. Now this is exactly the condition of a man under the influence of passions; for outburst of anger and sexual desires and other such passions do actually alter our bodily condition, and sometimes even produce fits of madness. Clearly, then, akratic people are like people who are asleep or mad or drunk ... That a man says knowledgeable things is no proof that he knows them. Men under the influence of these passions may utter scientific proofs or recite the poems of Empedocles, but they do not understand what they are saying.' Aristotle NE, Bk VII, Ch. 3, 1147a11.

44. Cottingham, 1998, Ch. 4, §7.
45. Kant, 1793.
46. Genesis 3: 6 (King James version).
47. Freud, 1916–17, Lecture XVIII.
48. Cottingham, 1998, Ch. 4, §6.
49. For this idea, see Cottingham, 2005, Ch. 7, §4, and Cottingham, 2006, pp. 401–20.
50. See Lacewing, 'What Reason Can't Do', p. 151, n. 55, and Cottingham, 1998, Ch. 4, §5, esp. pp. 131ff.
51. I do not, of course, mean that Rilke could pass exams in Freudian theory, but that his insights have the kind of resonance that is highly suggestive for anyone sympathetic to the psychoanalytic perspective on the moral and spiritual quest for the good life.
52. Rilke R.M., *Archaïscher Torso Apollos* [from *Der Neuen Gedichte anderer Teil*, 1908].
    I claim no great literary merit for my translation, only that it preserves the exacting rhyme and metrical scheme that was so important to Rilke's art, and which many modern 'poetic' translators blithely and self-indulgently ignore.
53. The inverted commas are needed for reasons Crisp concisely sets out in 'Meaning, Morality, and Religion', p. 172, n. 19.
54. See p. 61, above.
55. See Cottingham, 'The Good Life and the "Radical Contingency of the Ethical"', forthcoming, 2008.
56. St Augustine, *Confessiones* [*c*. 398], Book I, Ch. 1: '*fecisti nos ad te, et inquietum est cor nostrum donec requiescat in te.*' ('You have made us for yourself and our heart is restless until it finds repose in you.')
57. Pascal, *Pensées*, no. 131: '*L'homme passe l'homme.*'
58. Nagel, 1971, §VI. I discuss Nagel's position, and some connected view of Bernard Williams, in Cottingham, forthcoming, 2008.
59. Kant, 1790, Part I, Book I, §4. Kant's case may diverge from Hooker's because of complications about what is involved in the term 'intrinsic', but this does not affect my endorsement of the general thrust of his verdict.
60. Newman J. H., *The Dream of Gerontius* [1865].
61. Aristotle NE, Bk. I, Ch. 7, 1098a19.
62. For a useful survey of the recent debate, see Pereboom, 2005.
63. Cottingham, 2005, Ch. 2.
64. Cottingham, 2005, Ch. 2, §6, pp. 34–6.
65. Dawkins, 2006.
66. Hooker, 'The Meaning of Life', penultimate paragraph.
67. Cottingham, 2005, Ch. 7, §7.
68. Some non-naturalists of course regard moral properties as not wholly 'independent' of existing substances, but as depending on, or supported by, natural features of ordinary objects. Thus natural, pain-inflicting quality of an action is said to provide a 'reason' (in some cases a 'conclusive reason') for not doing it. (See for example, Stratton-Lake, 2002, p. 15.) However, if such reasons are taken to be objectively there, and somehow normative for the agents independently of their inclinations and motives, the worry about moral properties floating around independently of substances seems, sooner or later, to return.

69. To summarize very crudely: explanatorily vacuous because if the reason God commands X is that X is good, we are no nearer knowing what makes it good; morally counterintuitive because if the mere fact of God's commanding X makes it right, then we would have to say that torturing for fun is right if God were to order it.
70. See Cottingham, 2005, Ch. 3, §3.
71. Hebblethwaite, 2005, pp. 28–9.
72. There are, as Metz acknowledges, problems about whether such theories can account for normativity of moral truths, and also problems about whether the kind of 'necessity' involved might turn out, in the ethical case, to be species-relative; but he offers possible replies to both worries.
73. Cottingham, 2004, pp. 11–31.
74. Quintus Horatius Flaccus, *Odes* [*Carmina*, *c.* 23 BC], I, 31, final verse. (There are no rhyme requirements in Classical poetry, but my translation retains the Alcaic metre of the original.) The 'lute', traditional instrument of Apollo ('Son of Leto'), to whom the verse is addressed), refers to the joys of music but also symbolizes for Horace his hopes to continue his poetry; for my purposes it may be taken to include any creative endeavour.

Bibliography

Aristotle, *Nicomachean Ethics*, translated in J. Ackrill, *Aristotle the Philosopher* (Oxford: Oxford University Press, l981)

Cottingham J., 'Impartiality and Ethical Formation', forthcoming, in J. Cottingham, B. Feltham and P. Stratton-Lake (eds), *Partiality and Impartiality in Ethics*

Cottingham J., 'The Good Life and the "Radical Contingency of the Ethical"', forthcoming, in D. Callcut (ed.) *Reading Bernard Williams* (London: Routledge, 2008)

Cottingham J., 'What Difference Does It Make? The Nature and Significance of Theistic Belief.' *Ratio* XIX (4) December 2006, pp. 401–20, reprinted in J. Cottingham (ed.), *The Meaning of Theism* (Oxford: Blackwell, 2007)

Cottingham J., *The Spiritual Dimension: Religion, Philosophy and Human Value* (Cambridge: Cambridge University Press, 2005)

Cottingham J., '"Our Natural Guide ...": Conscience, "Nature", and Moral Experience', in D. Oderberg and T. Chappell (eds), *Human Values* (London: Palgrave, 2004)

Cottingham J., *On the Meaning of Life* (London: Routledge, 2003)

Cottingham J., *Philosophy and the Good Life* (Cambridge: Cambridge University Press, 1998)

Cottingham J., 'The Ethical Credentials of Partiality', *Proceedings of the Aristotelian Society*, 98 (1997–8) 1–21

Cottingham J., 'The Ethics of Self-Concern', *Ethics* 101, July (1991) 798–817

Cottingham J., 'Partiality, Favouritism and Morality', *Philosophical Quarterly*, 36 (1986) 357–73

Cottingham J., 'Ethics and Impartiality', *Philosophical Studies*, 43 (1983) 83–99

Dawkins R., *The God Delusion* (London: Bantam Press, 2006)

Descartes R., Letter to his editor Marin Mersenne, of 28 January 1641, in J. Cottingham, R. Stoothoff, D. Murdoch, and A. Kenny (eds), *The Philosophical*

Writings of Descartes, vol. III (Cambridge: Cambridge University Press, 1991), p. 172

Duff A., *Trials and Punishments* (Cambridge: Cambridge University Press, 1985)

Freud S., *Introductory Lectures on Psychoanalysis* [*Vorlesungen zur Einführung in die Psychoanalyse*, 1916–17], Lecture XVIII, trans. Riviere J. (London: Routledge, 1922)

Hadot P., *Philosophy as a Way of Life* (Cambridge, Mass.: Blackwell, 1995), originally published as *Exercises spirituels et philosophie antique* (Paris: Etudes Augustiniennes, 1987)

Harvey P., *An Introduction to Buddhist Ethics* (Cambridge: Cambridge University Press, 2000)

Hebblethwaite B., *In Defence of Christianity* (Oxford: Oxford University Press, 2005)

Heidegger M., *Being and Time* [*Sein und Zeit*, 1927], trans. Macquarrie J. and Robinson E. (New York: Harper and Row, 1962)

Jung C. J., *Modern Man in Search of a Soul,* Essays from the 1920s and 1930s, trans. Baynes C. F. (London: Routledge, 1933)

Kant I., *Die Religion innherhalb der Grenzen der blossen Vernunft* [1793], trans. Wood A. and di Giovanni G. (Cambridge: Cambridge University Press, 1998)

Kant I., *Critique of Judgement* [*Kritik der Urteilskraft*, 1790], trans. J. C. Meredith (Oxford: Clarendon, 1928)

Kant I., *Groundwork for the Metaphysic of Morals* [*Grundlegung zur Metaphysik der Sitten*, 1785], trans. Hill T. E. and Zweig A. (Oxford: Oxford University Press, 2003)

Mackie J., *Ethics: Inventing Right and Wrong* (Harmondsworth: Penguin, 1977)

Nagel T., 'The Absurd', *Journal of Philosophy* vol. LXIII, no. 20 (1971), reprinted in Nagel T., *Mortal Questions* (Cambridge: Cambridge University Press, 1979)

Pereboom D., 'The Problem of Evil', in Mann W. E. (ed.), *The Blackwell Guide to the Philosophy of Religion* (Oxford: Blackwell, 2005).

Stratton-Lake P. J., *Ethical Intuitionism* (Oxford: Clarendon Press, 2002)

Swinburne R., *Is There a God?* (Oxford: Oxford University Press, 1996)

Williams B., *Shame and Necessity* (Berkeley, CA: University of California Press, 1993)

Williams B., *Ethics and the Limits of Philosophy* (London: Collins/Fontana, 1985)

Williams B., *Moral Luck: Philosophical Papers 1973–1980* (Cambridge: Cambridge University Press 1981)

Williams B., 'Integrity,' in Smart J. J. C., and Williams B., *Utilitarianism: For and Against* (Cambridge: Cambridge University Press, 1972)

Index